REEL INDIA

Namrata Joshi is associate editor – cinema and a film critic with *The Hindu*. A member of FIPRESCI, the international federation of film critics based in Munich, she has been a member of its critics' jury at multiple film festivals across the world. She has also been on the selection committee for films at the International Film Festival of India, Goa, in 2008 and 2012. A Charles Wallace India Trust fellow and a Chevening scholar, she won India's National Award for Best Film Critic in 2004. Namrata has contributed pieces to various anthologies on Indian cinema, and currently resides and works in Mumbai.

Praise for the book

'This book is a rich mine of information for film scholars, historians, students or anyone else interested in cinema cultures in India. Joshi has archived a huge body of information and each chapter is worthy of an independent book.' – *Hindustan Times*

'Its true heart lies in its chronicling of magnificent obsessions like the ones quoted above: the obsessions of people who live outside the cinematic mainstream (or what city dwellers think is the mainstream) and engage with films in myriad ways, not seeking monetary benefit but doing things because they are compelled to; because cinema is so central to who they are.' – *Mint*

'Namrata Joshi's brilliantly written *Reel India* is one such book that captures the moods, dreams, aspirations and ambitions of those who religiously visit cinema halls and drown their worries, sorrows and sufferings for three hours.' – *Free Press Journal*

'There is a great celebration of what is in plain sight – the one experience of cinema uniting India, which clearly is a grand idea that binds it all, and it's ideal for readers who are just discovering the exotic offering called Bollywood. For a better part, *Reel India* manages to get everything as nattily as a dish inspired by the confluence of many cultures.' – *New Indian Express*

'The book inspires a range of emotions – amusement, nostalgia, respect and finally awe, at the sheer depth of Indian cinema's percolation into the ordinary Indian's life.' – *Tribune*

'The book is remarkable precisely because it brings to public notice the nature of this intense engagement, through a series of case-studies, covering different facets of popular cinema.' – *Book Review Literary Trust*

REEL INDIA

Cinema off the Beaten Track

NAMRATA JOSHI

hachette INDIA

First published in hardback in India in 2019 by Hachette India
(Registered name: Hachette Book Publishing India Pvt. Ltd)
An Hachette UK company
www.hachetteindia.com

This edition published in 2021

SRD

Hardback edition ISBN 978-93-5009-721-2
Paperback edition ISBN 978-93-91028-05-3
Ebook edition ISBN 978-93-5009-728-1

Hachette Book Publishing India Pvt. Ltd
4th & 5th Floors, Corporate Centre,
Plot No. 94, Sector 44, Gurugram 122003, India

Typeset in Minion Pro 10/13.5
by R Ajith Kumar, New Delhi

Printed and bound in India by
Manipal Technologies Limited, Manipal

FSC www.fsc.org
MIX
Paper from responsible sources
FSC™ C104740

For my parents, the reason why I am here
And my dear, darling niece Poorva, the keeper of my future

Contents

Introduction

Road Trippin' with the Movies

ALMOST TEN YEARS AFTER having first met her for a story I was doing for *Outlook* magazine, I went looking for Nandini Sehgal again. She belongs to the gang of women in Saharanpur – Manisha Malik, Shipra Sehgal and Kirti Malik being the other members – who had featured in my case study in understanding how small-town India was in the grip of Bollywood.[1]

Back then in 2008, the pretty, petite, soft-spoken and ever-smiling Mumbai girl had been trying to make a home in Saharanpur after her marriage. She never did spell it out in so many words, but I sensed that the move from India's Maximum City to a grungy Uttar Pradesh town of sugarcane, papermaking and wood-carving fame could not have been easy. No one looks forward to a downbeat curve in life, after all. She moved from living it up to the hilt as a college student in a city that never sleeps to a humdrum life, dictated by routine, in a perennially somnolent town, where social life is limited to activities within an often claustrophobic circle of neighbours, relatives and a few friends. From travelling freely anywhere in the big city, at any time of the day or night, to remaining largely confined within the four walls of home, life had certainly changed drastically. With no suitable jobs coming her way, Nandini was fighting interminable boredom in Saharanpur with only a television set and a remote control at her disposal to beat the blues.

When I first met her a decade ago, she had already found a new purpose in life with a little help from the feisty spirit of Mumbai that she still carried within her. Quick to realize that she had a lot of time on hand in Saharanpur and little to do, and having trained as a dance instructor and choreographer at a Bollywood dance class in Mumbai – because this art form had been one of her passions – she had decided to put her skills to good use by offering Bollywood dance lessons to local women and children. It was a small window to the world beyond her marital home, and it helped her breathe the fresh air of liberation, acquire financial independence and forge ahead on a path of self-determination while in a constricting, perhaps, even suffocating, world of small-town domesticity and conservatism. She never shared with me what her husband or in-laws felt about her initiative, never let on whether they approved of it or not, but it was evident in her smile and enthusiasm that she herself was loving it.

In a long, stark, rectangular, wood-floored room, with a mirror running along the entire length of a wall, so Nandini's students could watch their reflections as they danced to her tunes, it was all bump and grind, *jhatka matka*, twist and turn and thrust. Her classes began as early as 7.30 in the morning and went on till 9 p.m. Local middle-class women across all age groups – in their twenties, thirties, even fifties and sixties – who thronged the classes were also discovering, along with their teacher, an indescribable joy in this welcome break from the drudgery of household chores and a life harnessed to the dreariness of routine. Even if it remained within the confines of the room, dance was meant for their own pleasure and joy, rather than as entertainment to be presented to their conservative families and friends, who could well have eyed it as a dubious pastime and disapproved of it.

Yet, among them were the odd radical too, who stood out with their new, confident body language. In fact, one of them was even aspiring to audition for the television show *Boogie Woogie Mother's Special*, that too with the backing of her family.

'*Chhote chhote sheheron se, khaali bore dopaharon se hum toh jhola utha ke chale...*' ('Rucksack in hand, we're off and away, fleeing the small towns and their empty, boring afternoons...'), wrote Gulzar for a song that would feature in *Bunty aur Babli*, a 2005 film starring Rani Mukerji and Abhishek Bachchan, which went on to become a huge box-office success. Nandini's dance classes seemed emblematic of that escape. An hour of Bollywood song and dance could well have felt like being transported to the sets of the magical, make-believe world of films that helped turn Nandini's – and her students' – dreary monotony into a fairytale fantasy, even if for a fleeting span of time.

Meanwhile, Nandini's friends from her girl gang – Manisha, Shipra and Kirti – had found another getaway. Every other weekend, they would hire an Innova and set out from Saharanpur, heading for Delhi, some 180 km away, to catch a Hindi film in the comfort of a plush multiplex. These outings were for the big-ticket films (usually starring one of the Khan trinity) that weren't just movies, but events, celebrations. In a dusty town which lacked something as basic as a good children's park, Bollywood (besides television, of course) seemed to offer the only respite from the routine of their day-to-day lives.

'Our entire week is spent discussing the movie we have seen,' Shipra told me.

It didn't end there. In 2008, it seemed to me as if the entire city of Saharanpur that I had picked quite randomly, largely for its proximity to Delhi, was taking its cues for life from cinema. Its residents were, in fact, so steeped in Bollywood that they didn't notice it themselves. But it did catch the eye of an outsider to their world, like me. The interesting part was that this phenomenon cut across class divides. Even in the small, but more rarefied, classy section of Saharanpur society, parties and celebrations appeared to be inspired by *filmi* or film-influenced themes. At a party inspired by the 2007 release *Namastey London*, for instance, women were dressed in Western attire and men in traditional Indian outfits, because the film was about a rustic Punjabi, played by Akshay Kumar, falling in love with a girl born and brought up in London, a role tailor-made for Katrina Kaif, who enacted it. The women at the party seemed to be imbibing Bollywood in the way they dressed, spoke and behaved. Whether the trendy outfits and social graces and manners were indicative of a liberal, progressive outlook or masked conservative beliefs and practices on home ground was difficult to fathom. Katrina Kaif seemed to be the role model for the entire Meerut–Muzaffarnagar–Saharanpur stretch. At Vandana Verma's boutique, Saheli, the outfits most in demand were the black sari with a red border the same actress had worn in *Singh Is Kinng* (2008) and her balloon-cut dress in *Race*, a film that released the same year. At Kishi Sharma's She Tone beauty parlour, clients were asking for Deepika Padukone's retro look - bouffant hair, heavy eye make-up and pale lipstick - from *Om Shanti Om* (2007). Bollywood was taking them closer to a look they had been aspiring for, rather than the liberal lifestyle it symbolized on celluloid.

Bollywood's influence seemed to be ushering in a new, if restricted, freedom in the rich, but extremely conservative section of the larger west Uttar Pradesh region. It's a schizophrenia which is hard to pin down - inner as against outer conservatism. Dressing in Western outfits is more like an aspiration towards a desired look that need not indicate a concomitant liberalism in thought. Priyanshi Aggarwal and Pooja Awasthi, college students in Muzaffarnagar, told me how they chose the 2008 film *Jaane Tu... Ya Jaane Na*, starring Imran Khan and Genelia D'Souza, to introduce their orthodox parents to the mores of contemporary college life in metropolitan cities.

'They got to know that we can have [a] "healthy" friendship with boys,' Priyanshi explained.

On the way back to Delhi from Saharanpur, after meeting the two girls in Muzaffarnagar, I stopped by the town's Sri Ram College, where Reshu, a rather forthright student of management studies, shared the lesson he had learnt from *Guru*: it's okay to offer bribes if they help you get your work done. The 2007 Mani Ratnam film, with Abhishek Bachchan and Aishwarya Rai as the main leads, had clearly fired up his entrepreneurial ambitions. For this small-town boy with big dreams, the intuitive craftiness of the film's protagonist, Gurukant Desai, was a more assured way to success than, perhaps, the business theories outlined in his textbooks.

Ten years since my first visit, things seem to be much the same in Saharanpur. Shipra, Manisha and Kirti are still hooked to their movie outings.

'Cinema continues to be our weekend refresher,' Shipra tells me.

Only, they don't need to travel all the way to Delhi now for their film-oriented picnics. LX and SRS multiplexes have arrived in Saharanpur. I hear that fashions and trends have also evolved to reflect the popularity of more recent films and their stars. Now, the colours and kitsch, the song-and-dance routines at local weddings are all direct lifts from *Bajirao Mastani* and the big style icons are, predictably, Deepika Padukone and Priyanka Chopra. However, while *Bajirao Mastani* was a period piece, ethnic ('desi') dressing is out; it's the Indo-Western attire the stars and their rivals flaunt onscreen that appears to be much in demand.

'Kareena Kapoor's palazzos and short crop tops are selling the most,' says Vandana, the owner of Saheli boutique.

Kangana Ranaut, a small-town girl herself from Bhambla, Himachal Pradesh, has been at the forefront as the new role model for women. What makes her stand apart is the sophisticated, urban flair with which she dresses, the no-holds-barred manner in which she expresses her thoughts and the freedom with which she chooses to lead her life – on her own terms.

Meanwhile, Nandini's phone number has changed since I last met her; my contact in Saharanpur says she has, perhaps, gone back to Mumbai. But Ranjana Neb, who has been running Vaishnavi Nrityalaya, a dance school (for both classical and contemporary dance) in Saharanpur, for the past 25 years, also vouches for the steady popularity of Bollywood dance. And it isn't a prevailing trend in that town alone. Even in nearby Baraut, at a sombre and solemn event – the

Shatabdi Samaroh (centenary celebrations) of the staid Digambar Jain Inter College – held two years ago, it was Bollywood dancing all the way, besides classical and folk.

'It has no rules and restrictions; it is all about being uninhibited,' says Ranjana of Bollywood dancing.

I wonder if this could be one of the reasons why it holds such appeal in an otherwise reserved, often repressed society, and for women, in particular. For it is women who have taken to it big time – be it to beat stress, exercise in a fun way or just get away for some 'I, me, myself' time. Ranjana herself has been a winner of the women's freestyle solo category in the television dance reality show *Boogie Woogie*, in which she had danced to the song 'Bhumro' from *Mission Kashmir* (2000), a film starring Hrithik Roshan and Preity Zinta.

This encounter with Bollywood in Saharanpur left some niggling questions in my mind: Was cinema's hold on the public imagination in small towns like this one stronger, more far-reaching and more colourful and whimsical than in the cities? Or was that just a tendency in my urban mind to exoticize its appeal, fuelled by a sense of nostalgia? How does the small-town experience of movies vary from a metropolitan consumption of cinema? How has it changed with the advent of digitization, the proliferation of multiplexes, the ubiquitousness of television, the Internet and the mobile phone? What is unique about the vision of cinema outside the metros?

Moreover, what *is* a small town? With India's small towns growing in size and changing rapidly in the last few years, has their connection with cinema been undergoing a transformation of some kind as well?

Having grown up in Delhi, with one foot in small towns – thanks to the extended family we would visit from time to time – the Saharanpur jaunt took me back to the days of watching J. Om Prakash's Jeetendra–Reena Roy–Rameshwari–starrer *Aasha*, years after its release in 1980, in a ramshackle single-screen theatre at Holi Gate in Mathura. I can't recall its name now, only that it stood right opposite Shankar Halwai, our pit stop for *kachori–sabzi* and *lassi* before the screenings. The eatery is still there, though the cinema hall has since shut shop. But I still can't forget the clinking of the coins that would be thrown at the screen in appreciation when Roy, in a sequinned black oufit, sang, '*Sheesha ho ya dil ho, aakhir toot jaata hai*. Be it glass or the human heart, both shatter easily.' Equally heady was the experience of watching Yash Chopra's 1979 movie *Kaala Patthar* in an obscure theatre in Ajmer, with the packed house cheering with equal gusto at the initial enmity between Vijay (played by Amitabh Bachchan) and Mangal (Shatrughan Sinha in the role), and then their joining of hands to fight against the evil coal-mine owner. Much of that mofussil experience was replicated when I watched Shyam Benegal's *Welcome to Sajjanpur* (2008) at Kalpana Talkies in Saharanpur, complete with creaking chairs, whirring fans and the pleasurable anticipation of its interval, replete with the promise of a patties-and-cream roll treat.

I have come a long way indeed from those days when watching a film involved passion, spontaneity and a sense of deep emotional investment. Now, it is more about meditative musings on the finer aspects of movie-making. Perhaps, films don't mean as much to us – individuals living in an urban milieu – as they do to those for whom Saharanpur, Mathura or Ajmer is home. In metropolitan cities like the one I live in, they could even be something to engage with for a couple of hours over popcorn and a cold drink, and then be almost instantly forgotten, instead of being mulled over and absorbed.

Or perhaps not?

Saharanpur set me thinking, confused me and forced me to ask many questions to which clear answers weren't forthcoming. It also set me off on multiple journeys over the years to explore places and meet people with quaint, *filmi* associations. Some I accidentally bumped into while working on various office assignments; others I actively sought out. Friends, acquaintances, connections – many of them discovered online via Twitter and Facebook – offered pointers, extended a helping hand and got me the contacts I needed. I still don't have all the answers I set out to find. What I have gathered and cherish is a wealth of personal experience, the chance of witnessing lives and spaces at close hand, of being exposed to cultures, practices and even cuisines I wouldn't otherwise have had the good fortune to try out and savour. It has been, above all, a reassertion of the many-splendoured thing that is cinema.

Back to the question: What *is* a small town? Has it anything to do with the size and population demographic of a place? Is it a place that is not fully urban yet? Or the one that serves as a bridge between urban and rural India? Do we still define a small town by the census definition of those with a population between 500 and 10,00,000? Can I then claim that my travels in search of offbeat cinema stories have necessarily taken me through what can be strictly defined as small towns? Or are they now 'intermediate' towns, as they're currently being described? Moreover, even among small towns, aren't some bigger than others, while there are those that come across as decidedly more provincial?

It's not the place so much as the mindset that matters, a friend tells me.

It is a perspective shared by others.

'Small towns and big cities are not geographical. They are a mindspace,' observe Shabani Hassanwalia and Samreen Farooqui, makers of *Being Salman Khan*, a documentary on small-town fans of the macho Bollywood star.

'What are big cities, if not a collection of small towns?' asks Hindi film lyricist and writer Varun Grover.

'There is a small town in every big city,' Amitabh Bachchan had once tweeted to me, when I wrote about how different a world old Delhi was from the new areas of the city.

'Aren't Kanpur and Lucknow big cities? And aren't Trilokpuri and Seelampur like small towns within a big city?' asks media observer and critic Sudheesh Pachauri. 'There is no big city in India other than Mumbai. All others, including Delhi, Chennai, Kolkata, Bengaluru, Hyderabad are small towns,' says filmmaker Tigmanshu Dhulia of, what he considers, an omniscient provincialism at the heart and soul of India.

'There's, increasingly, not such a dramatic divergence; instead, there is a convergence between big cities and small towns,' says columnist-author Santosh Desai.

What used to be a small town yesterday may not be one today, what with easy access to television and the Internet, the growth of a standardized, ubiquitous townscape of malls and multiplexes, and a concomitant consumer culture.

'There is a new form of unification; there are the same reference points, [the] same role models, whether you are from a small town or big city,' Desai adds.

Then there is the larger context of a nation's relationship with cinema as a whole, which has been changing over the years. Films have traditionally been regarded as fantasy zones, and theatres, hallowed spaces where the audience escapes from reality and lives its collective dreams, desires and aspirations. Earlier, access to films was limited, especially in small towns and villages, which only intensified the desire for them. The stars, in turn, were creatures with a distinct aura about them, objects of awe and admiration for the viewers.

The fascination for cinema and its stars started changing radically in the 1990s, with the opening up of the economy. Economic liberalization and globalization were contributing factors in that transformation. Mainstream Hindi cinema moved away from the masses and rural themes to focus on Shining Urban India and the Non-Resident Indian. With stars becoming instantly accessible through print, electronic and, now, social media, their larger-than-life images began diminishing to some extent. Instead of continuing to be an end unto themselves, films and the stars they featured became objects to be consumed in the big metros, between periodic bouts of indulgence at food courts and in retail therapy at malls. In small towns, on the contrary, television emerged as the predominant medium for watching films and enjoying other forms of audio-visual entertainment.

The escapism that Bollywood cinema seems to encourage, along with its aspirational angle, might still hold true in small towns, even if they no longer do to the same extent in big cities. Culturally, there may now be a greater convergence between big cities and small towns, Desai maintains, but the chasm between fantasy and reality is much wider in mofussil areas. The love for films and the fascination with the stars is stronger and more unconditional.

'So they take their relationship with the stars a little more seriously,' he infers.

'Their affiliation with films and stars is much more emotional,' declares social anthropologist Shiv Vishvanathan, referring to people living in small towns.

But it's a dynamic, fluid relationship in a larger, ever-changing socio-economic and political world.

The question, therefore, arises: How, then, is cinema perceived in and responded to in a small town? There is no straightforward answer to such a question. An interesting development these days is the extent to which the backroom of Bollywood is filled with talent from small towns, a majority of such aspirants coming in from Bihar; writers, lyricists, assistant directors (ADs), directors – the list is unending. It's quite akin to their dominance in the civil services for some years now, or, for that matter, in any other public sphere. Bihar, once patronizingly described as a hapless and backward state, has seen its enterprising, industrious folk struggle, forge ahead and hold sway in various professions across India; Bollywood is no exception to this wave.

As lyricist Raj Shekhar once told me, it's an influx of aspirants from the remotest corners of the state, via Delhi University, to Aaram Nagar, the strugglers' hub in Andheri. So I thought, why not turn to friends who had grown up with films in the small towns of Bihar, to begin with? Perhaps the pointers could lie in their own intensely personal relationship with films?

These micro snapshots would, in fact, open up a macro experience for me.

Consider television journalist and anchor Ravish Kumar, who grew up in Motihari and Patna. Films, he acknowledges, were his dreams and the cinema hall was the home to these dreams.

'Mona, Pearl, Veena, Ashok, Roopak, Apsara, Regent... If these Patna cinemas were not there in my life, I would have had no heroes, no heroines, no dreams, no imagination,' he says.

He watched many films, sitting in the front stall and, at times, on broken seats; films like the critically acclaimed 1988 blockbuster *Tezaab* (when he got up and danced to '*Ek do teen*', the iconic 'item' number that Madhuri Dixit, the reigning star of the times, had immortalized with her nimble moves) and the Mithun Chakraborty–starrers *Disco Dancer* (1982) and *Dance Dance* (1987). He watched Rajendra Kumar's 1970 release *Ganwaar* innumerable times on a makeshift screen in a Bihar Cooperative Union hall, with rickshaw pullers and fruit and vegetable vendors for company, and *Ghulami* (1985), again starring Chakraborty, 10 times at Apsara. He caught the first show of Aamir Khan's debut film *Qayamat Se Qayamat Tak* at Mona in 1988 and went on to see it 18 times more. Since Kumar was quite an average student himself, the lyrics of the song from the film that was on everyone's lips at the time – '*Beta hamara bada naam karega*. My son will earn a name for himself'– hurt him to no end. He watched *Sholay*, the film that would become a legendary success despite a lacklustre public response to its release in 1975, not on a movie-theatre screen, but in the animated expressions of his friend Shiva, while the latter narrated the story to him. Ravish Kumar would, henceforth, make it a point to see Big B's films, first day, first show, even queueing up for another Bachchan-starrer *Agneepath* (1990) as early as 3 a.m. Watching films was a matter of right for him and he was determined to hold on to it at any cost in an era when cinema was not quite as socially acceptable as it has become today.

'My life doesn't extend beyond cinema,' he admits with unabashed candour.

Cinema, in turn, has made him understand life and society. He still regularly visits cinema halls, but feels that multiplexes, in both big cities and small towns, have robbed us of the community experience of watching a film, killed the social diversity the audience offered and homogenized the film-viewing experience itself.

According to author-academician Amitava Kumar, the best description of the experience of watching a film in a small town came from actor Manoj Bajpayee. Kumar had read the actor's account in a book and liked it so much that he used it in his novel *Home Products*, except that Bajpayee was called Neeraj Dubey in the novel. In an interview with a writer from London in the novel, Dubey says that if you really want to enjoy a Hindi film, you should go to a theatre in a small town in Bihar. He describes how small-town folks 'tear their shirts' open and throw coins at the screen in the excitement of watching a hit song or a titillating dance performance. For them, movies are not about fulfilling artistic expectations, as they are for many city slickers, but primarily about enjoyment, about letting themselves go.

'Small-town people... don't care a damn what people think,' Dubey tells the writer. 'If they want to cry, they cry or howl in the theatre... In small towns... they come to enjoy the film and if you betray them... and you can't hold them, then you'll see empty theatres the next day. They are extreme in their emotions; the city people aren't – I would say they don't know how to enjoy a Hindi film.'

Marketing manager Shashank Kumar, who spent his formative years (1991–99) in Pakur (a sleepy district in erstwhile Bihar, now Jharkhand, bang on the border with West Bengal), a land of granite kilns, stone chips and crushers, loads of trucks and dust, remembers watching films in two single-screen cinema halls – Suchitra and Mini Suchitra –with a crowd akin to the one described in the Amitava Kumar novel. Being the newer one, Mini Suchitra used to screen more recent releases (with a delay of at least two to three months) and Suchitra was happy playing films from the '70s and '80s, mostly of the '*maar dhaad aur* romance *se bharpoor* – replete with fights and romance' genre. The two big draws were actor Amitabh Bachchan and director Sooraj Barjatya. The average moviegoer for the action films, mostly starring Bachchan, was from the working class (comprising rickshaw pullers, handcart pullers, labourers and an immigrant Bangladeshi population colloquially known as '*Chaansa*') and he was the expressive sort. Cinema for this cross-section of society offered a spectator-sport kind of experience.

'Whistles, comments, catcalls and a general sense of din during action scenes made you feel that you were in a stadium and watching a sport; the hero used to be the home side,' recollects Shashank, adding, 'for small towns, cinema has been *the* most immersive form of entertainment and the awe with which the crowd approached the screen was inimitable.' That, he feels, is changing with time. 'I see a lack of fantastical connection. The dreamy-eyed glitter at the mention of their favourite film stars is going away. The young fans are now more realistic.'

Writer-filmmaker Aparajita Krishna also remembers watching films at Muzaffarpur's Shyam and Chitra Talkies. Those occasions were a ceremony of sorts. She had grown up in north Bihar's lychee land, famous for this juicy summer fruit, in the '60s. A few years earlier, in the '50s, the town's biggest high had been the visit of Prithviraj Kapoor, who had arrived to perform some of his plays at Chitra Talkies. It is a visit that is still remembered, generations later. In Muzaffarpur's hair-cutting salons, the 'Sadhana fringe', sported by the actress in her 1960 debut Hindi film *Love in Simla*, was the last word in women's coiffure; in tailors' shops, it was the 'Sadhana churidar-kurta', popularized by the actress in the Yash Chopra-directed film *Waqt* (1965), co-starring Sunil Dutt and Raaj Kumar, that came to be regarded as the ultimate feminine style statement.

'I can never erase the memory of a *sonar* [jeweller] of Muzaffarpur being taken to watch a Sadhana film to note the gold *jadau* jewellery set she was wearing, so that it could be replicated for a wedding trousseau,' Krishna admits.

In the '70s, Jaya Bhaduri, who would later marry Bachchan, her leading man in several films, left a lasting impression on middle-class Indian girls.

'She broke all the barriers of stardom,' Krishna observes,' in schools, colleges, *mohalla*s of Muzaffarpur. Girls would not only be dressing like her, but also laughing, giggling, talking like her.'

It is impossible to recapture that innocence and enchantment for cinema now.

'Film stars could not be accessed beyond their roles,' Krishna continues. 'They were not meant to be met in flesh and blood, but to be admired and worshipped from a distance. Their films and songs were the magnets that pulled the audience.'

Now, with technology, increased connectivity, television and live events, celebrities are to be found in every nook and corner of India. The unique connect that fans shared with their favourite film stars and their wonderment at their larger-than-life personas are almost lost in the churn and newfound aspirations of India's small towns, where progressiveness now rubs shoulders with old-worldliness, where the physical and mental landscapes of its residents reveal a duality that had been absent earlier.

In the 1990s, Amitesh Kumar, a Ph.D student at Delhi University, would watch movies at Dhruv, Kamal and Chitrangada Talkies in his hometown Bagaha in Bihar. Bordering UP and Nepal, the town had acquired some notoriety because of the region's infamous dacoities and was also known as 'mini Chambal'. The films viewed there – *Dil* (1990), starring the Indian teenager's new heart-throb Aamir Khan opposite Madhuri Dixit; *Hum*, a 1991 film with a multi-star cast headed by Amitabh Bachchan; Ajay Devgn's debut film *Phool Aur Kaante* (also released in 1991); the Bachchan–Sridevi–starrer *Khuda Gawah* (1992); *Beta* (1992), featuring Anil Kapoor and Madhuri Dixit, and *Hum Aapke Hain Koun...!* a 1994 Indian musical romantic comedy starring Salman Khan and Dixit, yet again – gave Kumar what he calls his 'archetypal images and impressions of cinema'. To cry during the emotional scenes and get excited over the action sequences was a perfectly acceptable response. For him, the viewers there, unlike those in the big cities, did not keep themselves at one remove from the hero and heroine on the screen. They immersed themselves, heart and soul, in the imaginary lives of imaginary characters, as though it was all true to life, real.

'We used to be one with the film and its characters. The atmosphere was alive and lively. Every film created its own mood and feeling,' he remembers.

According to Kumar, cinema in the small towns still has as an audience comprising the poor, the underprivileged and the subaltern group. They watch films with an involvement whose intensity is unmatched by that of the more privileged audience of the cities, for whom it is a consumer product like any other. In small towns, cinema has often been a major influence in life, even an inspiration.

'One of my friends was such a big fan of [actress] Divya Bharti that he performed a symbolic *shraddha* ceremony on her death and even fed the poor,' he recalls.

Till date, whenever Kumar visits a new town, he makes it a point to watch a film in one of the cinema halls there; it gives him a better understanding of the place.

Film journalist Ajay Brahmatmaj, who studied in Purnia, Darbhanga and Bettiah, saw films not just in the halls, but in makeshift tents set up during the various melas.

'There was an immense joy in watching films; it was like a festival,' he says.

Such was the audience involvement that a scene, song or dance would get replayed, again and again, on a viewer's request. The halls were often situated quite close to the railway station and bus stops, offering people a way to kill time before undertaking a long journey.

Media columnist and author Vineet Kumar, who lived in Bihar Sharif in Nalanda between 1982 and 1996, remembers how watching films, besides going to the theatre, had started becoming a community activity, with family, neighbours and the locality getting together to watch back-to-back films on a rented VCR and television set. He feels that cinema is no longer the addiction it used to be in Bihar Sharif, when for days on end, they would talk about a film, about the Simrans and Paros on screen.

'Cinema is no longer a fantasy,' he declares. 'People in small towns are as connected to cinema through TV as those in big cities. In fact, the small town–big city divide has given way now to [a] single screen–multiplex split.'

So, is going to the cinema in a small town still as distinct an experience as it used to be or just the stuff of nostalgia and memories? This was a question I kept posing to many as I went along. As opinions collided and concurred, I continued to travel across India in quest of film-related encounters. I realized that Bollywood slips in as a common thread in diverse narratives and discourses, especially in small-town north India. In every nook and corner, be it in the madrassas of Azamgarh or in the small villages near Gurdaspur, at the ghats of Varanasi or in the hole-in-the-wall hair-cutting saloons of Pushkar, there is something decidedly 'Bollywoodian' staring back at you. In Palitana, a Jain monk showed off a new temple to me, proudly declaring that Hema Malini had graced its inauguration with her presence, as though the star's visit had, somehow, validated the sanctum sanctorum's significance. A trip to Bharkunda village, 40 km from Ahmedabad, opened my eyes to a research project by IIM professor Brij Kothari, where subtitled Hindi film songs on the Doordarshan television programme *Chitrahaar* were being used to spread functional literacy in the villages of Gujarat; a cost-effective and fun mode of teaching. The last I heard of him, he was doing the same in the interiors of Maharashtra with television programmes that came with Marathi subtitles.

During the last general elections, my former colleagues at *Outlook* magazine hobnobbed with stars on their campaign trails across the country: from former Miss India and actress Gul Panag in Chandigarh to film director Prakash Jha in Champaran; from actor Paresh Rawal getting mobbed in Ahmedabad as Baburao Ganpatrao Apte (the memorable character he plays in the wildly popular Priyadarshan-directed 2000 release *Hera Pheri* and its sequel *Phir Hera Pheri*, directed by the late Neeraj Vora, released six years later) to actress Naghma drawing crowds in Meerut, where she was still remembered for her role in *Bewafaa Se Wafaa*, a 1992 release, with Juhi Chawla and Vivek Mushran as the main leads. Kolkata journalist Dola Mitra wrote about a fan screaming, 'Bappi-da, *ekta gaan hoyey jaak*!' from amidst the crowd that had gathered outside the Golden Inn Hotel in Dankuni, a small town in the Srirampur constituency from where the Bollywood music composer–singer Bappi Lahiri was contesting on a BJP ticket.[2] Not many commented on his credentials or credibility as a politician as he gamely sang the famous opening lines of his 1987 hit song, '*Chirodini tumi je amar, jugey jugey ami tomari*. You are mine forever; I have always been yours,' to an ecstatic crowd. Even Moon Moon Sen (who drew much of her name and fame from her legendary film-actress mother Suchitra Sen) was as much of a sensation in her off-white chiffon saris and pearl necklaces as Lahiri in her political avatar as the Trinamool candidate in the boondocks, a term that would appropriately describe much of Bankura district. Here too, vital issues were a mere afterthought.[3]

It set me thinking about the reasons why political parties were keen to rope in film stars for their campaigns. I wondered if the intention was to cash in on their glamorous, larger-than-life images and draw crowds. But did those crowds actually translate into votes? Did the stars' screen personae transcend into political roles? Not quite as successfully in the North, perhaps, but perceptibly so in the South, where political dynamics and fan-club culture seemed to go hand-in-hand, an assumption validated by the decision of film stars like Rajinikanth and Kamal Haasan to embark on the political path.

As I travelled further, what kept drawing me in and stirring my imagination was a trail of cinema stories that weren't quite about cinema, but something more. About places near and far, and people with a cinema connect we couldn't have ever imagined. About Salman Khan, whose image can evoke dramatically divergent responses in

Jodhpur, turning the town into a near schizophrenic space, divided, on the one hand, between his diehard fans with their blind adulation and unswerving loyalty, and the Bishnois, on the other, who continue to wage their bitter battle against the star in the blackbuck-chinkara hunting cases. About a town like Coimbatore that once housed some of the Tamil film industry's iconic studios, where many early classics were shot, but eventually surrendered its supremacy as Kollywood capital to Chennai. And about yet another town Madurai that has spun a whole genre of cinema around itself. The stories that hooked me were also about the way Bollywood could drive the economy of a small town like Wai and how distant towns could end up serving as convenient, fully equipped locales for shooting films. They impelled me to reflect on the cynicism over Bollywood inspiring places to spawn a cinema of their own and the role of technology in changing the way we view a film. Cinema stories that extend beyond cinema also offer insights into the expanding reach of film festivals, which are no longer the fiefdom of the big metros. They also expose the grim reality that in a country literally worshipping cinema for over a century, there are actually some states still struggling to access it. In Kashmir, for example, India's biggest dream factory may remain a distant dream for its millions. Looking at the book from a distance now, I get the sense that it hasn't turned out to be a wholesome one dish meal. Rather it's a typical thali, an Indian smorgasbord of distinct, diverse, and often, colliding and confounding flavours.

In our urgency to write about the films that make a mark, the stars who hog the limelight and the salacious gossip their real and imagined lives generate, we often overlook such stories that are at a tangent or on the periphery. At times, we even take them for granted. This book is an attempt to connect the less conspicuous dots and string a few of the stories together; some already known, others not quite as much.

Most have played out away from the metros. Mumbai, Delhi, Bengaluru, Chennai and Kolkata don't feature here. Some of the areas described in this book happen to be places few would ordinarily visit;

others may not even appear on maps or merit a mention in guidebooks. This book records my journey – both physical and metaphorical – through them, with cinema as my looking glass.

Is there a common human narrative threading its way through all these scattered tales? Yes, undoubtedly so. I also understood in the course of my journey that cinema is not merely a medium of entertainment or an art form, but an intensely personal engagement, and a significant sociological and economic constituent of some ordinary, unknown lives lived within commonplace homes and families in a few, rather unremarkable Indian towns.

I have also left out quite a bit of what I managed to unearth simply because more stories kept emerging from some corner of India or the other, leading to still more stories. Delving into each and every one of them would have entailed more time, travel and research, thereby prolonging the duration of an already long-drawn-out project. In fact, the very stories I have explored here constantly acquire new dimensions and open up fresh horizons.

Even as I call it a wrap, filmmaker Tigmanshu Dhulia informs me about the dacoit Balwanta in Gwalior, without whose inputs *Paan Singh Tomar* (2012), a biopic starring Irrfan Khan, might never have been made. Director Anurag Kashyap remembers a hall, somewhere close to Varanasi, that screens only old Dharmendra movies. Mahadev Toppo, a friend from the film-appreciation class I once attended at the Film and Television Institute of India (FTII), is helping tribals make films in their native Jharkhand. Meanwhile, I am still trying to verify whether there is, indeed, a Fulvadi tribe in Gujarat that imposes a fine on its people for watching films.

The journey I had undertaken has come to an end. Many more will hopefully begin now.

A Town Divided

IT'S A WET EID morning in Jodhpur. Driving out of the railway station, all you can see beyond the incessant drizzle are the ancient, imposing ramparts of the Mehrangarh Fort at a distance, a sea of men in crisp white kurtas and skullcaps walking towards Masjid Baitul Gafur for the morning namaaz, a posse of cops and, outnumbering them both, innumerable posters of *Kick* on the city walls, with its star Salman Khan staring purposefully back at you, as though exhorting you to watch his latest film.

'Bhai', as he is so fondly called by his fans, is plastered all over Jodhpur's townscape, decked in a shade of blue the way houses in Jaipur are painted a ubiquitous pink. Bhai is as omnipresent as the *mirchi vada*, *pyaaz kachori* or *makhaniya lassi* on offer at the streetside food stalls.

That Khan is the man of the day in Jodhpur, as he is every Eid, is proven to you a few hours later at the crammed New Kohinoor cinema on Chaupasni Road. When it comes to Bollywood, Eid celebrations are incomplete without Salman. For several years now, the festival has marked the arrival of his latest blockbuster.

'He and his films come to the theatres on Eid, like a feast after the long spell of *rozas* [fasts] during Ramzan,' declares his diehard fan and theatre manager Jameel Khan, a man with the manner and bearing of the stern, disciplinarian uncle who would forbid you from watching films instead of indulging your passion for Salman Khan.

Bhai's commanding presence and charisma are reflected in the swagger of the colourfully attired young men, who have gathered in large numbers for the matinee show of *Kick*. It's the kind of bluster that surpasses even that of their idol. They may bear little physical resemblance to him, but no one can stop them from imagining themselves as a chip of the Bhai block, as they sing out aloud in unison, '*Jumme ki raat hai, chumme ki baat hai*... It is Friday night, and we are deliberating over a kiss...' Conspicuously, there's not a single woman in the gathering to sing the song to.

'The first show on Eid is always full of this *chiller* [riff-raff] crowd, who come here to spend their *Eidi* [money gifted on Eid]. Women and family trickle in much later,' says Jameel.

Had it not been raining, the fans would have come to the theatre with a band playing Salman's hit songs, he tells you, adding, 'At the time of the release of *Tere Naam*, they even came in his get-up, sporting his distinct hairstyle from the film.'

It's 1.15p.m. and the crowd is already becoming impatient and unruly, waiting to buy the 3 p.m. show tickets. The queue is growing longer by the minute as the rain beats down harder. The filmgoers are restless and raring to go, even as cops are out with their batons to keep the roaring mob in control. The aggression is intimidating and the delirium, scary. It is apparently like this for a Bhai film every year. In fact, in 2003, on the day of *Tere Naam*'s release, there had been an accident at the theatre; the star's fans nearly broke an iron fence, injuring a few.

In stark contrast to this hysteria and frenzy unleashed in Salman fans at every one of his film releases is the distant, frosty reaction of the town's Bishnoi community, for whom protecting the environment is part of their religious doctrine. A deadpan Ram Nivas Budhnagar and an ever-smiling Puneet Jangu, two leading members of this prosperous and influential group of Vishnu worshippers, may look like a study in contrast, but are united in their unwillingness to forgive the film star for the environmental crimes he is believed to have committed in the city, back in 1998. He is alleged to have shot dead shy, harmless chinkaras and blackbucks – the hunting of both is banned in India under the Wildlife Protection Act of 1972 – in three separate incidents while he was in Jodhpur for the shooting of *Hum Saath Saath Hain*. Actors Tabu, Saif Ali Khan, Sonali Bendre and Neelam were named the co-accused in one of those incidents that had allegedly taken place on 1 October 1998 at Kankani village in the Guda Bishnoiyan area. Moreover, on two other occasions, on 27 September and 29 September 1998 respectively, Salman and his co-actors, including comedian Satish Shah, had allegedly gone hunting and killed a couple of chinkaras in Bhavad and another at Ghoda Farm House near Mathania village. Twenty years have passed, but the legal battles over these cases are still on and far from reaching any resolution.

Twenty years is a long time. Long enough for a memory to fade, long enough for marking a closure. But even 20 years later, Jodhpur is a town still deeply conflicted over the onscreen Bhai and the off-screen Salman Khan, with a long list of transgressions pinned to his name. On one side are his fanatic fans; on the other, the steadfast, dedicated Bishnois.

The Bishnois revere animal and plant life; in their world view, killing an animal or felling a tree is a sacrilege, punishable only by death. You can encounter their peaceful and unhurried world on the Jaipur highway, 20 km from Jodhpur. The ashram and temple of Jambeshwarji, the 15th-century patron saint of the Bishnoi community, are situated in Jajiwal Bishnoiyan in the Banad area. Jambeshwarji espoused 29 principles from which his disciples are believed to have derived their name: Bishnois, or the 'twenty-niners'. The drive through long stretches of *bajra* (pearl millet) fields feels more like a wildlife safari. The only sound one hears is the plaintive call of the peacock. Here, deer, blackbuck and chinkara, along with jackal, rabbits and nilgai, roam as freely and fearlessly as grazing cattle, even ambling into the ashram during the evening *arti*, looking for food. It's these protected deer that Salman Khan is alleged to have hunted, incurring the wrath of the Bishnoi community and leading to his initial arrest on their insistence.[4]

As soon as the first shot was fired, Salman was in trouble. Bishnois living close by rushed out of their houses and chased the actor's vehicle, a Gypsy, with seven of them astride three motorcycles. They noted down the Gypsy's number and have been relentlessly following the case ever since. In the absence of a definitive verdict, however, their frustration is mounting and they are, understandably, a trifle despondent.

'The court just keeps offering one date after and another and justice keeps getting delayed, but we are sure he will eventually be punished,' says Ram Nivas, alluding to Salman and the cases against him. 'It's a long struggle, but there is light at the end of the tunnel.'

Although five years have passed since I met him in 2014, I have kept in touch with him, following every new turn and development in the cases.

Four separate cases related to blackbuck and chinkara poaching had been filed against the actor. In the Arms Act case, he was accused of using two firearms with allegedly expired licences, but was acquitted. The appeal subsequently filed in the High Court by the Rajasthan government is pending at the time of this book going to press.

In the two cases in which Salman Khan was accused of killing a pair of chinkaras in Bhavad on 27 September 1998 and a third one in Ghoda Farm House in Mathania on 29 September, he was acquitted by the High Court. The state government subsequently filed a special writ petition in the Supreme Court.

The judgement on the fourth case, in which he was charged with hunting two blackbucks on 1 October 1998 at Kankani, was delivered on 5 April 2018, with a local court sentencing Salman Khan to five years' imprisonment. The court acquitted the co-accused, four other Hindi film actors – Saif Ali Khan, Tabu, Neelam and Sonali Bendre – and a local travel agent Dushyant Singh for lack of sufficient evidence.

A large number of Bishnois reportedly gathered outside the District Court in Jodhpur and raised slogans against the Bollywood actor when the judgement was announced. Some of them burst crackers, shouting that justice had been delivered, never imagining that they were, perhaps, celebrating their victory too soon. The sentence has since been suspended, pending appeal in the High Court.

At the time of my interaction with him in 2014, however, Ram Niwas has no way of foretelling these developments. He sounds hopeful as he says, '*Hum nigraani kar rahe hain.* We are keeping a watchful eye. We are working with the state government and Forest Department [on the pending appeals and the writ petitions] so that no effort is spared. We won't let go of Salman till the very end. We will fight till the end. We are not disillusioned.'

There is pride in his voice as he speaks of the Bishnois' passionate involvement with environmental issues and the effective information system they have in place to track down offenders who flout wildlife-protection laws. Almost every Bishnoi has a mobile phone handy and every family owns a motorbike. A couple of hundred members of their group can congregate in a jiffy on hearing of any hunting or poaching incident in their territory. Lawyers from the Bishnoi community come forward to help fight cases involving such incidents, free of charge. Politically, they dominate three of the eight Assembly constituencies in Jodhpur: Phalodi, Lohawat and Luni. Hence, their word can't be taken lightly.

Interestingly, the Bishnoi stronghold Luni, where Salman Khan was staying when the incident took place in 1998, had appealed to the actor so much that he wanted to build a house there. The case filed against him seems to have changed his perspective, however. He has come back to Jodhpur only for the hearings. Of course, the unforgiving Bishnois wouldn't have allowed him in otherwise. They had, in fact, protested, when he was invited as the state guest in Jaipur for a marathon in 2011.

'He has been an offender of the state and its people. So we protested against the move,' Ram Nivas tells me three years after that incident.

'If somebody destroys your house, you can't invite him over as a guest and be hospitable.'

Eventually, the star did arrive to flag off the marathon, but left almost immediately afterwards, without participating in the run.

The Bishnois insist, though, that there is nothing personal in their feud with Salman. Despite their anger over his poaching, no attempt has ever been made by the community to stall the release of his films in Jodhpur. Their only contention, it seems, is that he has flouted an environmental law and must be punished for it.

'He has been a repeat offender,' Ram Nivas firmly declares. 'There was direct evidence of his violation of the law. What Salman did was premeditated and planned, for thrills and fun.'

He makes no effort to hide his intense dislike of the star. He can't accept Bhai and the goodness he projects on screen. Forget watching his films in theatres, Ram Nivas switches channels if he sees Salman on television, even if it is in some obscure advertisement.

'I can't accept him as a good human being on screen when he has committed such crimes. I can't accept the show of artificiality he puts up on the screen,' he says, grim-faced and dour.

Puneet Jangu still regrets having watched the 1998 SRK–Kajol–Rani Mukerji–blockbuster *Kuch Kuch Hota Hai*, because he didn't know Salman would make a special appearance in the second half. There is an unmistakable note of glee in his voice as he shares the general perception in his circle that Nawazuddin Siddiqui, a consummate actor, had stolen Bhai's thunder in *Kick*.

Both the Bishnois are concerned about the message Salman sends out to his admirers.

'He is a public figure. His fans worship him. When they see him hunt, they get inspired to do the same,' Puneet observes.

Puneet may not be too wide of the mark. Mohammad Afzal, the head operator at the New Kohinoor, claims that the hunting cases have, ironically, made the star more popular in Jodhpur and helped him widen his fan base.

'The fact that he has been coming here occasionally for the hearings keeps him in the news and makes us connect more strongly with him,' he acknowledges.

The fandom surrounding Salman Khan was at its peak back in 2007, when the courtroom drama involving these cases was going through its most gripping phase. Every detail of the unfolding show was being discussed on Jodhpur's streets – from the colour of the *chikan* kurta Salman's then girlfriend Katrina Kaif had worn to the stubble on his brother Arbaaz Khan's face. Speculation was rife on how the actor would bear the oppressive heat in his cramped prison cell or whether he had struck up a rapport with his lifer cellmate Kishore Parekh. There was much concern over how he was managing to get by on basic meals of dal-roti and *chana-gur* in jail, how he would have to sleep on the floor and swat away mosquitoes under a single fan on a hot summer night. His bodyguard, Shera, had become the sleepy town's new superstar by association, so much so that he himself had to be provided with security personnel. And just about every Jodhpuri could identify the Khan family's official vehicle – the black Hyundai Terracan.

The Bishnoi's loathing of the superstar may seem as irrational as the unquestioning love his fans reserve for him, but Salman Khan is just the kind of star who evokes such extreme responses. It's evident in the catcalls and whistles you hear while watching a scene or two of *Kick* from New Kohinoor's projection room. There's not an inch of space in either of the two halls in the twin theatre, as extra benches and chairs have already been provided to accommodate the spillover crowd. His fans obviously see this enigmatic bad boy in an entirely different light. I ask a group of them about what they think of the hunting incident. The excuses exonerating Salman fly thick and fast: the media has been too harsh, he is not a professional hunter or poacher, he was a soft target for his detractors, because he is a celebrity, he was inveigled into hunting, he didn't shoot the animals at all... What do they like so much about him, I enquire, probing further. This time, the answers are equally prompt, equally impassioned: his well-muscled body, the way he delivers his lines, his dance moves, the way he fights... Quite clearly, everything about him!

'*Mazaa aata hai uski* filmein *dekh ke*, break *milta hai* life *se*. His films are fun to watch, and offer respite from the drudgery of day-to-day life,' says Narayan Singh, an autorickshaw driver who has Bhai's posters adorning his vehicle.

'His mix of action, comedy and dialogue *baazi* works big time in the small towns,' explains Shailesh Kapoor, CEO and founder, Ormax Media, a Mumbai-based media consulting firm.

Though he is as much a darling of the upper-crust, urban, elite, multiplex crowd, Salman Khan has traditionally been the undisputed hero of the so-called B- and C-centres, the star loved by the masses.

'Someone had once told us that people in the metros consume Salman as kitsch. They enjoy his unabashed honesty, his [apparent] lack of public finesse. He makes city folk feel liberated, because he is never scared of being who he wants to be. But they'll never be him. In the smaller towns, we felt the connection is much more visceral, as if he's a blood relative,' say Shabani Hassanwalia and Samreen Farooqui, directors of *Being Bhaijaan*, a documentary on Salman Khan's mind-boggling stardom in outlying Chhindwara and Nagpur in Madhya Pradesh, when I interview them for the article published in 2014 for *Outlook*.[5]

'A very large slice of Salman's traditional fan-base is comprised of those for whom the changes unleashed by the forces of globalisation did not accrue any immediate benefits. Provincial towns, suburban areas, urban slums and mohallas are spaces where Salman reigns,' writes Shohini Ghosh, professor at the AJK Mass Communication Research Centre, Jamia Millia Islamia, in *Caravan* magazine.[6]

'He is *hamara banda* [our man], the *nukkad* king of India,' social anthropologist Shiv Visvanathan is quoted as saying in *Outlook*.[7]

'He has been the dream of every adolescent from the marginalized quarters,' columnist-author Santosh Desai observes in the same article.

No wonder the troubled hero has often been called the icon of the 'lumpen proletariat'. Jodhpur, the second-largest town in Rajasthan, which is on the cusp of giant changes, with multiplexes and malls mushrooming all over, still retains a foothold in its more mofussil past and is one of the many pockets where Salman rules the roost. The only other actors who come remotely close are Ajay Devgn and Akshay Kumar.

The New Kohinoor audience, consisting largely of local, not so well-off Muslim youngsters, brings another facet of Salman's fandom to light. At a time when Islam seems to be a religion under scanner and its followers, loyalties are perpetually questioned, Salman has an added resonance among the lower middle-class and working-class mofussil Muslims. Shah Rukh Khan may have embraced his Muslim identity more openly in *Chak De! India* (2007), *My Name Is Khan* (2010) and the more recent *Raees* (2017), but it's Salman they seem to identify with.

'The anxiety suffered by the ordinary Muslim – who could be randomly targeted for interrogation, torture and incarceration merely on the basis of suspicion – found reflection, as it were, in the unpredictable vicissitudes that beset Salman Khan. Salman's ability to survive the odds may explain why among his billion fans, under-privileged Muslims form a devoted constituency,' writes Shohini Ghosh in the *Caravan*.

Referring to the actor's films in the same essay, she writes: 'Straddling the borderlines of legality and criminality, the protagonists in these films confront a world of moral anarchy.'

They either live in a moral vacuum or are themselves tainted. In innumerable comedies like *Maine Pyaar Kyun Kiya* and *No Entry*, both 2005 releases with Salman in the lead, the protagonist is the naughty man-child or man-boy, whose jokes border on the risqué and the offensive; but somehow, he gets away with all his trespasses on the strength of his cheekily charming smile. Then there are the violent action turns. Take rowdy Radhe Mohan of *Tere Naam* (2003), who is so addicted to violence that even while romancing his lady love, he adopts strategies that are geared to intimidate her. Relentless in his efforts to win her over, he even abducts her and eventually, she responds to his overtures. But fate intervenes and he becomes a victim of violence himself, ending up in a mental health institution.

Given the huge success of *Tere Naam* and the near cult status the character enacted by Salman Khan acquired after its release, even inspiring his young male fans to flaunt the same long, lank hairstyle, it is hardly surprising that when the actor played the lead in *Wanted* (2009), his character was also called Radhe. Here again is a man whom a girl would hesitate to associate with, let alone take home to her parents. Yet, Radhe, a hired killer, mysteriously manages to attract the heroine. Such 'moral anarchy' on the character's part and the easy leeway he gets, despite all the hideous crimes he has committed, holds true as well for the real-life persona of the actor who plays him. Salman Khan's on-screen identity is often mirrored in his bad-boy image in real life.

'[E]ven at the best of times, Salman Khan walks a risky tightrope. There is no telling when he will slip and fall,' writes Ghosh.

Ultimately, the key to his star persona lies, perhaps, in his unpredictability, in the bundle of contradictions he seems to represent.

'His stardom is a collage of confusions,' says Shiv Visvanathan in *Outlook*.

He's ruthless, yet affectionate; intimidating, yet caring. On the one hand, the actor might drive rashly and (allegedly) kill a person sleeping on the pavement; on the other, he runs Being Human, a Mumbai-based charity for the underprivileged. Salman is known to charge a royal pay packet for his various public appearances, but none of it supposedly goes into his own account; it allegedly funds his social work. He can endear himself to women with his protective nature and put them off just as easily by cracking an unseemly joke on rape. Take his tumultuous relationship with Aishwarya Rai, who had claimed that he was harassing her after their breakup in 2002. Things came to such a pass that a police complaint was lodged against him. Along with fame, notoriety has been his constant companion.

'The dark side of him represents the complexity of our times,' Ghosh writes in the *Caravan*.

'He's primordial and flawed,' says Visvanathan in *Outlook*.

'It is this imperfect, flawed persona of Salman that attracts his fans,' say documentary filmmakers Hassanwalia and Farooqui in the interview I conducted for *Outlook* in 2014. '[It] Makes him more human, more accessible. He has made mistakes, risen from failure and conquered. And we, especially in India, have always worshipped and forgiven our gods and leaders. Salman is yet another example.'

So while the split between the Bishnois and his fans in Jodhpur may come across as extreme, it is the attendant ambivalence that makes Salman Khan the star he is. More so in mofussil India.

Fans and Fandoms

JODHPUR MIGHT BE DIVIDED on the real–reel binary in Salman Khan's life and persona, but an individual in Lucknow has been steadfast in his devotion to Shah Rukh Khan, regardless of whether the actor acknowledges – let alone reciprocates – the affection or not.

Ordinary Joe Vishal Singh is actually quite extraordinary. His mobile ringtone is '*Tujhe dekha toh yeh jaana, sanam, Pyaar hota hai deewana, sanam.* The moment I saw you, my love, I knew that love was sheer madness' – one of the many popular numbers from the 1995 SRK–Kajol–starrer *Dilwale Dulhania Le Jaayenge* (*DDLJ*) that went on to become a huge box-office success and led to the stars being paired opposite each other in many more romantic films. The exteriors of Singh's three-storeyed house and his two cars are plastered with posters of the latest Shah Rukh Khan film. We had met him when *Happy New Year*, a 2014 heist film with an ensemble cast featuring the actor, was just around the corner. Not only were the Diwali lights adorning the walls of Singh's home arranged to spell out 'Happy New Year', those bedecking the house itself were similarly strung. In the course of time, it would have got a *Dilwale* and *Fan* upgrade in keeping with the star's subsequent releases in 2015 and 2016. At the time this book was being written, the Singh residence was awaiting a fresh facelift with the arrival of *Raees* in 2017, the next SRK release co-starring Pakistani actress Mahira Khan. He also sends me pictures of the residence and the car that have been done up with the posters of *Zero*, a 2018 release with, naturally, SRK in the lead.

Vishal Singh's love story with his wife, Ruchi, has also had its SRK moments. He wooed her *Deewana* style, right down to using that famous line the character played by Shah Rukh resorts to in a bid to win over Divya Bharti, in the role of his lady love: '*Kya Karoon? Jaan de doon?* What should I do? Lay down my life for you?' At Ruchi's brother's wedding, Singh asked her parents for their daughter's hand in marriage and won them over by going into *DDLJ* mode. The honeymoon involved a long drive from Lucknow to 'Mannat' – SRK's home – in Mumbai to meet the star. Singh named his son Raj Aryan, combining SRK's most-popular onscreen avatar with the name of the star's own son, and his daughter's name Simran was inspired by the character Kajol plays in *DDLJ*.

Every year, this ardent SRK fan waits enthusiastically for 2 November. Singh celebrates the day, like he would a festival, with his family and friends.

'It's my Eid, Diwali, Christmas, Holi, all rolled into one,' he says happily.

All because it is Shah Rukh Khan's birthday. The day's rituals are fixed: Singh performs a havan in the morning, praying for the star's long life, and rounds it off by cutting a cake in the evening.

'My only request to god is that Shah Rukh should always remain the King Khan of Bollywood, and his films should keep breaking box-office records,' he says.

There's not an inch of space in his life – physical or emotional, personal or official – that hasn't been taken over by Shah Rukh Khan. Even his online existence, be it on WhatsApp or Facebook, is entirely dedicated to SRK; there is precious little about Singh himself. His internalization of SRK's identity is scarily complete to the extent that Singh has even legally rechristened himself 'Vishahrukh'.

'Call me Vishahrukh,' he insists.

We do.

Singh confesses to having had it tough in life. He was forced to leave home in Hardoi, UP, when he was very young and still doesn't have much of family support to fall back on. Somewhere, SRK seems to have turned into a surrogate family for him, that offers him long-distance succour and has added a splash of Eastmancolour to his otherwise humdrum, black-and-white existence.

Singh's SRK obsession was born in the late '80s, while watching the actor in television serials like *Circus*, *Fauji* and *Dil Dariya*. *Deewana* (1992), the actor's debut film, in which he played the second male lead – the first being Rishi Kapoor – opposite the late Divya Bharti, took the fan's fixation to the next level.

'I loved his hairstyle,' Singh reminisces. 'I used to put a music system in my bike and play, "*Koi na koi chahiye hum pe marne walla.* I need someone who will love me to death," while driving. Just like he sings in *Deewana*.'

The initial craze has now grown into something of a personal faith and philosophy. Singh is convinced there was something uncanny and miraculous about the fact that his wife was expecting their daughter at the same time that SRK's wife, Gauri, was pregnant with Aryan. He strongly believes that even the cancerous growth on his kidney that was detected some years ago was cured thanks to his unwavering faith in the star.

'He is the sun of my solar system. I keep getting my energy and strength from him,' he maintains. 'Twenty-four years of my life have been devoted to him and I have never let my dedication fade away.'

Enter Singh's house in Lucknow and SRK's presence becomes all-pervasive – to the exclusion of every other person or object. The last time I visited his house in 2013, Singh had over 20,000 photos of the star on display. They stare back at you from the walls, the ceiling, the fans and the lights, even the television set and the swimming pool-sized bathtub in his children's room. The kitsch here is larger than life and more surreal than what you might see on a 70 mm screen. The SRK bubble he lives in and his complete identification with the star is not merely disconcerting; it's eerie.

The whole house is a monument to love, a Taj Mahal, as it were, dedicated to none other than Shah Rukh Khan. Singh calls it, predictably, Shah Rukh Palace. The mansion's top-floor hall has been converted into a mandir of sorts, where the presiding deity is the star himself.

'It will be a museum where I will store every little thing that has anything to do with Shah Rukh,' says the fan.

All he wishes and hopes for is that the star should come and visit some day, and approve and bless his home.

Though Singh has made SRK the crowning glory of his life, he isn't quite the star's lookalike the way Gaurav of *Fan* was. Neither in appearance nor in his mannerisms. There is no attempt either to be so. He isn't about to make a living out of parroting the famous 'K-k-k-k-Kiran' line from *Darr* (1993), a Shah Rukh Khan–Juhi Chawla–Sunny Deol starrer, in which SRK, an obsessive lover, has a distinctive stammer. Vishahrukh Singh is not the kind of guy you could pick out in a sea of humanity. In one word, he is nondescript, like the millions of others on the streets of India. And yet, he is a Lucknow celeb, featured among the Page 3 glitterati of the City of Nawabs, all because of his SRK *bhakti*. At one time, the organized group of SRK fans in and around Lucknow used to consist of approximately 100 to 150 members. Under Singh's stewardship, however, the group has grown almost sixfold over the years.

'With WhatsApp and Facebook, my SRK fan community has grown into the thousands,' he says proudly.

Contemplating his almost religious zeal for anything to do with SRK, you can't help but wonder if that is what being truly, madly and deeply in love is all about.

However, Singh is quite precise in spelling out the difference between being a fan and a clone. There is an obvious pride in him having an identity of his own, albeit under SRK's looming shadow.

'I have my own business and a successful one at that,' he says.

The innumerable boxes of the Reckeweg homeopathy medicines that Vishahrukh Singh has a wholesale business of are inscribed with Shah Rukh Khan's name, and his own company is called Shah Rukh Force. Singh recently launched a production house, also called Shah Rukh Force, to make a movie on the star and his impact on people. Tentatively titled *Hum Bhi Shah Rukh*, it will feature interviews with a host of Lucknow-based theatre artistes and capture their views on how much the star has influenced them.

'Even my CA and banker friends talk about how they are inspired by his energy and six packs at the age of 50,' Singh confides.

He was hoping to organize the film's mahurat on a large scale in the presence of the star and Akhilesh Yadav, who as chief minister of Uttar Pradesh had been promoting Bollywood film shoots in the state during his tenure. Yadav has subsequently been succeeded by Yogi Adityanath as the state's CM.

Though Singh watched *Fan* four times, one show after another, on the day of its release with 120 other SRK fans for company in Lucknow's Wave multiplex, he isn't happy with the portrayal of the fan as an obsessive creature. Nor can he wrap his head around the fact that in the film, the star doesn't save the fan, but lets him pass into oblivion.

'If it were for real, Shah Rukh Gaurav *ko bacha lete.* Shah Rukh would have saved Gaurav,' he states with conviction.

Vishahrukh Singh had quite clearly seen himself on screen as he watched the film and is taking the piece of fiction too personally.

'*Hamari chahat mein farq hai.* There is a difference in our love for the star,' he is at pains to point out. 'The fans can never turn negative.'

The day I visit him in Lucknow, Singh is feeling spurned by the star. As I get to know him better over the years, I will come to realize that this is a running thread in his love story.

Though Singh had met the star several times in the past, both in Mumbai and when Shah Rukh Khan came to Lucknow for film promotions, there have, in recent times, been many attempts on the fan's part to meet his idol – all unsuccessful, due to the apparent lack of cooperation from the actor's staff. Perhaps, something has annoyed the star, Singh wonders aloud, when we meet at Shah Rukh Palace. Or is he, the fan, getting too possessive and irksome for the star to handle, I speculate silently. He recalls his last meeting with SRK, when the star had come to Lucknow to promote *Don 2*, a 2011 release. Singh had tried to spend almost every waking moment with him, posed for pictures with him wherever he went in Lucknow. But the star had still not visited his Shah Rukh Palace.

Then there was his failed attempt to meet SRK in Dubai at a live concert on 1 December 2013. Reaching the star's associate and friend Karim Morani was as close as he could get to the man himself.

'*Kadam kadam pe saath hote hue bhi nahin mil paa rahe hain.* So close and yet so far,' Singh sighs, wistful and dejected.

For a long time, it had been almost as if Krishna were eluding his Meera or Radha. Life had been all about *viraha rasa*. Of separation and yearning. Of not being able to meet his deity, but worshipping him from afar. Singh, however, corrects me on the analogy, likening himself to Sudama in his relation to SRK's Krishna and laying claim, thereby, to a certain equality in his equation with the star; which he regards as friendship, rather than the more obvious fan–star connection, where his position is a subservient one in the hierarchical order.

I speak to Vishahrukh Singh a few days before SRK's 50th birthday on 2 November 2015.

'It'll be like a once-in-a-lifetime event, a *maha kumbh*, for me,' he says.[8]

Fifty of the star's fans are intending to party in Lucknow on 1 November, right up till midnight. The party menu? Chilli paneer, fried rice, chowmein, chocolate cake and Frooti, a brand SRK endorses.

Vishahrukh Singh tells me that he is packing his suitcase to fly to Mumbai after the party with a 42 foot-long foldable birthday card that he plans to unfurl outside SRK's home, Mannat. Made of paper and vinyl, it will contain messages for the star and his fans' best wishes, along with an invitation to visit Singh's home in Lucknow. In the evening, he will meet the star personally at Taj Land's End in a fan event organized by the film trade magazine *Box Office India*.

Singh calls up again after leaving Mumbai. He is, indeed, one of the many fans whom SRK met. However, that exclusive one-on-one that could have made him feel special, that could have elevated his status to that of the fan above all other fans, remains elusive.

'*Unse milne ki chaah mein boodhe hote jaa rahe hain.* In my hankering to meet him, I am getting older by the day,' he says, sounding a bit forlorn.

A year later, out of the blue, I get a call from him again. He is in Mumbai with his wife and two kids, staying in a hotel on Hill Road in Bandra, that is as close to Mannat as he could possibly get. Most of his days, evenings and nights are spent in the Barista at Bandstand, waiting to get a call from the star to meet him. He is using anybody and everybody he knows – from SRK's wife Gauri's *mamaji* (uncle) to the security guard – to gain access to the star. Doesn't the fact that he is being denied a personal meeting for so long now rile him, I ask, a little frazzled myself at the actor's persistent denial of an audience. Doesn't it make his faith in SRK waver? It does hurt, Singh concedes, but he prefers to blame the situation on the actor's staff, rather than on the man himself.

'*Bhagwan tak aapko pujari hi toh le jaata hai, na*? It's the priest who leads you to god, right?'

'What is a fan?' I ask Shah Rukh Khan in an interview before the release of *Fan*.

'The one who will love me no matter what I do,' he replies promptly.

Vishahrukh Singh seems to fit the bill. He finds something positive even in being denied an audience with King Khan.

'It has made me meet so many people, increased my social circle,' he says of his efforts to gain access to his idol. 'Otherwise, I would have remained a frog in the well in Lucknow.'

Then, one fine day, just before he is about to board his flight back to

Lucknow, I get a WhatsApp message from Vishahrukh Singh. The star has met him, signed on an especially designed T-shirt, posed for family pictures and even agreed to work in the film that his fan is planning to make on him. Singh quotes a few words, summing up what he has been telling me since we last met; it is apparently something that Shirdi Sai Baba had told his followers: *shraddha, saburi*. At the altar he has set up in praise of SRK, all that's stood Singh in good stead is faith and patience. And then he adds an SRK layer to it.

'Didn't he say in *Om Shanti Om* that "*Agar kisi cheez ko shiddat se chaho toh puri kayanaat tumhein usse milvane par lag jaati hai*? If you desire something with all your heart, the universe conspires to bring you together"?'

The latest from him is a round of images sent on WhatsApp. SRK met him and his family again when he was in Lucknow for the promotions of *Zero*. The star couldn't, however, visit Shah Rukh Palace, the Taj Mahal that Singh has built in his honour. Is this finally the happy ending to the star–fan saga I have been a witness to over the years that I have known both? Or is it one of the many ups in the ongoing tale? Watch this space.

Pondering over the story, I have to confess that for a rational person like me, Vishahrukh Singh is someone to look askance at. Is his obsession with SRK the outcome of a misplaced sense of self, I wonder. Or is he transferring his own consciousness on to the film star? All I can deduce is that obsession or not, his reverence for Shah Rukh is innocent, unquestioning and sustained by nothing more than a desire for a nod, an acknowledgement from the star.

'Otherwise,' Singh sighs, 'who would care for a homoeopathic medicine dealer in Lucknow?'

My meetings with Singh leave me wondering if the model of fandom he embodies is uniform across India, or even the world, cutting across class, caste, religion and other divides. How does a fan in Lucknow vary from one in Mumbai? The question plays in my head as I travel on to meet another fan in Bhopal.

There is great confidence and certitude in the manner in which Moin Khan guides me to our meeting place.

'There is the famous Afghan Hotel in Peer Gate in Old Bhopal. You get off there and ask anyone. *Saara sheher mujhe* "Purane Bhopal ke John" *ke naam se jaanta hai.* The whole of Bhopal knows me as "Old Bhopal's John Abraham",' he says, playing on the iconic line yesteryear actor Ajit had delivered in his role as the villain in the 1976 Shatrughan Sinha–starrer *Kalicharan*: '*Saara sheher mujhe* Loin *ke naam se jaanta hai*.'

From the unmistakable swagger in his stance, it is clear that Moin fancies himself as the provincial version of Bollywood action hero John Abraham.

His confidence in his fame is not misplaced, I discover. Hunting out a stranger in an unfamiliar city had never been as easy for me as it is in tracing 'Old Bhopal's John'. The very first person I bump into at Peer Gate leads me to him.

Soon enough, I find myself staring hard at him, unconsciously trying to spot the differences – and the similarities – between him and the actor he has modelled himself after.

'My side face is just like him, isn't it?' he asks rhetorically, showing me his profile.

Is he projecting the star in himself? Is it Abraham's borrowed face that gives Moin his identity and his local fans, I wonder cynically, while admitting to myself that the resemblance is, indeed, uncanny.

Well, not quite. While Moin might look like the actor, he doesn't necessarily want to follow in his footsteps.

The Bhopal resident's love for John (whom he said 'hello' to and shook hands with briefly when the star was in town) doesn't manifest itself in mimicry or impersonation.

'*Bheed mein pehchaan di hai* John *ne.* Thanks to my resemblance to John, I stand out in a crowd,' says Moin. 'But I don't want to be an actor like him.'

John Abraham might be his calling card, but there's more to Moin than merely being the actor's doppelgänger. It makes this star–fan equation a refreshing departure from the usual formulaic one etched in my mind (and embodied, to an extent, by Vishahrukh Singh): of blind faith and worship, of seeking an alternate reality and refuge in the star, away from his own all-enveloping shabby reality. The star is more like a proxy friend here. The one who, as Moin puts it, 'adds more colour to my life'.

The vast, bare hall where we are now sitting is the place where he practises his passions: catwalk and body building. Having been crowned Mr Bhopal thrice, Moin prefers to be what John started off as: a model. He has modelled for Levis and Bajaj events, appeared in shows, and launches in and around Bhopal, and also in Raipur and Bilaspur. He walked the ramp at Dehradun Fashion Week. Even here in Bhopal, it's not the big ticket he is gunning for; small, provincial fashion assignments will do.

'Rather than struggle [to achieve success] in big cities, I want to be the king of my small town,' he says.

With John as the guru and guide, of course.

'He inspires me to do good work,' Moin acknowledges.

There's a certain contentment and cheerfulness about him that stem from a secure financial background; from the fact that modelling is more a hobby than a means of livelihood that puts dal and rice on the family table. For that, there's the family business. Afghan Hotel, set up by his grandfather 56 years ago, is famous in Bhopal for its fried fish and has recently expanded its operations by opening three more branches in the city.

'All thanks to Allah,' says Moin, adding cheekily, 'and John.'

A few more days in the town and I realize that Moin is not the only John Abraham lookalike; Bhopal is teeming with them. The cult surrounding Abraham started with a film released in 2004: *Dhoom*. Which is around the time Moin also obtained his membership to the fan club.

'I already had long hair like John then. I just got them [it] straightened,' he recalls.

But why *Dhoom*, of all the Bollywood blockbusters, I enquire, intrigued. Bikes, is the curious answer.

Bhopal is a city obsessed with motor sports; that is, bike and car racing. Also, for long, it has been the capital of auto modification and customization; jeeps, cars and bikes are given magnificent makeovers in Bhopal. So John, as Kabir, the mobike-riding baddie in *Dhoom*, clicked instantly with the audience here. Since then, it has inspired many youngsters to take to bike stunts. Bhopal's biker gangs – Four Star Bikers India, Bhopal Biker Boys, among others – have mushroomed across the city, performing stunts around midnight on the road running around the local lake. They have even left their prints online as Facebook fan pages, fetching thousands of 'likes'.

Babar Khan, a big name, was part of *MTV Stunt Mania*. Syed Adil Kazmi went on to appear on the television show *Emotional Atyachar* on UTV Bindaas. Both Babar and Adil, like Moin, are photocopies of Abraham. It may have no particular significance, but there is surely something noteworthy in the fact that all three men, along with most of the others struck by the John-'n-Bike mania, are Muslims. Locals tell me that 95 per cent of those who get their jeeps customized are also Muslims.

'It's like a tradition and [a] hobby with them,' says Sushil Shukla, the Bhopal-based editor of the famous children's magazine *Chakmak*.

On the face of it, they seem more obsessed with films and stars than the city's other communities.

Moin explains it in greater detail. Most of these Muslim boys come from rich, landed families. Business is good and there is no dearth of money.

'But we get to study in Urdu-medium schools. Our education leaves a lot to be desired. So we end up with other passions,' he elaborates. 'These hobbies then become a way of asserting ourselves. *Kisi tarah se toh naam kamayein*. At least, we should try and stand out, be noticed in some way.'

So as to have an impact beyond the narrow confines of the neighbourhood and the city of Bhopal.

As for Vishahrukh Singh, for Moin too, the star himself and the fandom he has inspired are conduits to the larger world that would otherwise have been out of reach. On that note, he shows off his two R15s (in cherryred and yellow), a white ZMR and a new white CBR 250.

'All I want now is a Hayabusa,' he declares.

God – and John – willing!

Local Lore

NO GOOD RELATIONSHIP CAN ever be a one-way street. If mofussil India looks up to Bollywood for its role models and for more than just a willing suspension of disbelief, Mumbai's Tinseltown has had its own robust connection with the grass roots. More than just telling the stories of characters from small towns and bringing them alive, it has brought some hitherto obscure, unknown places into the limelight by turning them into iconic locales for popular films. Like the Apta railway station on the Panvel–Roha route of Central Railways. It was on this very platform that the famous last scene of Shah Rukh Khan's *Dilwale Dulhania Le Jayenge* (1995) was shot. The Kareena Kapoor–Shahid Kapoor–Fardeen Khan–starrer *Fida*; *Swades*, with SRK in the lead; *Once Upon a Crime*, starring Shahid Kapoor, Kareena Kapoor and Akshaye Khanna – all 2004 releases – *Bunty aur Babli* (2005), a commercial success with Rani Mukerji and Abhishek Bachchan in the lead roles, and *Rang De Basanti* (2006), with Aamir Khan heading the ensemble cast, are the other films that have been shot in Apta. Its centrality to Bollywood endures. In fact, in the financial year 2015–2016, it earned the highest revenue – ₹32 lakh – for the Central Railways through the film shoots of 18 productions.[9] Close to Mumbai, yet not crowded, and quite affordable – it costs ₹50,000 to ₹60,000 per day to shoot there, a mere pittance compared to the ₹1.25 crore a day that a film unit could run up for shooting at the bigger stations – it has become the favourite location for shooting train/platform sequences. In fact, the last film to have been shot here was Tiger Shroff's *Baaghi* (2016).

Just as perfect casting can make the performances in a film and, in turn, the film itself come alive, so can the right location. Most often, getting the location right can be an important reason for a film and a place to become famous, and fit each other like a hand in a glove. Like *Sholay* and Ramanagaram (also called Ramanagara).

It's only after having beaten Bengaluru's infamous traffic, all the way from the airport to the Mysuru highway, that our driver, Ravi Kumar, now relaxing over a breakfast of *chow chow bhaath* and filter coffee, introduces his little town Ramanagaram.

'It is the place where *Sholay* was shot,' he announces proudly.

He was yet to be born then and had only recently viewed the classic. But Ravi Kumar is familiar with all the key spots where the film was shot. It's almost like a piece of folklore in his family, passed down from one generation to the next. At the 5 km milestone, he slows down, cautiously edging the car to the left of the road, and points out the Ramdevara Hill, a group of rocky outposts in the distance to our right.

'Those are the *Sholay* hills,' he says proudly.

There is a practised precision to this act; you know right away that he has done the same with every outsider he's ferried into town.

There is a small town by the name of Ramgarh near Ranchi, but filmmaker Ramesh Sippy chose Ramanagaram, 50 km south-west of Bengaluru (then Bangalore), for his fictional Ramgarh. The entire village – the Thakur's house on the top, the water tank, the Holi maidan, the Shiv mandir – was set up there, and *Sholay* became the first Hindi dacoit film to have been shot in the South (previously, all shootings for similar films had been confined to the Chambal ravines or Rajasthan's dunes). In *Bollybook: The Big Book of Hindi Movie Trivia*, Diptakirti Chaudhuri identifies the references to the real places in *Sholay* – Jabalpur, Meerut, Moradabad. So though the film was shot in a fictional Ramgarh set up in Ramanagaram, its presumed location was the badlands of Uttar Pradesh.

There is a fascinating account in Anupama Chopra's book *Sholay: The Making of a Classic* about how art director Ram Yedekar spent an entire month in the South in his car, with his driver and cook for company, scouting locations for the film. The final toss-up was between Tumakuru and Ramanagaram.

'"It captured my imagination," he [Ramesh Sippy, the film's director] says. "I was fascinated." [Cinematographer Dwarka] Divecha cast his eagle eye on the location and confirmed the decision.'

As you approach the town, you begin to understand why it was the chosen one. Quite obviously, the topography. The looming rocky hills, the granite outcrops, the daunting boulders and the flat, desolate stretches – nothing else could have created a more menacing den for Gabbar Singh; no other locale could have so vividly represented the endangered home environment of Thakur and his villagers. But in making a reel Ramgarh out of the real Ramanagaram, director Ramesh Sippy also had to construct a road all the way from the highway into the then poorly connected rural town. After all, you need a place to be accessible enough to shoot there.

In becoming the face of Ramgarh, Ramanagaram obscures the importance of another noteworthy film. Ramdevara Betta, aka the '*Sholay* hills', had also served as the location for David Lean's *A Passage to India*. Small entrances were blasted in the rocks to simulate the openings to the caves for the key sequence involving Dr Aziz Ahmed (played by Victor Banerjee) and Adela Quested (with Judy Davis in the role), leading up to the accusation of rape levelled against Aziz. The guides point out those openings to you on the climb up. The crevices in the rocks are the nesting sites for the rare long-billed vultures. The Ram temple on the way has 1,000-odd steps to huff and puff on all the way to the top.

Other than that, there is nothing particularly remarkable to soak in. Late Bollywood actor Raaj Kumar's farmhouse lies in the vicinity; well-known south Indian film actor Prakash Raj's is just a kilometre away – the nuggets of information keep coming as you take the '*filmi*' walk. Had it not been for this special connect with films, Ramanagaram would have been just another blink-and-you-miss-it town that you zipped past while driving along the highway. Unlike the approach to it through landscape that comes across as brooding, even menacing – an appropriate locale for Gabbar Singh's hideout – the physical ordinariness of the town itself is compensated for by the colourful stories and out-of-the-ordinary lore that emerge from it.

But there is more to Ramanagaram than *Sholay* and *A Passage to India*. Headquarters of the Ramanagaram district, the town is known for sericulture and has been nicknamed 'Silk Town'. With its seven hills, it is also a centre for adventure sports, like rock climbing, mountaineering and trekking. Waters sports happen around the nearby Kanva Dam. We see crowds of youngsters in small groups making maximum use of their weekend by taking to the many sports on offer. Watching them, I wonder if they aren't too young to even know of and understand the magic of *Sholay* that had brought me there.

With the film in mind, it's only fit that I should chance upon a stunt school blooming in the shadow of the hills: Sahasa Kala Shikshana Kendra, established in 2006.

'What better place to have a stunts academy!' declares its owner-manager Hassan Raghu, an ex-defence personnel and former stunt master of south Indian films, who began his career as a stunt master in 1980 with veteran Putta Kanagal's *Ranganayaki*. He did the action sequences for those portions of Sanjay Khan's television serial *The Sword of Tipu Sultan* that were shot in Mysuru and was given a special award by the Karnataka government for his stunts work in the 1985 film *Accident*, directed by the late Shankar Nag. A landmark Kannada film, its plot is eerily similar to the real-life hit-and-run case involving Salman Khan.

Though the academy offers all-round comprehensive training to actors, stunt artistes and fight masters, along with theatre artistes and defence and police personnel, anyone who wants to learn martial arts is welcome to enroll for admission here. The focus is on indigenous martial-arts forms, like *kushti*, *kalari*, *malla khamb*, and so on. It's a rustic set-up. No fancy equipment here at all. What you do find is the *akhada*s. There are also free hostels for tribal kids from economically weaker backgrounds. Moreover, the centre organizes a national Shaurya Diwas every year and hopes to become a deemed university soon. A show is quickly put up for us by the team; it involves combat with canes, poles and chains. Pehelwan Anand breaks a solid rock with a one-hand chop and then pulls a jeep forward with his teeth. You gape at his feats and ask Raghu if such stunts aren't the reason for too much violence in our films.

Pat comes his reply: 'It is not about blood and blasts and flying cars; it is about artistry and thrill. It is an art form like music and dance. Otherwise, *Sholay* would not be the classic that it is.'

Ramanagaram is not the only place to gain popularity post *Sholay*. Most often, film locations, especially those used as a backdrop for the song-and-dance routines, turn into instant tourist destinations for curious viewers.

The Athirapally Falls have been much sought after in the wake of

Mani Ratnam's 2007 film *Guru* that was ostensibly inspired by the life of industrialist Dhirubhai Ambani, and starred Abhishek Bachchan, Aishwarya Rai, R Madhavan and Vidya Balan, among others, and the same director's Abhishek Bachchan–Aishwarya Rai–Vikram–starrer *Raavan*, that released in 2010.

Chapora Fort in Vagator, Goa, became the go-to place after the 2001 release of Farhan Akhtar's *Dil Chahta Hai*, an Aamir Khan starrer that was a stupendous box-office success.

Pangong Lake in Ladakh began attracting Indian visitors because of the song '*Satrangi re*', picturized in another Mani Ratnam film *Dil Se* (1988), and the Bollywood blockbuster *3 Idiots*, with Aamir Khan in the lead, which was partly shot there, helping boost tourism in the region. In fact, several 'Rancho' restaurants (named after the lead character played by Aamir Khan) are reported to have sprung up after the film's release in 2009.

The stepwells in the 2006 Shah Rukh Khan–Rani Mukerji–starrer *Paheli* prompted people to take an interest in Hadi Rani ki Baori in Todaraisingh, which is approximately 140 km from Jaipur.

Some places are still mining the movies to drive tourism. Every juice and snack stall in Goa's Dona Paula is named after Rohit Shetty's Ajay Devgn–starrer *Singham*, released in 2011. The film's famous action sequence of cars being blown away was shot here. However, the location's first brush with *filmi* fame had come much earlier, with *Ek Duuje ke Liye*, a tragic love story in the Romeo-and-Juliet format, starring Kamal Haasan and Rati Agnihotri. Large chunks of the film that would become one of the top grossers of 1981 were shot in Dona Paula.

'Today movie show: *Octopussy*. Tomorrow: *Octopussy*' is a common message on billboards in the cafés around Udaipur's Lake Pichola. Significant segments of the James Bond movie *Octopussy* were shot in Udaipur in 1982 at the Lake Palace Hotel, Shiv Niwas Palace Hotel, Jagmandir Island Palace Hotel and Monsoon Palace Hotel, and it is still shown every evening at these cafés. The idea is to be introduced to the locations in the movie and then take a guided tour through them to experience the reality behind the reel world.

Quite like Ramanagaram after the release of *Sholay*, Bhadwai, a small village in Raisen district, 70 km from Bhopal, caught the media's attention on 'becoming' Peepli village in the Aamir Khan–produced *Peepli Live*, Anusha Rizvi's directorial debut in 2010, that featured an actor who would take another two years to become a much-sought-after face with the Vidya Balan–starrer *Kahani*: Nawazuddin Siddiqui. Chosen after seven days of location hunting through 35 villages, Bhadwai was found to be a perfect fit for Peepli. Home to 1,500 people – mostly farmers, labourers and daily-wage earners, both Hindu and Muslim – it was discovered to be suffering from deprivations and facing dilemmas similar to those depicted in the film. It appeared to be a perfect microcosm for the film's theme. Though just hours away from the state capital Bhopal, I discovered that Bhadwai had no proper access roads. Here, electricity played truant for much of the day and there were no taps for water to flow from, because residents had been unable to fork out the ₹1,000 that was required as the installation charge. Higher education remained a distant dream for most girls in Bhadwai because for kilometres around there was no institution where they could continue their schooling after Class VIII. As for local healthcare, a stark picture of the lack of medical facilities emerged when I spoke to villager Kishenlal for an article for *Outlook*.[10]

'If you are seriously ill,' he quipped, his characteristic black humour intact, 'you go all the way to Bhopal; and if you die on the way, you just take a U-turn back to Bhadwai.'

Later, while in Bhopal in 2014, location manager Anoop Joshi remembered the shooting of the film as a community experience, in which the cast, crew and village participated together.

'It wasn't about stars locking themselves up in their vanity vans, but mingling with each other and the villagers,' said Joshi.

Some, like Raghubir Yadav, would sit by the Bhadwai pond for hours together. A man of the soil himself, he regularly had his meals with the villagers and sang along with the local *bhajan mandali*.

'Every person and household was involved [in] some way or the other with the film,' Joshi recalls.

No extras were used and the villagers filled in instead. However, they were not aware of being integrated in the shots. Even their colourful '*bhat-sooar*' (the local name for a 12-seater passenger tempo) found a place in the film.

Much work was done while the crew was around. The narrow lane leading up to the village was widened and tarred to provide access for heavy trucks and equipment into the village. A dilapidated madrassa was renovated to fill in as a base camp, and makeshift bathrooms were built for the crew, to be used later by the villagers themselves.

I found the residents of Bhadwai touchingly nostalgic about those two months when the film unit had taken over their village and their lives, giving them more to look forward to than just the daily grind. Eagerly watching the film's promos on television and hearing its songs on FM, they were also hoping against hope that *Peepli Live* would do what the government and the administration had not been able to for generations – change their lives for the better. Alas, it didn't. The film turned out to be a pipe dream for them. And the villagers' brush with modernity and progress was short-lived. No wonder they call cinema a 'dream factory'. You have to wake up from dreams eventually, and see the real behind the reel.

At first glance, Wai feels like an open-air Filmistan or Mehboob Studio. Get off the Mumbai–Satara bus and it's like you have landed straight on to a busy film set: a man running with the lights here, another rushing off with a camera there. Reflectors, bouncers, diffusers and boxes full of expensive cinema equipment that a layman would be clueless about lie casually on the roads. Several film shoots are on, I'm told, the biggest of them being Prabhu Deva's untitled production with Shahid Kapoor, which, much after my Wai visit, gets released as *R... Rajkumar*.

Wai town, in the Satara district of Maharashtra, is said to have come into existence in the 1700s, and the Pandavas, of Mahabharata, are believed to have lived here. In those days, it was called Viraatnagari. The 17th-century warlord from Bijapur, Afzal Khan, is believed to have made his first halt here on his way to battle it out with Shivaji. In fact, till date, Wai celebrates Krishnabai Utsav, a festival to mark the Maratha warrior king's victory over Khan. There's also a remnant of the place's colonial past: a beautiful old bridge built by the British nearly 125 years ago.

Present-day Wai is characterized by the usual chaos and dirt of the town centre and the natural beauty of the surrounding villages, with the Sahyadri hills visible on the outskirts.

The day of our visit, a film crew has taken over the town entirely. As they apparently do every single day. No hotel rooms are available. Pearl, the best hotel in town, is booked for months together; Sanai Residency, on the outskirts, with a giant *3 Idiots* bum bench occupying pride of place in the reception area, does have a vacant room, but is just too far away from the 'lights, camera, action'. Fortunately, the *Gulaab Gang* cap-clad Mandar Shendye, a Marathi theatre professional, who coordinates and line produces the many film shoots in Wai (including Soumik Sen's recent *Gulaab Gang*), manages to find me a room in Annapurna Lodge, right in the heart of town. Whichever way you look, there is no escaping cinema in Wai. Even my hotel room's window quite appropriately faces the town's New Chitra Talkies, which is showing the Vidyut Jammwal–starrer *Commando: A One Man Army* (2013). To accommodate me at the lodge for a day, Mandar has moved the assistant director of one of the films out to another room. But the big, bold board on my door remains in place. 'AD,' it announces to all who pass by. The other doors on my floor bear similar insignia, identifying their rooms' occupants: choreographer, camera assistant, gaffer, set designer. For one day in my life, I can pretend to be part of a film unit, even though I know nothing about filmmaking.

What I do get to know is that it's a hierarchical world out there – quite like it is in other walks of life. These modest lodges, like the one I have been put up at, are where the second leads, assistants and crew members are accommodated. The big stars and directors keep their distance from the hoi polloi, staying 12 km away in the genteel seclusion of Panchgani or in the luxurious comfort of a hospitality address in Mahabaleshwar, 30 km away.

'Ravine Hotel is the favourite of the stars,' Mandar confides.

He asks one of his assistants to show me around. Immediately after checking in, I am whisked away in an autorickshaw for a day-long guided tour of Wai and the surrounding villages. The purpose is just to show me the famous spots for film shoots. I go wide-eyed as I recognize the significance of a commonplace village home in Warkhadwadi, complete with its tulsi plant growing right in the middle of the courtyard. It had, after all, represented the house of Kaveriamma (the nanny of the character played by SRK) in *Swades*. Under normal circumstances, I would, most probably, have passed it without a second glance but now, given what I know, I immediately decide to capture it on camera for posterity.

There are several such moments ahead, which I encounter in between wolfing down *vada-pav* and *misal-pav*, and drinking *solkadi* from the innumerable *rasvanti griha* (refreshment houses) that proclaim: '*Thandgar solkadi milet.* Cold *solkadi* is available.' There's the iconic well (chosen, it seems, after rejecting 70 to 80 of its kind in the region) that featured in the philosophical, lyrical and heart-rending *Vihir*, the Marathi film on death, loss and its acceptance. There's also the barren, dry and dusty mountainous area where the rough-and-tough village set of Vishal Bhardwaj's 2006 film *Omkara*, starring Ajay Devgn, Kareena Kapoor and Saif Ali Khan, was pitched. The quiet backwaters of the Dhom Dam served as the setting for the famous boat scene featuring an introspective Shah Rukh Khan in *Swades*; and the water tank that was built for the crucial power-generation sequence in the same film is pointed out to me from a distance when I visit Pasarani village.

'It's not in use, but the residents felt there was no point in destroying it,' Mandar explains. 'So they have kept it as a memento.'

But, much against my wishes, what stays out of the zone of my lens is the elaborate and gaudy set of a small south Indian town centre for Rohit Shetty's then under-production SRK–Deepika Padukone–starrer *Chennai Express* (2013). Since the last schedule of the film, a 10-day 'patchwork' shoot, is still to take place, the security guard on duty warns me almost threateningly against reaching for my camera. But I do get to feast my eyes on the temple at the centre, and the kitschy streets and shops around it. When the film is eventually released in 2013 and I get to watch it on the big screen, those very same things leap out at me with a unique urgency.

Wai makes eminent sense as a choice shooting destination for Bollywood. It is close to Mumbai, has the requisite infrastructure and backup, and facilitates quick clearances to help complete a film shoot fast, in just a few long outdoor schedules.

'Any permission [that needs to be granted for a film shoot to proceed] is just a phone call away,' declares Hemant Zore, a theatre artiste turned shoot coordinator.

Known as Dakshin Kashi, or the Varanasi of the South, Wai's seven ghats – Gangapuri, Madhi Aali, Ganapati Aali, Dharmapuri, Brahmanshahi, Ramdoh and Bhimkund – along the Krishna River have served onscreen as those of Varanasi itself. Not just the ghats, there are more than a hundred temples, old houses and villages that are regularly used as backdrops for films. This is a no haphazard exercise. It is handled with professional competence. Mandar hands us a pen drive containing pictures and videos of all the possible locations. Such pen drives are given out to film-production houses to help them find suitable locales without having to travel on extended 'recces'. There seem to be many favourite locations: the Dholya Ganapati Temple, the haveli of Peshwa Nana Fadnavis and Menawali Ghat, with its beautiful rocks. The haveli is dilapidated and crumbling, and only its exteriors are now used for shooting. While we are in Menawali, carpenters and painters are busy putting together a garish set with cut-outs of cows and elephants. It seems to be all about reality and fantasy existing together harmoniously in the same frame.

Wai is famous in Maharashtra and in Bollywood, specifically – though not quite as much in the world outside – as the go-to place for film shoots. One of the earliest films to have been shot there was in the late '50s: Vijay Bhatt's Rajendra Kumar–starrer *Goonj Uthi Shehnai*. There was K. Vishwanath's *Sargam* in the '70s, starring Rishi Kapoor and Jaya Prada, and Raj Kapoor is also known to have canned a few shots of his swansong, the Mandakini–starrer *Ram Teri Ganga Maili*, right here in 1985.

'Earlier, there were just one or two filmmakers who used to come here to shoot a song or a few romantic scenes,' says Mandar.

Filmmaker Prakash Jha single-handedly changed all that. He turned Wai from a mere location into a Film City of sorts – the integrated film-shooting destination it has become today. Jha came here for his National Award–winning film *Gangaajal* (2003), with Ajay Devgn in the lead. Not only did he use the lanes, mandir, ghats, colleges, hospitals – the Ganpati Ghat, the Gangapuri area and the Kisan Veer Mahavidyalaya, that was turned into the police station – he also involved the locals in crowd scenes.

'The villagers who came with their own lunchboxes were given ₹150 for a day of [the] shoot and those who ate the food available on location were given ₹120,' Mandar recalls.

Jha is not the only one to have homed in on Wai. It has also become a Rohit Shetty favourite, with him shooting *Singham*, *Bol Bachchan*

(2012) and *Chennai Express* here. Directors Ashutosh Gowariker and Priyadarshan have been the other regulars.

Now shoots – of Hindi and Marathi television serials, films and advertisements – contribute significantly to Wai's economy. Reeling off figures that I am unable to verify, Mandar claims that 50 per cent of the population works in the farming sector (namely sugarcane, wheat, cotton and turmeric farming) and 30 per cent in the Maharashtra Industrial Development Corporation. Twenty per cent makes a living from what can be called the film-shooting industry. A few years ago, due to the construction of the Dhom Dam, many villages and fields were flooded and remained submerged under water. The residents were forced to leave their homes and relocate to another area. They also had to find alternative sources of employment. That was when cinema shoots came in as a boon. Hotels, eating joints, caterers, transporters – the film shoots would also create several jobs in the secondary and tertiary sectors.

'Even a sweeper stands to gain from them,' Mandar maintains.

I have the famous *poori-bhaji* breakfast at Nirmal Hotel, a hole-in-the-wall place opposite the police station. Its owner Jeetendra Dev also does catering for visiting film units – sometimes, for five or six of them at a go. He has two helpers in the café, but during the shoots, his entire family and 13 village women come together to help prepare the meals.

'At times, I have to shut down the hotel to just cater to the film units,' he says.

When the shooting of *Gangaajal* was in progress, there used to be only four or five lodges in the town; now there are over 22. There's a 180-strong contingent of vehicles ready for renting, including such as Qualis, Tavera and Innova.

'Eighty cars were taken on hire for 50 days for [the] *Chennai Express* shoot alone,' Mandar volunteers.

The kind of film shoot-related jobs that paid people ₹100 each just a few years ago now fetches them ₹1200 – Mandar throws these very approximate figures at me in a bid to explain the local growth in income.

'Our lifestyles have changed for the better. We have better mobile phones now. I couldn't afford a pair of jeans in college. Now, at 45, I am living it up,' he says.

There are six or seven coordinators in town, quite like Mandar, each with a posse of assistants who run the show smoothly and seamlessly, like a professional event-management company, complete with Samsung smartphones wielded like walkie-talkies. They, however, compare film shoots to '*beti ki shaadi* [a daughter's wedding]' that needs to be handled with meticulous care. They don't see them as work.

'It feels like [a] picnic with friends; we don't even know how time flies and the day passes by at the shoots,' Mandar muses.

What began as a mere hobby has become a full-fledged profession for him. Theatre professional though he is, Mandar has worked for 10 films as an assistant coordinator and 10 more, independently, as a coordinator. He has also worked in 12 ads and 25 serials. And all this within two years.

Coordinators like him not only facilitate shooting, but also source the crowds and junior artistes. Every village has a coordinator who rounds up a group of 50, as and when required. At the drop of a hat, a crowd of 500 can be cobbled together by them.

'If you tell me this evening, I can get you a crowd of 2000 tomorrow at 7 a.m,' boasts Mandar.

What's more you don't even need to guide the crowd. Such has been the power of film shoots that Wai residents themselves have become cinema savvy.

'They know the camera, what's a top-angle shot or a close-up,' says Mandar.

Wai doesn't go all moony-eyed over glamour; Bollywood is a part and parcel of life here, a routine. So you won't find star-struck fans crowding around shoots or film stars, the reason why shooting in Wai has zero nuisance value.

Cinema apart, Wai occupies a position of immense significance when it comes to Marathi culture. It is the place where the Marathi Vishwakosh (encyclopaedia) is compiled. Moreover, it has the Govardhan Sanstha, an institution that is more than a century old and is dedicated to the care and rehabilitation of the cow, an animal sacred to Hindus.

Apart from film shoots, there are two other things I encounter in Wai that typify it. What hits me most is the caste obsession. We may have pushed it into the shadows in our urban environments, but in Wai, caste seems to be key in the daily lives of its inhabitants. The locals are quick to read mine from my surname and, at every juncture, I am told for no apparent reason, and without provocation, 'This is a Brahmin lodge; that one is a Brahmin eatery.' I am directed to the spotlessly clean Bandu Gore Bhojanalaya – not simply because of the home-style, fresh, delicious and must-eat thali it offers, but because it is run by a Brahmin family. And, as an afterthought, also because Vidya Balan had her meals there while shooting for *Ishqiya* in 2010. Khamkar Sweet Home is also a must-visit because of the caste connect and the fact that all visiting film stars pick up the orange, strawberry, mango, *anjeer* (fig) and the many other fruit-flavoured *barfi*s from here to take back home.

The other omnipresent reality is water, or rather, the lack of it. In village after village, you can read the posters: '*Jethe asati jalache sathe, tethe swarg hi une vaate...*' or '*Jalsandhaaranaat keli kasoor, jal tanchaichaprashn bhesur.*' Roughly translated from Marathi, the messages mean: 'A place with enough water is more heavenly than heaven'; and 'Without sufficient conservation, dreadful water shortage is your destination.' It's obvious that despite the existence of the Dhom Dam, the region is reeling under a severe water crisis. You can see the water barely trickling out of the community taps in the villages, as girls crowd around them to fill buckets to take back home. Film shoots have been roped in rather uniquely by the villages in their fight for water. For every villager sourced for a crowd scene in a film or even as a junior artiste, the producer has to pay a small additional token amount to the recruit's panchayat. The money thus made by the gram panchayats is channelled towards supporting water-conservation efforts in the area. In one of the villages, it was even used for laying a water pipeline.

In Wai, film shoots, therefore, aren't just about money and prosperity, income and economy, but also about the environment, conservation and welfare.

But, most of all, as Mandar puts it, 'They have given our small town an identity.'

A town that would, otherwise, have been hard to spot on the map.

Even as Wai attracts a range of films and filmmakers from Mumbai, Rajpipla in Gujarat is the favourite shooting location for low-budget Bhojpuri films. Avijit Ghosh in his book *Cinema Bhojpuri* writes of a variety of locales available to shoot in – hills, lakes, rivers (the Narmada and the Karjan, for instance), waterfalls (Jerwani, Junaghata and Ninai, to name a few), a couple of palaces, the Sardar Sarovar or Narmada Dam, and several temples along the riverbanks – that are all charming and easy on the pocket. The rustic ambience is as close as it can get to the villages of eastern UP and Bihar. According to an article titled 'Bhojpuri Plot' by Uday Mahurkar in the November 2008 issue of *India Today*, shooting in Rajpipla is about 40 per cent cheaper than it would be in and around Mumbai. The place is just 60 km from Bharuch, a mainline railway station on the Delhi–Mumbai line. By road, it's seven hours from Mumbai. The first Bhojpuri film to have been shot here was *Ganga Jaisan Mai Hamaar* (2001).

Interestingly, Prakash Jha has, in the meantime, shifted his focus from Wai to Bhopal. It's his new go-to shooting destination, with his more recent films *Raajneeti* (2010), *Aarakshan* (2011), *Chakravyuh* (2012) and *Satyagraha* (2013) having been canned there. A slew of other filmmakers – from Anusha Rizvi for *Peepli Live* to Sai Kabeer for *Revolver Rani* – have followed Jha's footsteps. And while it is true that films like Vishal Bhardwaj's *Maqbool* (2003) and the Mani Ratnam-directed *Yuva* (2004) had already been shot in Bhopal many years ago, the consolidation of business, akin to Wai's a decade ago, is happening only now, though on a much smaller scale.

The latest Bhopal-bound filmmaker is Tigmanshu Dhulia, who was shooting *Yaara* in the Madhya Pradesh capital at the time of my visit.

I discover Bhopal's equivalent of Mandar Shendye in Anoop Joshi. Better known as 'Bunty' in Mumbai, he is Bollywood's go-to man in this town and not only shares the Wai coordinator and line producer's roots in theatre, but is more firmly entrenched in the world of stage performances.

Bunty started off as a drum player and musician in the orchestras organized for religious festivals like Ganesh Utsav and Durga Puja.

'Studies were my last priority, even in school,' he remembers.

He was busy participating, instead, in the theatre group Rangsheel and learnt *chhau*-based ballet at the Little Ballet Troupe, associated with the iconic Uday Shankar Academy. He joined Bharat Bhavan in 1985 and was involved with its repertory for almost 16 years. A time well spent, because it brought him in close contact with doyens like B.V. Karanth, B.M. Shah, Prasanna and Bansi Kaul.

'My whole life has been only about theatre,' he says.

No wonder the crisis button in his life got pushed in 2001, when the repertory shut down and there was only one way out: to head for Mumbai in search of acting assignments.

But apart from theatre, the other thing which has served as Bunty's life force is his hometown: Bhopal.

'It's wonderful, unique, a town of artistes, writers and painters. Seventy to 80 per cent of the residents are not originally from Bhopal, but those who came from outside and didn't want to go back,' he tells me. 'It's a town with which you end up forming a lifelong relationship.'

No wonder he eventually decided not to head for Mumbai, but let the city reach out to him – through film shoots. One of the earliest projects he handled was Pravesh Bhardwaj's television serial *Shaheen*, aired on Sony Entertainment Television (India) from September 1999 onwards. Sudhir Mishra's 2005 release *Hazaaron Khwaishein Aisi* (in which Bihar was recreated in Bhopal), starring Kay Kay Menon, Shiney Ahuja and debutante actress Chitrangada Singh, is the one film that taught Bunty a lot, because it was a tough shoot, filled with financial and logistical uncertainties. Over the years, he claims to have created his support structure, bit by bit. Simple things like his professional association with a shop called Virasat, where furniture is available on hire and from where Bunty helps film-production crews source items for shoots, to his own small, but sincere team – Raj Kumar, assistant for art, lightman Sanjay, who can also assist as cameraman, dressman Sabir and spotboy Shahid, a make-up man and continuity coordinator – all drawn from the Bharat Bhavan talent pool.

It is Bunty who takes me on a tour of the Noor Us Sabah Hotel. Once owned by Saif Ali Khan's family (apparently, its flaghouse is still the actor's property), it's the town's preferred hospitality address for Bollywood A-listers. I am shown a special suite, complete with a 5000 sq. ft private terrace, lift, special gym, and a personal cook and valet, that was reserved for Amitabh Bachchan during his numerous stays while shooting for Prakash Jha's *Aarakshan* and *Satyagraha*. I also visit the furniture supplier, Virasat, Bunty had mentioned. Proudly displayed and up for sale – or should we say, auction? – are a bed and a rocking chair, which Bachchan had used during his stay. The star and veteran actor is not the only one to have patronized the hotel. The Noor Us Sabah has been a home away from home for almost all of Bollywood – Ranbir Kapoor, Ajay Devgn, Manoj Bajpai and Arjun Rampal, among others, have all stayed there while on extended shoots lasting nearly two months.

But why, I wonder aloud, has Bollywood taken a shine to Bhopal, in particular, when it could easily have headed for any other town?

'Because Bhopal has *adab*, *tameez*, *tehzeeb* and *mehmaan-nawazi*,' Bunty observes simply, referring to the inherent breeding, refined manners and tradition of hospitality that are said to define the city's residents.

I silently ponder that it could also well be for Bhopal's beauty – its hills, lakes, parks and greenery, on the one hand, and its fine old architecture, on the other. But I do understand the import of a place where the people's artistic bent of mind and their involvement in professional theatre can mean an easy availability of local talent for a film crew to rope in as part of the cast. The other advantage is that Bhopalis are disciplined and cooperative, and allow film shoots to proceed uninterrupted.

Bunty corroborates this fact.

'For the shoot of *Raajneeti*, there was a crowd of a thousand just 20 feet away from Katrina Kaif,' he recalls. 'But there was no disturbance; no problems whatsoever.'

His reasoning is that it's to do with the kind of people Bhopalis are: introverts, rather than outgoing exhibitionists; less keen on film stars and glamour than on theatre, *mushairas* and *qawwalis*, and partial to pastimes like fishing and games like chess and cards.

And why is Bollywood so fond of Bunty, in particular? Perhaps, because he never compromises on his commitments and always comes up with a solution to a problem. Even when it involves sourcing an unusual item like a lizard. Bunty recalls how the creature was required for a film shoot (the name of the film eludes him, however), but unavailable with any local animal supplier. His attempts to whisk one off the wall of his own home also failed. It struck him then that he had read in *Dainik Bhaskar*, a Hindi-language daily, about a boy who supposedly ate lizards. Bunty tracked him down and sourced one *chhipkali* (lizard) from him. Says he, 'My attempt is to make Bhopal the ultimate comfort zone for Bollywood.'

Meanwhile, his individual efforts may soon find an institutional resonance. The government master plan allocates a 400 acre plot for a proposed Bhojpuri Film City, while Prakash Jha has 23 acres of land on which he is planning to build a film institute (these plans are still pending as we go to press). A case of Bollywood calling Bhopal, as well as Bhopal calling Bollywood.

In the Nawab's Court

LUCKNOW, THE CAPITAL OF Uttar Pradesh, is not a small town like Wai. It's not even old-world in a way that nawabi Bhopal continues to be. A hotbed of politics, caste, sectarian issues, and day-to-day skirmishes, crime and violence, much like any other burgeoning city, Lucknow has, over the years, lost much of its *nazakat* and *nafasat*, its *adab* and *tehzeeb*, its grace and dignity, while evolving from a small town into a big city. A journey through its Bollywoodian heart makes you realize, however, that in its connect with Hindi films from the past to the present, it still manages to offer a glimpse of the graciousness, the leisurely lifestyle and the laid-back manner that once defined the loveliness of the little town it used to be. In a city in transition, it is Bollywood that has kept the nostalgia intact, the memory of Old Lucknow alive.

Not unusual, then, to find that legendary music composer Naushad Ali still lives on in Lucknow, and in a most unlikely place too. It's an obscure shop called Allan Saheb & Sons on Aminabad's Gautam Buddha Marg. The oldest in Lucknow for sales and repairs of all kinds of musical instruments, Allan Saheb was set up in 1925. And it was in 1937 that the 18-year-old Naushad ran away from his conservative family home in Lucknow to pursue a career in music in the film industry in Mumbai (then Bombay). In the intervening years, it was Allan Saheb in Lucknow that served as one of Naushad's 'musical' homes, where he repaired, tuned and ran his fingers over many a harmonium. The shop still has a clutch of black-and-white photos of the music composer, including a lovely one of him conducting an orchestra, displayed alongside the various instruments up for sale.

Its laconic owner, Azeem Azmatullah, recalls how it was his grandfather who had given Naushad his first harmonium.

'*Ladakpan mein yahan baithte the. Apna* harmonium *khud theek kiya karte the*. In his youth, he [Naushad] used to sit in the shop and repair his harmonium himself,' he says.

Azmatullah has many other stories to tell: how Naushad began his career as an orchestra artiste in Lucknow, playing the harmonium as part of the live background score for the silent films that were screened at the Royal Talkies (later rechristened Mehra Cinema); how musicians were so disdained in those days that his orthodox future in-laws were told at the time his marriage was being negotiated that he was a tailor, so as not to put them off the prospective groom altogether; and how Naushad's conservative father, who despised films and film music, was quite unaware that the songs being played at his son's wedding were the very ones the young man had composed for various films.

Apart from Allan Saheb, the other significant musical training ground for Naushad is also in the vicinity of Lucknow: the dargah of Haji Waris Ali Shah in Barabanki's Dewa Sharif. While his family's religious faith took him regularly to the dargah, it was the Sufi *qawwal*s there who struck a musical chord within him and became his earliest gurus.

Naushad is not, however, Luck's only musical connect to Bollywood. Lucknow has also been home to a host of playback singers for films – from Talat Mahmood to Anup Jalota and Baba Sehgal. Talat Mahmood, a resident of Nazarbagh, had apprenticed under Pandit S.C.R. Bhat at Marris College of Music (now known as the Bhatkhande Music University) and, in his initial days, sang ghazals on All India Radio, Lucknow.

The city has also given Hindi cinema some of its biggest names. Old-time actress Bina Rai was from Lucknow. So are filmmakers

Sudhir Mishra and Muzaffar Ali, who belongs to the city's royal family of Kotwara.

It is clear that multifaceted Lucknow – the city of nawabs and courtesans, the artistic, aesthetic and political hub of north India, the architectural home of diverse heritage buildings, ancient mosques, *imambaras* and *baradaris*, the motherland of Kathak dance, chikan embroidery, mushairas, *sher-o-shairi*, thumri, *dadra*, ghazals and Begum Akhtar, the acme of our syncretic and secular culture, India's Ganga–Jamuni *tehzeeb*, and a place obsessed with games like *patangbaazi* (kite-flying contests) and *baterbaazi* (a sport that pits one Indian quail against another) – has had a long-standing relationship with Hindi cinema. And the exchange programme is still going strong between the country's most cultured city, as many believe it to be, and its cinema capital.

Their glory days may well be behind them, but the nawabs still take their Lucknow very seriously. I go calling on the most media-friendly of them all (though some claim he is no nawab at all, but a fake): Sheesh Mahal's Nawab Jafar Mir Abdullah. Bollywood, I am told, calls on him regularly; he is, apparently, the one-stop shop for any kind of Lucknow-based research. His home is a museum of sorts. A host of ornate utensils, antique pots and pans, and priceless paandaans occupy pride of place alongside dusty furniture, fading upholstery and several photographs and books highlighting Lucknow's Bollywood connection. Along with paan, he offers me the choicest stories and I am content to just listen, without pausing to question their veracity.

I am told how the palki that legendary yesteryear 'Tragedy Queen' Meena Kumari used in the 1972 Indian cult classic *Pakeezah* was sourced from Lucknow; that the enormous blue stone ring – the famous Nishapuri Shajri Feroza, apparently – that actor Farooque Sheikh wore in *Umrao Jaan* (1981) is actually Nawab Sahib's family heirloom, chosen from the many priceless curios in his collection which are ostensibly used in Bollywood films. He claims handing out '*saaman aur mashvire*', objects and advice, to several filmmakers for their film shoots in response to their requests. He goes on to tell me how he had helped Muzaffar Ali with the biopic on Lucknow courtesan Umrao Jaan at the behest of Ali's father, Raja Syed Sajid Hussain. Why, he himself had appeared in a sequence in *Umrao Jaan*, as the host of a music *mehfil*.

'You can see me seated next to Farooque Sheikh in the "*In aankhon ki masti ke*" ("By the lust of the eyes") *mujra*,' he says.

Recently, he and his younger brother, Nawab Masood Abdullah, were visible in the famous *bent-baazi*/mushaira scene of Abhishek Chaubey's *Dedh Ishqiya* (2014), a tale of two crooks, with Naseeruddin Shah, Arshad Warsi and Madhuri Dixit in the lead roles, that was steeped in Lucknow's culture. Earlier, the aristocratic siblings had appeared in the popular '*Jhalla vallah*' item number in *Ishaqzaade* (2012), Habib Faisal's UP gangland version of Romeo and Juliet, shot in Hardoi–Lucknow, with debutants Arjun Kapoor and Parineeti Chopra cast opposite each other.

The nawab remembers almost each and every scene of *Umrao Jaan* – even some of those that were eventually edited out – as he does of Anil Sharma's 2001 period film *Gadar: Ek Prem Katha*, with Sunny Deol and Ameesha Patel in the lead, where Lucknow was apparently depicted in the film as Pakistan, specifically Lahore. The famous scene involving the uprooting of the handpump was shot inside the La Martiniere College grounds. The thumri '*Aan milo sajna*' ('Come and meet my love') was performed in the *baradari* of Lucknow Zoo. The Taj Hotel lobby and the La Martiniere School were the other important locations used in the film.

As with *Umrao Jaan* and *Gadar*, Lucknow has served as the backdrop for several movies that have highlighted its well-known sites and localities, the nawab tells us, right from the Residency in Subodh Mukherjee's 1957 Dev Anand–Nutan–starrer *Paying Guest* to Aminabad in H.S. Rawail's *Mere Mehboob*, a 1963 Muslim social with Rajendra Kumar and Sadhana in the lead that went on to become a huge box-office success; from Kaisarbagh in M. Sadiq's Urdu-language top grosser *Chaudhvin ka Chand* (1960), starring Guru Dutt and Waheeda Rehman, to Husainabad in his 1967 film *Bahu Begum*, where legendary heroine Meena Kumari, Pradeep Kumar and Ashok Kumar played the main leads. *Chaudhvin ka Chand* even featured a song that was an ode to the city: '*Ye* Lucknow *ki sar zameen*' ('This is the birthplace of Lucknow'). The song '*Chalo, dildar, chalo, chand ke paar chalo*' ('Let's go beloved to the other side of the moon') in Kamal Amrohi's *Pakeezah* (1972), another Meena Kumari classic and the last film she would act in before her premature death that very year at the age of 38, was shot with the Gomti River in the background.

The more famous Lucknow films include Satyajit Ray's *Shatranj ke Khilari* (1977), with Sanjeev Kumar and Amjad Khan in the main roles, and Shyam Benegal's *Junoon* (1978), where Shashi Kapoor was cast opposite debutante actress Nafisa Ali, a former Miss India and national swimming champion. Both films are set during the 1857 Sepoy Mutiny when soldiers of the East India Company rebelled against their British masters. Another film shot in Lucknow is James Ivory's 1965 ode to a travelling theatre – *Shakespeare Wallah* – the star cast of which included Madhur Jaffrey, a young Shashi Kapoor and his sister-in-law, British stage actress Felicity Kendal.

While Bollywood's love affair with Lucknow hasn't lost its intensity despite the passage of time, I come to learn during my stay in the city that even Hollywood had pitched its tent there, with Craig Gillespie shooting his biographical sports drama *Million Dollar Arm* (released in 2014) at the Amausi airport and within the Lucknow University campus. Incidentally, years ago, another Hollywood film had been shot on the La Martiniere School grounds of the same city: Errol Flynn–starrer *Kim*, released more than six decades earlier.

'It's a beautiful city and the locations haven't been overexposed yet,' says Nawab Jafar Mir Abdullah in the course of our conversation, offering insights into why it continues to appeal to filmmakers from Bollywood.

It stands to reason why, in recent times too, there has been a string of films set in contemporary Lucknow. Chandan Arora's *Main, Meri Patni aur Woh* (2005), which featured Kay Kay Menon and West Bengal's National Award–winning actress Rituparna Sengupta, had Rajpal Yadav's character working at Lucknow University. Maneesh Sharma's 2011 romantic comedy *Ladies vs Ricky Bahl* had one segment set in *tehzeeb*-steeped Lucknow and left the audience with, among other things, the memory of a classic line inspired by the city's kite-flying obsession: '*Ungli mein saddi ke tarah lapetna.* Wrap around the finger like a kite's string.' Tigmanshu Dhulia's 2013 Saif Ali Khan–starrer *Bullett Raja* was based in a UP rife with political games and gang wars, while also giving a nod to the state's vicious casteist reality; and Habib Faisal's 2014 romantic comedy *Daawat-e-Ishq*, with a Lucknawi khansama for a hero (played by Aditya Roy Kapoor), threw the town's tantalizing kababs, biryani, *shahi tukda*s and *phirni*s at the audience. However, it was Kabeer Kaushik's *Sehar*, a 2005 crime drama starring Arshad Warsi and Mahima Chaudhry, that took the most incisive look at the UP-based mafia – the dons who fight for railway tenders, network with arms dealers and align themselves with political parties during elections to further their own ends. Into this well-entrenched 'system' steps Gajraj Singh (played by Sushant Singh), a new don who will be satisfied with nothing but total control. It's up to the honest cop SSP Ajay Kumar (with Arshad Warsi playing him) and his force to clean up organized crime in the area. Clichéd as Kaushik's story and characters may be, it's the UP–Lucknow context that makes the film stand apart from others in its genre. *Sehar* succeeds in creating an authentic feel of the city and the state as they are today, a virtual dystopia where things rarely function smoothly, and law and order are flouted too often for comfort. It is vital, throbbing, real. And much of it also has to do with the film's lingo – *shuddh* (chaste) Hindi, complete with all the fine turns of phrase that lend it its distinctive character and class, a bow to the Lucknawi *zubaan* (tongue).

Until today, Bollywood's rapport with Lucknow is as strong as ever. Abhinay Deo's new Irrfan Khan–starrer *Blackmail* (released in early 2018) is a dark comedy about a middle-class Lucknow man. Sudhir Mishra returned to the scene with *Daas Dev*, his Lucknow version of *Devdas*, that was also released in 2018.

Moreover, the lure of the state government subsidy of ₹2 crore on offer under the administration of Chief Minister Akhilesh Yadav for filmmakers willing to shoot at least two-thirds of their films in UP had been attracting more and more Bollywood teams to the state and to Lucknow, in particular. In fact, Muzaffar Ali had, reportedly, applied for the grant for his new film *Jaanisaar* not so long ago.

With Yogi Adityanath having succeeded Yadav as chief minister, the UP government has modified the the state's policy on films to extend the cash incentives available, so that they cover not only movies made in Hindi and UP's regional languages, as had been the case so far, but also those in English and in any Indian language. The facility has also been extended to overseas Indian filmmakers (who hold Overseas Citizenship of India, or OCI), provided that their films are based on Indian issues, have received the official stamp of the Central Board of Film Certification and are screened in India.

An increase in the number of film shoots has resulted in an interesting side effect: it is not just the historic monuments and iconic sights like the Residency, Rumi Darwaza and Musa Bagh that have become the focus of interest as shooting locales, filmmakers also are seeking out interesting private properties like kothis and havelis. As a result, letting them out for film shootings has become a lucrative business for their owners.

Malihabad, a town in Lucknow district, is well known as the home of poet Josh Malihabadi. It was also in Malihabad's palaces that Shyam Benegal shot his film *Junoon*. These days, however, Padma Shri Kalimullah Khan, who took to mango cultivation in 1957 shortly after failing his Class VII exams, is the town's most famous resident. The man has grafted and grown more than 350 varieties of mango – from the bittergourd-shaped Karela to the heart-shaped Asroor Muqarar – on a single 100-year-old tree. Like Malihabad, the palaces of Kakori (famous for its kababs and the 1925 Kakori Conspiracy, related to the Indian Independence movement, engineered by Ram Prasad Bismil, Chandrasekhar Azad and Ashfaqullah Khan) have also featured extensively in Hindi films, the most famous of the sequences shot there being the '*Aankhen teri*' ('Your eyes') song from Manish Jha's 2007 film *Anwar*, starring Siddharth Koirala, film star Manisha's brother.

There are many such palatial homes in Lucknow that lend themselves as ideal locales for shooting films: Salempur House, Khajurgaon Palace, Jahangirabad Palace, which might soon be turned into a heritage hotel... I visit one such haveli, in particular, that looks like a miniature white palace, standing in quiet isolation on the busy road and has been a favourite location for recent Bollywood filmshoots – Dr Rishad Rizvi's Ahmad Manzil. A physician by profession, Rizvi belongs to one of Lucknow's oldest families. I meet him at his famous ancestral home in the Akbari Gate area. Built in 1922, it originally belonged to tobacco merchants Ahmad Ali & Sons. It was in the 1940s that it came to Rizvi's ancesters.

Having been active in theatre himself, Rizvi has many friends in the television and film industry. One of them is filmmaker, actor and television host Roshan Abbas. Initially, in the little time he could spare from his medical practice, the doctor would merely help out the film crew in town. Now that he has become deeply involved in film-related activities, however, his entire schedule has turned topsy-turvy and his priorities have changed.

'Managing film production seems to have become a profession and medicine, a hobby,' Rizvi confesses.

Initially, a few small projects for Doordarshan had been shot in Ahmad Manzil. It is, therefore, no surprise that the first few full-scale film shoots were enough to throw the Rizvi family out of gear.

'I hadn't bargained for 250-odd people all over the place,' Rizvi recalls.

Now, to protect his privacy, he lets out only certain portions of his sprawling family home. The production teams of *Tanu Weds Manu* (2011), starring Kangana Ranaut, *Ishaqzaade* and Salman Khan's *Dabangg 2*, the 2012 sequel to the star's 2010 smash hit *Dabangg*, have all dropped anchor at Ahmad Manzil. Why? I get my answer as I take a walk around the property, with Rizvi acting as guide.

'It encompasses different kinds of locations – all in one property,' my host explains. 'There is an architectural variation and a difference of ambience in the various portions of Ahmad Manzil.'

As he leads me around the property and shows me passageways which can work for chase sequences, I realize that left on my own to navigate its vast expanses, I could easily have lost my way. Rizvi points out one site within the property which looks like an old factory, and open areas that can be adapted to serve as a marketplace on screen. The absence of homogeneity in its architecture and the versatility of the space it encapsulates are the property's unique selling propositions. Rizvi himself doesn't know how the architectural wonder came about, since it was handed over to his predecessors by another family.

He is well aware, though, of private property owners cashing in on the frequent film shoots taking place in the city. Earlier, the star-struck owners would be happy to let their homes out to filmmakers for a nominal fee if a photo or chai–coffee session with a star were thrown in. Now, with experience, they have become more professional; they want to be paid more, at times, justifiably so, for the maintenance and upkeep of the property, and to cover the cost of damages during the shoots.

'A few years ago, a 10-day shoot would cost the production house around ₹50,000. Now that amount is charged for just a single day of shoot. In fact, it could even go up to a lakh for a day's shoot,' Rizvi tells me.

In comparison, the Archaeological Survey of India has been far more reasonable: when we went visiting five years ago, it was charging ₹10,000 as the security amount and ₹5,000 for a day's shoot at the city's heritage buildings. The rates haven't gone up, we are assured by industry insiders, in keeping with the UP government's initiative to encourage shoots in the state.

With Rizvi, it's also a case of 'buy one, get one free'. Not only is his house a perennial presence in contemporary Bollywood films, he himself has become a cameo specialist of sorts. He played Jimmy Sheirgill's father in Anand L. Rai's *Tanu Weds Manu* and stepped in as the father of the groom in a wedding scene in Tigmanshu Dhulia's *Bullett Raja*. He has done cameos in Maneesh Sharma's *Ladies vs Ricky Bahl*, Kush Bhargava's production *Monica* (2012), with Divya Dutta in the lead role, and Roshan Abbas' *Always Kabhi Kabhi* (2011), a Shah Rukh Khan production, as well.

Unlike Rizvi, Raja Amresh Singh and his wife, Abha, of Khajurgaon Palace didn't have much of a rapport with the film world. In fact, they had been using their huge heritage property to host royal Awadhi dinners and cultural evenings, complete with Kathak, ghazals and thumris, for foreign tourists in order to give them a taste of the lifestyle favoured by Lucknow's Hindu royalty. Then, *Bullett Raja* was shot in its courtyard. Khajurgaon Palace is now on Bollywood's most-wanted list, along with other such properties.

It's not hard to understand why it would stir a filmmaker's imagination. Built in 1896, the palace bears a very strong British influence, along with elements of native Awadhi architecture. Located in Naka Hindola, a busy, clamorous wholesale market of electrical goods, the entrance to Khajurgaon Palace is a narrow, easy-to-miss lane between two shops. Inside, though, it's an entirely different story;

one of unimaginable opulence, as you behold a magnificent mansion, complete with a beautiful fountain, Belgian chandeliers, sweeping Italian marble staircases, ornately crafted wrought-iron windows and balconies, and a Darbar Hall with hand-painted murals. The owners, however, are fastidiously selective when it comes to choosing who they will allow to shoot on the premises and in which specific areas of the property. Heritage, conservation and cultural tourism still remain their priority over Bollywood.

Lucknow's *filmi* connect goes beyond its locales and mansions. Good actors continue to thrive in the city because of its active theatre scene, and many of them travel to Mumbai as and when films come calling.

Like Dr Anil Rastogi, a scientist with a doctoral degree, who recently retired as head of the biochemistry department at the Central Drug Research Institute (CDRI). A much-awarded theatre veteran, Dr Rastogi has acted in over 80 plays in the last 50 years. The *filmi* connect goes back to Sudhir Mishra's *Yeh Woh Manzil To Nahin* (1987), with Pankaj Kapoor and Naseeruddin Shah in the lead roles. *Main, Meri Patni aur Woh* (2005) and actor–director Rajat Kapoor's *Chintu Ji* (2009) were thrown in later. Dr Rastogi's most recent appearance was in *Ishaqzaade*, where he played Arjun Kapoor's stern grandfather.

'But I never went to Mumbai to seek offers,' he is at pains to clarify.

Though he has a flat in Mumbai, he visits the city only when a challenging role comes his way. Otherwise, Lucknow has enough to keep the actor in him engaged.

'We want work on our own terms and conditions, and not get lost in the sea of strugglers in Mumbai,' says Jugal Kishore, who has flirted with Hindi films like *Peepli Live* and *Dabangg 2*, and has acted with superstar Nirahua in Bhojpuri films as well. But his heart continues to be firmly lodged in theatre. A product of the Bhartendu Academy of Dramatic Arts and its former head, his focus has been to bring traditional and dying folk forms of theatre into the limelight. Films happen on the side.

Farrukh Jaffar's energy and vivacity belie her 80-plus years. The first announcer of All India Radio, Lucknow, when it started its broadcasting service in 1963, she still recalls her first announcement.

'*Hum* All India Radio *ke* Lucknow *kendra se bol rahe hain. Ye hai* Vividh Bharati *ka panchrangi karyakram*... This is All India Radio, Lucknow, bringing you Vividh Bharati's variety programme...' she says. '*Hawa main pehli awaaz jo ubhari thi woh hamari thi.* The first voice to come on air was mine.'

Hugely popular in the town, Jaffar gained countrywide fame more recently for her portrayal of the crotchety old 'amma' in Anusha Rizvi's *Peepli Live.*

Born to a zamindar family in Jaunpur, Jaffar moved to Lucknow following her marriage to eminent journalist and freedom fighter Syed Muhammad Jaffer. She wrote and acted in several radio plays, and also did a brief stint on stage with Ebrahim Alkazi in Delhi. Her first foray into films happened with Muzaffar Ali's *Umrao Jaan*, where she was cast in the role of the courtesan's mother. She calls it '*filmi duniya ki sair ka pehla jeena* – the first step in my journey through the world of films.' Prakash Jha's *Chakravyuh*, Anand L. Rai's *Tanu Weds Manu* and Kabir Sadanand's *Fugly* (2014), featuring Jimmy Shergill, among others, followed. When we meet her, she has just wrapped up Buddhadeb Dasgupta's *Anwar ka Ajab Qissa* (released in 2013), with Nawazuddin Siddiqui, and Praveen Morchhale's *Barefoot to Goa*, a challenging film, surely, for a loquacious woman like her, because she has no dialogues in it.

According to her, what sets the actors in Lucknow apart is their impeccable enunciation.

'We can pick up the language and *lahza* [accent and intonation] of any part of the world very easily and flawlessly,' she declares proudly.

A reason, perhaps, why some of them are also much sought after by the film industry for dubbing.

Indeed, Lucknow's most significant influence is evident in the language of Hindi films. Dr Yogesh Praveen writes in his book *Aapka Lucknow* that the language and diction of characters in films need to be clear, precise and effective tools for communication.

'And Lucknow is the richest when it comes to this treasure,' he adds.

No wonder the *sher-o-shairi* of Lucknow, its Hindi, Urdu and Awadhi *boli* have lent gravitas and dignity to Hindi films or, as Nawab Mir Abdullah puts it, given them a touch of *tehzeeb*, *saleeka* (etiquette) and *nafasat* (artistry).

'The script, screenplay, dialogue writers and lyricists down the years have worked with Lucknawi language and enunciation as their ideal,' writes Praveen.

'Lucknow writers gave a literary flavour to the stories, dialogues and songs in cinema,' said poet Malikzaada Mansoor Ahmad, who was seen along with Anwar Jalalpuri reciting poems in the mushaira scene in *Dedh Ishqiya*. Both Ahmad and Jalalpuri have passed on since our meeting with them in 2013.

Not to be left behind, the literary world of Lucknow has had a foot in Mumbai as well. Novelist Amritlal Nagar wrote Uday Shankar's *Kalpana* (1948), among other films. Years later, his daughter Achala Nagar would write the scripts of several films, including B.R. Chopra's *Nikaah* (1982), starring Raj Babbar, Deepak Parashar and Pakistan-born debutante singer–actress Salma Agha, and Ravi Chopra's 2003 release *Baghban* that was critically acclaimed and a huge commercial success, despite bringing together Amitabh Bachchan and Hema Malini – paired romantically, decades earlier, in Bollywood films – in character roles. In the intervening years, Munshi Shams Lucknawi had written V. Shantaram's *Dahej* (1952), *Parchhain* (1952), *Subah ka Taara* (1954) and *Sehra* (1963). In fact, *Dahej* was set in Lucknow's Thakurganj area. Mirza Wajahat of Lucknow is credited with writing the iconic dialogues of K. Asif's *Mughal-e-Azam* (1960), starring the once real-life romantic pair Dilip Kumar and Madhubala. The film went on to break all box-office records. Famous writer Babu Bhagwati

Charan Varma's novel *Chitralekha* was adapted for the screen twice, with Meena Kumari in the lead in the 1964 version. K.P. Saksena wrote the dialogues for Ashutosh Gowariker's *Lagaan* (2001), an Aamir Khan starrer, which won much critical acclaim and several awards. Many lyricists – Hasan Kamal, Majaaz Lucknawi, Yogesh, actress Shabana Azmi's father, Kaifi Azmi, Neelesh Mishra, Majrooh Sultanpuri, Jan Nisar and his son, Javed Akhtar, and Amitabh Bhattacharya – have all had their roots in Lucknow.

For all these success stories, however, and the mutual love and affection shared by Lucknow and Mumbai, there are also tales of fiascos, of aborted ventures and *filmi* dreams dying young. Our Lucknow trip comes to a close with one such sad, untold and undocumented story of a film called *Kirchhein* (Shards), written by Anwar Nadeem Kaisar Bari, nephew of the Pakistani poet Josh Malihabadi; a film that was launched and relaunched, but never made.

Anwar Nadeem confesses that he was always interested in movies, in writing songs and spinning stories, but was just as sceptical about taking the train from Lucknow's Char Bagh railway station to Mumbai, to forge a career in the Hindi film industry. He wanted films to come home to him. For a while, it seemed as if his dream would actually turn into reality.

In 1971, he met Satyanand Rao, who hailed from a village in Andhra Pradesh and wanted to make a film that was set in Lucknow. Nadeem's *Kirchhein*, about a woman who tries to bring her sister out of the *kotha-tawaif* (courtesan) world by marrying her off to her own lover, caught Rao's fancy. Three songs were recorded in Bombay (now Mumbai), among them, a rare Muhammad Rafi gem: '*Chaahoon bhi to soch na paaoon mera mann kya soch raha hai*. However much I try, I can never tell what my heart is feeling.' A unit came down to Lucknow from Bombay for the shoot. But things got stalled even before they could start in earnest. A production of Mehfil Films, launched by Nawab Jafar Mir Abdullah in the '80s, *Kirchhein* never saw the light of day for lack of finances – or so the nawab claims. A decade later, Rao tried to relaunch the film with a new name – *Thakan*. A new theme song was also recorded for it. A unit came down from Bombay again. And yet again, things ground to a halt for the same reason – lack of finances.

Nadeem refuses to talk much about it. All you can sense is a deep cynicism and an irreparable fissure in his relationship with the nawab. But even as it lies unmade, the film's script has been published as a book. Does he anticipate the possibility of the film eventually being made, now that Lucknow is buzzing with film shoots?

'No,' comes the curt reply. 'It's about a culture whose tracks have been erased. It's about the past that no longer exists.'

It's about a city that is lost in time, even as another Lucknow thrives today – in Bollywood films.

CineMadurai

I'M ON A LATE-NIGHT bus from Coimbatore to Madurai. It will drop me off at the temple town in the wee hours of the morning. That I'm arriving in an unfamiliar place at around 3 a.m. is a cause for concern among my well-wishers. They fear the worst, in ascending order, from the more predictable and relatively harmless possibility ('You could get fleeced by the auto driver,' and 'The guy might drive you around in circles, instead of taking you straight to the hotel') to the downright sinister: 'You could get mugged by the rowdies and beheaded with an *aruval*.' An *aruval*, of course, is a sickle, a harvesting tool for farmers and a weapon quite commonly wielded by gangsters, I am told.

Such menacing, even gory pictures and the apprehensions they feed all stem from what Madurai seems to stand for in their minds: a violence-prone town, with belligerent, bloodthirsty residents brandishing sickles at the very whiff of a brawl. It's this fearsome image that lingers in my mind as I head towards it, further heightened by the clutch of violent 'Madurai films' that I have watched earlier. '3M movies,' as a friend describes them – about murder, mayhem and morbidity in Madurai.

Is it Madurai's intrinsic violence, rooted in its politics and society, that comes through in the 'Madurai films' or is it the bloodshed shown onscreen that has created the myth of Madurai violence? These are the questions that have played on my mind, as they possibly would for an outsider to this world, its politics, culture and cinema.

Unfortunately – or should I say, luckily – my first impression of Thoonga Nagaram, 'the city that never sleeps', as Madurai is often described, doesn't quite live up to its tainted reputation. The early morning auto ride goes off without a hitch. I encounter no unsavoury individuals during my hiccup-free stay. Nor do I become embroiled in unpleasant incidents. In contrast to the Madurai of the movies, the real one feels surprisingly innocuous and quite safe.

However, friends living in the South are still not ready to give Madurai the benefit of the doubt. It's a tourist's perspective, say some, commenting on my point of view. Perhaps, argue others, it's because I have arrived on a very auspicious day. It's the Poornima of the Shravan month – Raksha Bandhan – after all, the day on which pious south Indian Brahmins are known to change their *poonal* (the holy thread), preferably in a ceremony conducted at a temple.

Leaving the blood and gore aside, a great many other cinema-derived images of Madurai come alive for me as I peer out of my hotel window: loud songs blaring in the narrow streets, people in shrill, piercing parleys (I don't know about what), the rhythmic beating of drums and Madurai *malli* (jasmine flowers) on sale at every corner, with the imposing presence of the magnificent Meenakshi Amman Temple in the background.

To complete the coming together of the reel and the real, I am told that my hotel on West Perumal Maistry Street is right next to where the grand Thangam Theatre, once the largest in South Asia, used to tower over its surroundings till it was razed to the ground in 2011. Built in 1952, it could seat 2,563 persons and was spread over more than 52,000 sq. ft. Family disputes and ownership battles led to its closure and eventual demolition, and it has now made way for a block of residential flats.

Movie theatres may come and go, but cinema in Madurai and the stars animating it are very much alive in the local imagination, so much so that the popular delicacy – the flat and fluffy 'Kushboo idli' – is supposedly named after Khushbu, the award-winning star of many a south Indian film, my hotel owner tells me. I bite into this unsolicited information unquestioningly.

The crucial question that needs to be addressed, above all, is: what exactly is a Madurai film and what are its implications?

There are places in films that are imagined. Then there are the real ones in which films are set. Madurai is that rare town that has gone beyond merely being the milieu and has inspired a whole genre or sub-genre of modern Tamil cinema, complete with its unique codes and conventions, which had film critic Baradwaj Rangan coin the term 'CineMadurai' – a distinction few cities in India can boast of. Among them is north Chennai. In the last few years, Kollywood has increasingly become obsessed about telling stories revolving around north Chennai neighbourhoods and showcasing protagonists based there. Even filmmakers in the North acknowledge CineMadurai's influence on their works. In the opening credits of *Gangs of Wasseypur*, for example, filmmaker Anurag Kashyap acknowledges the 'Madurai Triumvirate' of filmmakers Bala, Ameer Sultan and M. Sasikumar.

'It's an original and rooted genre created by the new-age Tamil filmmakers, who have not been influenced by the narratives of the West,' says filmmaker Srinivas Bhashyam.

'It's all about young, independent filmmakers, who branched off the mainstream,' observes film historian Theodore Baskaran.

Branched off and veered away from the big cities and Chennai, I gather, to take cinema to a rural home in Madurai.

Yes, Madurai itself is a big town, but the settings of its films are the ruthless streets, its ugly underbelly, the urban villages within the city and the rural hinterlands beyond.

But how does Madurai – a city – have a genre of cinema named after it that is rooted in the rural? How does a devout, temple town birth films that are all about blood and gore, murder and mayhem? How do these polarities reconcile? How is a compromise forged between the two extremes?

Srinivas tells me that if I were to live in Madurai for a while (rather than swoop in and out like a tourist), I would be able to witness how the worlds have already merged.

'Unlike cities like Bengaluru, Delhi or Mumbai, the outskirts of Madurai bleed into the town itself,' he explains. 'The violence, the value systems, the machismo, the male attitude and patriarchy of the small towns on the margins are present in the city centre as well.'

So unlike Delhi, where a Greater Kailash may have no connect whatsoever with a Meerut, things are starkly different in Madurai. There might be a KFC in one particular area and not in another, but an average inhabitant would have the same ideas and beliefs as one living a 100 km away.

'It is the cinema of the entire region than just Madurai,' Srinivas sums up.

I subsequently learn that for him, CineMadurai is also about certain powerful, landed, patriarchal communities like the Thevars and the Gounders. In fact, apart from the geographical location and the setting, it has grown to be identified with certain genre conventions as well. CineMadurai has grown beyond Madurai.

'It has ethnic roots; there are portrayals of folk culture, music, festivals and village rituals,' Baskaran adds.

The hero is almost always rough and scruffy (read 'unshaven') and the heroine perennially sweet and innocent (read 'without make-up and deglamorized'). But there are no pastoral idylls here. On the contrary, there is graphic violence – gang wars and/or family quarrels, street brawls and lots of bloodshed – and love stories that end in tragedy, often with the harsh and cruel reality of caste discrimination and poverty as an underlying theme.

'And the fights don't involve guns, but *aruvals*,' Baskaran clarifies.

Yes, those very sickles that I had been warned of! Watch a CineMadurai film and you'll end up believing that every Madurai resident has one tucked away in his *veshti* (dhoti), ready to be whipped out at the drop of a hat.

'CineMadurai marks the return of the native; it harks back to the native land,' observes filmmaker, writer and professor K. Hariharan, former director of the LV Prasad Film and TV Academy in Chennai.

But, according to him, the slice of life it represents may well be just a notion of reality, much like the 'created' villages in Hindi films.

'Like the UP of *Ganga Jamuna*, where Bhojpuri is spoken,' he elaborates, adding, however, that 'the Madurai films did bring the deep-set frustrations of the people to a boil'.

A reason, perhaps, for their immense popularity.

'It's feel-bad cinema that initially felt very appealing, meaningful and real, almost a relief, as opposed to the urban middle-class movies of Vijay and Vikram, and the saccharine-sweet fantasies of Hindi cinema,' Srinivas tells me.

It all started in 2004 with Balaji Sakhtivel's *Kaadhal*, a powerful love story about a Madurai mechanic and a rich liquor baron's daughter. Srinivas feels, however, that the seeds of the genre were sown all the way back in the early '70s in Bharathiraja's Sridevi–Kamal Haasan–Rajinikanth-starrer *Pathinaaru Vayathinile*, a film which was also remade in Hindi in 1979 as *Solva Sawan*, with Amol Palekar and Sridevi, marking her debut in Bollywood. Though *Pathinaaru Vayathinile* is technically not a Madurai film, it laid the grounds for the formula that came to dominate it.

'It was entirely set and shot in a village, brought the rural ethos alive,' Srinivas informs me. 'However, Bharathiraja's aesthetic was raw, rustic and realistic, but not bloody, like the contemporary Madurai movies are.'

Thevar Magan (1992) was another film that focussed on Tamil Nadu's rural south and its Thevar community, long before the term 'CineMadurai' was coined.

Yet another film that Srinivas feels belongs to the genre (though it has never been formally acknowledged as such) is *Virumaandi* (2004). Written and directed by Kamal Haasan, he also played the lead in it. About two prison inmates from Madurai, Kothala Thevar and Virumaandi, the film interplays their individual perspectives on the same story. It was the first movie to have featured the rough game of *jallikattu*, or bull taming, played in Madurai during Pongal (but banned by the Supreme Court in 2014, a decision which would be upheld again in 2016). The sets, however, were recreated in Chennai.

According to Hariharan, it was filmmaker Bala who gave a fillip to the genre with his debut as a director in the Vikram–starrer *Sethu* (1999). It earned the actor the nickname 'Chiyaan', after the name of the character played by him in the film, and was also remade in Hindi as *Tere Naam*, with Salman Khan playing the lead. Both the original and the remake proved to be big hits.

The recent rise and rise of Madurai movies started off with Ameer Sultan's *Paruthiveeran* (2007), an intensely moving, brutal and tragic love story from the boondocks, starring Karthi in his feature-film debut. Prabhu Solomon's *Mynaa* (2010), starring Vidharth and Amala Paul, was yet another heart-rending story, where the objections of the family to the relationship beween the lovers and unfortunate misunderstandings that crop up along the way keep the young man and woman apart. Set in the arena of rooster fights, Vetrimaaran's *Aadukalam* (2011), with Dhanush and Taapsee Pannu in the lead, dealt with the game of one-upmanship between a mentor and his pupil. The omnipresent brutality, bloodshed and aggression are offset by a tender love story that plays out on the side and the end leaves you with an overwhelming sense of loss and waste.

However, it is M. Sasikumar's *Subramaniapuram* (2008) that could, arguably, be considered the best film in the genre. A dark, gritty story about youth unemployment and unrest in 1980s' Madurai, it was made on a shoestring budget with a relatively unknown cast, except for Sasikumar himself in a pivotal role. Involving love and friendship, betrayal and revenge, poverty, politics and crime, the story is set in the streets of one of Madurai's working-class neighbourhoods.

'It is set in the time when rowdyism entered politics,' Sasikumar clarifies, referring to the increasing infiltration of political parties and polls by lumpen elements that have been used to manipulate the masses through intimidation, instead of addressing their concerns, and have turned governance into a self-serving vehicle furthering the interests of certain political leaders, rather than working for the greater good of the people.

According to him, all of Subramaniapuram is a character in the film; the locality is the real hero. The filmmaker spent time researching the areas in Madurai where the gangs operated – Subramaniapuram, Jaihindpuram, Vazhaithoppu, and more. But many of those street scenes had to be shot in Dindigul, rather than in Madurai, because Sasikumar no longer senses the restless, throbbing energy at its core that had caught his interest earlier.

'Things have changed in Madurai now,' he says.

He feels that the geography and topography, the very look and the incipient, bustling energy that defined the streets seem to have gone missing for reasons he cannot fathom.

I meet Sasikumar in the quiet, picturesque environs of the Heritage Hotel, far removed from the madness and chaos of the main town, and ask him the question topmost in my head: why this fascination for Madurai? Perhaps, he replies, because a good number of Tamil cinema's new wave filmmakers have come from Madurai or grew up and studied there (though there are a few exceptions, like Chennai boy Vetrimaaran). The city's vibe, its culture, is something they are familiar with.

'It's a place we know best and are confident about tackling on screen,' Sasikumar explains. 'There's a sentimental attachment to it.'

He calls *Subramaniapuram* a story that was 'born from the seeds of my native soil'.

Anand Pandian, who edited the English script of *Subramaniapuram* for Tranquebar, a literary imprint of Westland Books, describes his experience of watching the film at Cine Priya theatre in Madurai: 'The movie hall erupted in a cacophony of whistling when the characters in the film watch a movie themselves, *Murattu Kaali*, the 1980 film starring Tamil celluloid deity Rajinikanth. On the screen I could see another Madurai movie hall packed with roaring bodies, also teetering between jubilation and aggression, another hall that felt and looked so much like this one. It was suddenly impossible to distinguish the whistling of loudspeakers from the sound of those around me. Realist cinema had spilled into the world of real experience.'

Madurai is significant for the Tamil film industry, because, as Baskaran puts it, 'It's a city sold to cinema.'

The audience is known to fight tooth and nail to buy tickets for the big films, often climbing over the shoulders of people ahead of them in the queue to reach the ticket window before anyone else can. It was a very similar scene that Sasikumar would recreate in *Subramaniapuram*. The theatre shown was supposedly the historic Thangam, but the scene was actually shot in Central cinema.

'It's not just about watching films. People also discuss them endlessly and, in the industry, it's always asked as to how a film is doing in Madurai,' says Sasikumar.

If it works in Madurai, the entire south of Tamil Nadu is sure to bring in huge profits.

Madurai is, after all, the state's third-largest city, the centre of Tamil language, literature, history and culture, and the state's educational, industrial and manufacturing hub.

What does Sasikumar have to say about its violent image?

He brushes my question aside. 'There are good and bad people everywhere,' he says.

'Madurai is a fertile, rich, moneyed land that holds on to its pride and culture,' Srinivas explains, offering a different interpretation to the town's fearsome image. 'Valour and machismo are valorized. People are proud and assertive, like the Punjabis or Haryanvis of the North.'

It is a town so bound by certain codes of honour that people would not hesitate, even today, to kill or take their own life to uphold a principle.

As a viewer, you are also aware that cinema has a way of inventing its own mythology, whereby, instead of accepting a city the way it is in its starkly real setting, you often end up absorbing its essence, filtered through the prism of a screen.

'It's like all the Jats get identified with the *khap panchayat* and honour killings,' says Hariharan. 'It's about isolated, real examples of violence getting exaggerated on screen.'

There's more to Madurai than machismo, I am assured.

Indeed, underplayed though it may be, there is a softer, non-violent, nurturing side as well to this rather harsh portrait of the city. Surprisingly, that too has a cinema connect, albeit an indirect one. As I get ready to set out on my onward journey to Chennai, *The Hindu* journalist Soma Basu tells me about film star Katrina Kaif's mother and stepfather – Sussana and Jesse Joseph – who are involved in social work aimed at improving the health, well-being and status of the girl child in Pudupatti and a dozen other villages in the Usilampatti taluk, an area otherwise notorious for female foeticide and infanticide. The couple had arrived in India in 2004, making the long journey from London to Chennai to organize relief work for those whose lives and homes had been destroyed by the tsunami. They stayed on to work for the welfare of local children. They helped rebuild Claretian Mercy Home for abandoned children in Azhagusurai village, 30 km off Madurai, and now call the temple town their second home. The locals pitch in as well, lending a helping hand to the outsiders.

Such examples of compassion and philanthrophy notwithstanding, many insist that there is a grain of truth in the culture of violence, even though I may have mercifully been spared a first-hand glimpse of it. It has always been a politically volatile place. At the time of my visit, it was represented by R. Gopalakrishnan of the All India Anna Dravida Munnetra Kazhagam (AIADMK), but it was M.K. Alagiri, the second son of the former chief minister of Tamil Nadu and head of Dravida Munnetra Kazagham (DMK), the late M. Karunanidhi, who had been holding sway over the region. Karunanidhi was said to prefer his younger son, M.K. Stalin, which led to widespread clashes between the latter's supporters and those of Alagiri. The land mafia was in cahoots with local politicians in the game of money and muscle power. Things grew more intense in the surrounding villages. Acts of revenge, murders and land-grabbing had become de rigueur, said the bureau chief of a local newspaper.

'If you look at the Tamil newspapers, it seems that all the riots, fights and murders are happening in Madurai. All issues seem to get resolved there through violence,' says film historian Baskaran.

Journalist Subha J. Rao reinforces this impression by harking back to patterns set in the historical past.

'Then too, Madurai has seen bloodshed,' she points out. 'Legend has it that King Koon Pandiyan allegedly got 8,000 Jains massacred in Samanatham, a village in Madurai, in the seventh century.'

When it comes to cinema, however, there is only that much 'feel-bad' that a market can take; a reason, perhaps, why Madurai films have been losing their sheen of late – on their home turf as well. Also, the filmmakers who had created the genre and given it its special niche ended up letting people down with their subsequent mediocre work. As I travel around in Madurai, the CineMadurai genre itself appears to have moved on to its moment of reckoning. Its abiding conventions have begun to feel like familiar clichés and easy stereotypes. The more recent films have hit the low end of creativity. So while north India may still not have discovered it fully, the core audience in the South is wondering: where will it go from here?

The answer, in all likelihood, lies in *jigarthanda*, which may well be the next step up in the evolution. Madurai's signature drink, a drink to 'cool the heart', *jigarthanda* inspired the title of 2014's most crucial Tamil hit, directed by Karthik Subbaraj. A 'funny' Madurai film about the making of a Madurai film, this gangster comedy about a young filmmaker Karthik travelling to Madurai to make a film on 'Assault' Sethu, the local don, tried to broaden the scope of the 'Madurai film'. This 'Madurai-ception', to describe it in one word, was seen as the next step in the evolution of the genre beyond the code of pure, in-your-face violence, despite remaining quite well-entrenched in it.

Right from the 'Madurai song', '*Malarnthum malaratha*' ('Like a blooming flower') from Shivaji Ganesan's *Pasamalar*, and its street food – those delicious banana *bajji*s – to portraying the town's passionate cinema culture, *Jigarthanda* is a homage to Madurai. It belongs to, yet strays away from CineMadurai. About gangsters and gang wars, it involves copious amounts of bloodshed. It refers to a violent Madurai neighbourhood like Jaihindpuram. Why, it even gives a nod to a CineMadurai admirer – Anurag Kashyap – and brings filmmaker Vetrimaaran, one of its practitioners, into the picture.

But, as Srinivas puts it, 'It is clever, postmodern, entertaining, with a sense of humour, [and] plays with the storytelling.'

Jigarthanda has an inventive, unusual story; and, most of all, it is not 'indulgently feel-bad'; in fact, it is hilarious and entertaining. It's as much about belly laughs, as it is about shootouts.

'It's self-reflexive filmmaking. It enquires into the Madurai cinema genre,' Hariharan observes.

Yes, the *aruval* is omnipresent in this film as well, but refreshingly, it isn't just a weapon. It is, hilariously, also the decoration for a dreaded don's birthday cake. That he cuts with – guess what? An *aruval*.

Long after my Madurai visit, in March 2019, Anurag Kashyap organized a special screening of *Subramaniapuram* in Mumbai. Young film buffs lapped it up. I spoke to one of them – film professional Anup Pandey – who gushes about 'the milieu, the visual treatment, the play of emotions and the incredible, incipient energy'. Despite the lack of subtitles, he claims that he 'got' the film. And leaves me wondering: How can a genre that is well past its glory days still hold interest? That too for an outsider to the world?

According to Srinivas, CineMadurai might be on the wane now, but it has left a deep impact on Tamil and other cinemas of India.

'It flows in the bloodstream of a lot of our cinema. It has percolated and is getting carried on in different ways in the work of a cross-section of young filmmakers, often without them even realizing it,' he observs.

For him, even a film as recent as Vetrimaaran's *Vada Chennai*, though located in north Chennai, takes its aesthetic from CineMadurai.

'He has cleverly urbanized it,' says Srinivas, adding that if we were to do reverse engineering, a lot of contemporary stuff – from a Marathi film like *Sairat* to a web series like *Mirzapur* – would owe a lot to the game.

In fact, for him, *Mirzapur* is the 'north Indian great-grandson' of the Madurai films. But without an *aruval* in sight.

The Trouble with Spoofs

ABOUT A YEAR AFTER having met him for the first time in 2014, I receive a reproachful email from Mohammed Farogh Jafri.

'*Maine aap ko* mail *kiya tha*,' he writes. '*Aapne jawaab nahin diya – uska afsos nahin hai. Par meri* amma *ke intekaal ki khabar par bhi aap ka koi* reaction *nahin aaya – is ka afsos hai. Aap logon ke liye* mail *sirf ek* official medium, *ek* technology *ka tukda ho sakti hai, magar hum toh dil nikal ke rakh dete hain aur uske baad bhi agar koi asar na ho toh phir*... I had mailed you. That you sent no reply did not dishearten me. What did was your failure to even react to the news of my mother's demise. For people like you, an email might be an official medium of communication, a mere piece of technology, but we pour our hearts out in it and if even that leaves others unmoved, well...'

Farogh's email, informing me of his mother's death, may have got lost in the virtual world, but in his subsequent reproach, I could find a pointer to the persona of the man, one of the most famous residents of Malegaon, a small town in the Nashik district of Maharashtra, which lies on NH 3, connecting Mumbai to Agra.

A leading writer of the town's famous spoof-cinema industry, Farogh is constantly thinking films. When I meet him, it's *Malegaon ka James Bond 007.5* that's preoccupying him. The way he describes things and expresses himself – never simple and direct, but dramatic and forceful or poetic and tangential – makes it seem as though he were quoting certain lines or describing compelling scenes from his own film scripts, rather than having conversations about life's vicissitudes. Hear him talk of his first love for a girl in school and all the other great love stories will instantly pale into insignificance.

His inclination to presume familiarity with near strangers like me can, at times, lead to awkwardness or even a feeling of uneasiness, especially when he takes it upon himself to share his intensely private thoughts and relationship issues. Or – much to my discomfiture – recites *shayari* to me in his flamboyantly romantic style, with his wife, children and even mother looking on. However, the reason for his almost intrusive friendliness is quite transparent. Every personal connect established, every new rapport struck up holds a promise for him – the hope of a way out of Malegaon and into Mumbai, specifically, Bollywood. The City of Dreams lies just 296 km away, but even though Farogh is in his early 40s when I meet him, he hasn't been able to bridge this distance and find a foothold in the Hindi film industry.

Will I, with my supposed Bollywood connections, show him the way, he wonders. He is certainly hopeful. I know I have little to offer him, other than a few phone numbers.

Farogh is clear about his direction in life: he wants to write scripts for Bollywood films. For now, the stepping stone towards it is television. It is clear that whatever else he may lack, it certainly isn't confidence in his potential.

'*Bahut* great master artwork *karunga*,' he declares. 'Inshallah *Buniyaad, Tamas, Rajani* ke standard *ke* serial *likh aur bana kar dunga.* God willing, I will do great work. I will write and make serials of the same quality as *Buniyaad, Tamas, Rajani*.'

He doesn't bat an eyelid as he refers to these long-running television serials of the '80s, directed by stalwarts like Ramesh Sippy, Govind Nihalani and Basu Chatterjee.

Farogh does have talent; he can convey a great deal in just a few words. But the pattern of failed attempts in making it to Bollywood also stems from his own personality. He is a complicated individual, living inside his own mind, sunk in introspection, instead of being canny and enterprising. Moreover, his pride in his own talent is unshakeable, his self-confidence almost verges on arrogance and he has an overwhelming sense of superiority.

'*Mujhe bacha kar shayad aap* Urdu literature *ka kuch faayda kar sakein.* By giving me an opportunity to prove myself, you will, perhaps, be doing Urdu literature a favour,' he writes to me.

His deeply melancholic nature could well be a defence mechanism against the insecurities and vulnerabilities stemming from life's inequities. He comes from a family of intellectuals, who probably deserve far better than the shabby environs they are holed up in. Their home is in an overcrowded ghetto, with small clusters of houses lining narrow lanes. Overflowing drains run alongside.

'*Kabr se thoda hi bada* room… A room hardly bigger than a grave,' is how he describes his little space.

It is a room full of books and films. From a tome on Israeli politics to Syd Field's screenwriting Bible – he has them all.

Farogh's mother was a primary-school teacher. His father used to bring out an eveninger called *Shaamnama*.

'Javed Akhtar saab *se milti julti rahi hai meri zindagi*. My life resembles Javed Akhtar's,' he says, referring to his progressive family.

His parents married for love in an era when it was almost unheard of and his mother, who apparently hadn't a care in the world, used to be a quite a fashionista, 'sporting three-inch heels'.

I sense Farogh's guilt over his failure to take his family out of the rut. His daughter is doing a diploma in education. He wants her to work for a while, before marrying her off with all the pomp and show expected of a respectable family.

'*Achcha beta nahin ban saka, par achcha baap banne mein meri madad keejiye.* I could never be a worthy son, but help me become a responsible father,' he implores.

You can sense an incredible political awareness in him and this doesn't apply to his insights on Malegaon, Maharashtra and India alone. He offers well-reasoned critiques of America and the Islamic nations as well.

'*Dono quamon ke taane baane se kapda ban raha hai, is sheher ki* economy *chal raha hai*. The textile mills and the town's economy are run by the shared effort and contribution of the two communities,' he says, emphasizing the need for Hindu–Muslim harmony in Malegaon.

These aren't empty words. It was he who took the lead and was part of the street-theatre groups who performed to promote peace and harmony in the wake of the 2001 riots in Malegaon.

Farogh's knowledge of films is just as extensive. Camera angles, framing, lighting, script-writing – he has learnt them all on his own from films, foreign and Indian.

He knows that he deserves better than Malegaon, a dreary industrial town. His life here may be less than banal, but in his mind, he still lives it on a 70 mm scale, strutting about like a thespian on the stage of his own destiny. Farogh's persona is striking in its propensity for theatricality and flourishes. And you can't help feeling that he is a character who deserves a film on himself.

In many ways, Farogh personifies Malegaon and its film industry. He represents a perspective from which you can study the odd town, its people and its industry. An economically feeble and socially fragile town, its unique spoof-making enterprise is the rare spot of sunshine in its otherwise wasteland-like landscape.

Much has been written about and made of Malegaon's spoof-cinema industry – from Manu Joseph's 21 July 2003 piece in *Outlook*[11] to Faiza Khan's popular documentary *Supermen of Malegaon* that helped familiarize the town for many across India. But visiting the place in person opens your eyes to certain realities you were probably unaware of. This little, Muslim-dominated (the community constitutes roughly 75 per cent of the population) town continues to move along rather shakily on two different wheels – powerlooms and projectors. It is in its dark, depressing factories that the local youth earn their daily wages as weavers or welders, and it is in the local cinema halls that they escape from their dreary reality.

Malegaon is a town which potable water, sanitation, education and even decent medical facilities have bypassed. Electricity supply is intermittent, forcing power looms to remain shut, unless the owners can afford generators. It may have many cinema halls (Kidwai, Upkar, Subhash, Deepak, Mohan and now a multiplex called Cinemax Sandesh), but not a single public park. Yes, there's the famous Arvind ice-cream stall, which provides the only other recreational 'outing', apart from films, to Malegaon residents. And, of course, Poornima Hotel, famous for its dosas, where the spoof-cinema industry took root and the first Malegaon spoof was hatched. It is also where I meet the folks from the industry.

Spoofs of Bollywood movies, like *Malegaon ke Sholay*, the hilarious spoof of *Sholay*, released in 2000, are unique to Malegaon and have brought fame to this nondescript industrial town. With no leading public figure as patron, no political, economic or social support, no mentor or guide to show the way, spoof cinema in Malegaon has risen like a grass-roots mass movement of sorts, the agent provocateur being a small businessman and film buff Nasir Sheikh, whose family used to run a cinema hall in Malegaon, where his own dreams of filmmaking took root. It was Sheikh who would turn the collective obsession with cinema into Malegaon's calling card.

Back in 2000, he borrowed ₹50,000 from his brother, gathered the town's Dharmendra, Big B and Sanjeev Kumar lookalikes, shot with them on a handycam and made an inventive parody of the Ramesh Sippy–classic *Sholay*, in which the fearsome Gabbar was called Rubber and the irrepressible Basanti answered to the name of Basmati, the slender-grained, fragrant rice served in many homes during the main meals. While writing an article ('Sirens of Malewood, *Outllook*, 11 May 2009) I got to to know that the wacky film gave Malegaon's residents reason for a hearty laugh, earned more than double its investment and set off the local trend that would lead to a flourishing alternate spoof-cinema industry in Malegaon. Every Friday, the town gathered to watch its own quirky 'of the people, by the people, for the people' video films in friendly neighbourhood video halls. Nasir followed in the footsteps of Sippy, yet again, to make *Malegaon ki Shaan*. Others were inspired to emulate him and churned out burlesque versions of *Mughal-e-Azam*, *Don*, *Karan Arjun*, *Rangeela* and *Lagaan*.

Initially released in Malegaon, these Hindustani language (a mix of Hindi and Urdu) films soon found their way across India in the form of CDs and are now available on YouTube. Nobody I talk to has a logical explanation for the growth of the phenomenon. Nasir's success lit the spark, driving many youngsters to try his formula; and now, spoof cinema seems to have given Malegaon residents an identity they are loath to relinquish; a legacy of sorts they feel impelled to live up to. These spoofs were neither made to earn money nor to provide a platform for the maker's artistry and talent. I get the feeling that Malegaon's brand of filmmaking has provided its residents with an escape route from the drudgery of their day-to-day life and a unique sense of pride, apart from allowing them to celebrate the sheer joy of cinema. They may be eking out a living by selling vegetables or working in factories, running eateries or tea stalls. They could be electricians and cycle mechanics of modest means. But they will still make films with whatever little spare money and time they have at their disposal. They are all shockingly resourceful. Actors – and the crew – are willing to work for free for the sheer glory of being involved in such an enterprise. Local shops provide the costumes, wedding videographers turn cinematographers for the occasion and fields nearby become 'outdoors locations'. Improvisation is everything. For the crane shot, the camera gets mounted on a bullock cart, the cameraman sits on one end and the crew pushes the other end to make it go up, rather like a see-saw. The camera is placed on a bike and carted around for trolley, zoom and pan shots.

A few years ago, this booming enterprise was badly hit by a crackdown on unlicensed video parlours. Moreover, the 2001 riots, the bomb blasts in 2006 and 2008, terror-driven activities, the communal divide (with Hindus and Muslims living on opposite banks of the Mausam River, on either side of the Mausam Pul, with one side relatively prosperous,the other utterly impoverished) and the economic downturn took their inevitable toll. As a result, power cuts lasting between eight and 10 hours are now a part of life in Malegaon and have become its new calling card. To further compound its problems, the town was in the news again, some years ago, for the first offence reported after the new Maharashtra Animal Preservation (Amendment) Act, banning beef slaughter in the state, came into effect. Three people were booked for allegedly slaughtering a pair of calves. But curiously enough, in the midst of all the bad news and business setbacks, a few people continue to make films and seem to find in them some respite from life's harsh realities. The hype, hoopla and attention the industry gathered during Nasir's time, not just in the town, but even beyond Malegaon itself, however, seem to have abated. There is a downswing, but no perceptible signs of giving it up entirely.

It isn't until you visit Malegaon, as I do, that you realize that all the previous writings on this industry are yesterday's stories. Just as old trends give way to the new in Bollywood, every now and then, they do the same in Malegaon. I find, during my visit in 2014, that a lot has changed in this town since 2000. I discover that the spoofs of Bollywood and Hollywood films have given way to spoofs of Salman Khan movies and original horror flicks. The minute a Salman film is announced in Mumbai, someone or the other in Malegaon starts working on one with the same title, but based on an original idea. Malegaon's versions of *Ek Tha Tiger* and *Dabangg 2* have just been released in the form of CDs, even as the original Bollywood versions are showing in theatres while I am there. And work has started locally on Malegaon's own versions of *Kick* and *Jai Ho*, titled what else but *Malegaon ki Jai Ho* and *Malegoan ki Kick*?

Meanwhile, one of Malegoan's filmmakers, Raj Tribhuvan, is also working on an original film, a psychological thriller called *Dot Dot Dot*. In fact, they all want to go original now. Writer-director-actor Khursheed Siddiqui sells vegetables for a living, but that doesn't stop him from wanting to make a movie on the life of Meena Thackeray, wife of the late Bal Thackeray. In this quest to fulfil his dream, he has sent a letter to their son, Shiv Sena supremo Uddhav Thackeray, asking for permission.

But, however original the intention, the references are still squarely Bollywood, as I discover when I am introduced to 'Malegaon *ka* Salman' in the famous Poornima Hotel. His real name is Mubeen. But he calls himself Mubeen Salman and makes an entry into Poornima Hotel quite like the star, in a floral shirt and tight pants, with the swagger intact. A man of few words like his idol, Mubeen barely mumbles a sentence or two, but is acutely aware of his muscular physique as he struts around the hotel. There is also the singer Ashok Jadhav, better known as 'Malegaon *ka* Suresh Wadkar' after the famous playback singer, because his voice and singing style are reminiscent of Wadkar's. Word has got around of my presence in town and they all decide to meet me together to discuss the state of their industry.

They have better resources to work with now, they tell me. With the advancement of technology in general and easier access to it, more sophisticated cameras, lights and reflectors are used.

Some of their claims do seem a bit exaggerated, though.

'Mumbai actors are willing to work in our films,' says Tribhuvan.

When I prod him further, however, urging him to come up with a few names, he concedes that they aren't the top-of-the-league guys, but little-known supporting actors and those working in television.

VCR-to-VCR editing has given way to computers. An electronics shop owner, Shahid Jamal, who uses 'Pinnacle 8/7', is a leading editor. So is Zahir Hussain, who runs a television repair shop and has 10 films behind him. A tiny music-recording studio has come up as well. Despite the setbacks suffered due to political and communal issues, the group insists that budgets have gone up now, with financiers – often from outside the town – with more money at their disposal stepping in to back a few projects. Most significantly, a Mollywood or Malegaon Film Association, with some 300 members, has also been registered. But there is a flip side to each of the success stories. It's not quite *achche din* (good days), however much they may claim otherwise.

Firoz Tarzan, who made *Malegaon ka Ek Tha Tiger*, owns a plastic factory. He had made the film on a budget of ₹4.5 lakh, but it recovered only ₹2.86 lakh. However, like a few others in the Malegaon industry, he continues to see life through rose-tinted glasses. He is not worried. Unlike the other small-time producers, he has the means and money to throw away. Filmmaking for him is an indulgence and a hobby.

But despite the divide – between the small Malegaon films that are in the majority and the few new big-budgeted ones – some things remain much the same. The film plots are still crazy, peppered with local issues, idioms, images and, of course, the inimitable local sense of humour. Every film comes loaded with social messages, as usual. The majority of the people working in the industry are still Muslims (Deepak Shivaji Ahire and Raj Tribhuvan are exceptions, however) and, as has been the norm so far, Malegaon's women don't work in the movies. Heroines are imported from nearby Jalgaon. And there is an unwritten rule Malegaon's films continue to abide by: no bold, sexy scenes.

'Malegaon *ki* films *ka naam kharab nahin karna hai*. We don't want to give our films a bad name,' they tell me in unison.

Meanwhile, the Dadasaheb Phalke of Malegaon – Nasir Sheikh – the man who started it all, has since managed to get a foothold in Mumbai and made a Chaplinesque silent serial for Sab TV called *Malegaon ka Chintu*. Its second season, *Chintu Ban Gaya Gentleman*, the title a take-off on Shah Rukh Khan's 1992 romantic comedy *Raju Ban Gaya Gentleman*, took Nasir around the globe.

I meet him in his own store in Malegaon, the legendary readymade-clothes showroom that was once a video hall where he saw and screened his personal favourites – Jackie Chan and Jet Li movies, and Charlie Chaplin's *Modern Times* and *City Lights* – among others.

I had last met Nasir at Tonic, in Delhi's Siri Fort Complex, where he was buying me a meal for writing an article on the Faiza Khan documentary *Supermen of Malegaon*, on his – and the town's – first Hollywood spoof *Malegaon ka Superman*. It was this very article that had brought him into the limelight and this was his way of acknowledging his gratitude. Incidentally, Khan's documentary that had won several awards across the globe, including at the Asian First Film Festival, the Golden Apricot Yerevan International Film Festival and the Vesoul Asian Film Festival, was one of the earliest documentaries to find a commercial release in Indian theatres.

Sheikh, along with his cast and crew, had been invited to the International Film Festival of India (IFFI) in Delhi for the screening of *Malegaon ka Superman*, only to be stopped at the entrance, as they didn't 'look' like people who'd be making or watching festival films. He was hurt, but excited, nonetheless. It was his first film festival, his first stay in a hotel and his first plane ride, and it was certainly the furthest he had gone away from his hometown. Now, having seen the world – Shimla, Kulu Manali, Kashmir, Goa, Ahmedabad, Germany, Italy, Switzerland, Singapore, Hong Kong, Macau and Thailand – all he wants to do is drop anchor in Malegaon.

'*Mujhe toh* Malegaon *hi raas aata hai. Din ginta hoon ki kab wapas aana hoga*. It's only in Malegaon that I feel completely at home. When I'm away, I keep counting down the days till my return,' he says, when I meet him in Malegaon.

He realizes that the industry he founded has grown and newer faces have taken over the reins. After Superman, he wants to make a send-up of Spiderman. His Spiderman will be fat.

'When he hangs from the web, he will fall to the ground,' he explains guffawing. When I last met Farogh in the summer of 2018, his life seems to have taken a different turn. He has married off his daughter, and made a documentary called *Ye Zaroori Hai* on a Muslim powerloom worker fighting for children's right to vaccination. But he still dreams of making it big in Bollywood one day.

You can take a Malegaon *mulga* (boy) out of Malegaon, but not the spirit of Malegaon out of the same *mulga*.

Malegaon's spoof cinema doesn't exist in isolation. It is the king of a unique world consisting of small, local film industries that many wouldn't have even heard of; yet, far though they may be from Bollywood's limelight, they are flourishing in a parallel sphere of their own.

For a few years now, locally made low-budget video films have been flooding almost the entire northern, eastern and western regions of India. There is no disputing the fact that Malegaon is the country's video-film capital. The video-film industry is not one big monolith, however. It assumes various shapes and manifestations in different regions.

Consider its presence in Ahmedabad, for example, in the form of Sindhi films, though my introduction to their most well-known maker is, curiously enough, through a sweet shop in the city.

Like most Sindhi confectioners, Mahalakshmi Sweets in Ahmedabad's Kuber Nagar is proud of its customary *tosha* – fried flour rolls dipped in sugar syrup – and *sev ki barfi*, a delicacy made with unsalted fried strings of gramflour and reduced milk. The shop's heavyset, gregarious and hospitable owner, Chander Danwani, is proud of yet another creation he dishes out regularly – Sindhi films.

Three generations of the Danwani family have been involved in the business of sweets in Ahmedabad. For three generations, they have also been part of a Sindhi theatre group called Jai Bhavani. It wasn't just love for the stage, however, that drew the Danwani family into the world of performance from their usual place in the business of sweets, but a desperate attempt to keep their mellifluous mother tongue alive.

'Day by day, the Sindhi language is dying a slow death,' Danwani sighs.

A bit of culture, some entertainment could, perhaps, keep it going, had been his idea when he made his foray into theatre.

Apprehensions about its imminent extinction made him branch out further, from theatre into the more popular zone of filmmaking – all in the hope of luring the younger, film-obsessed generation to the use of the Sindhi language.

'We thought it would help attract the young. who are speaking in Hindi and English, more than [in] Sindhi, even in their homes,' he says. 'And almost no one knows how to read and write in the language any more.'

Not that Danwani has anything against the use of Hindi and English. His primary concern is that his own lingo, culture and identity should not fall by the wayside. Films are his way of giving it a leg up. As it is for a handful of other Sindhi film producers.

Danwani does not deal in big-screen, commercial feature films, but in friendly neighbourhood video films. Since 1981, he has made 57 of them. His partners are 25 other small businessmen like him: the local grocers, and fruit and vegetable vendors. No wonder the budget of the films on an average is not just modest, but minuscule: between ₹30,000 and ₹50,000. Danwani and his partners make about two such films a year. The money from their theatre, especially when they travel with their shows, subsidizes the cost of production, but they do look actively for advertising, sponsorship and financiers. The camera of choice is the basic, hand-held one, 'the one used for shooting wedding videos,' I'm told. To avoid intrusive location sounds and to cut down on the subsequent cost of dubbing that outdoor shoots would thus necessitate, most films are shot in the relative peace and quiet of indoor locations. A few films, however, have been shot outdoors in Mount Abu, Ajmer and Indore. And, of course, Ulhasnagar, aka Sindhunagar, that has the largest population of Hindu Sindhis outside Sindh (5,06,098, according to the 2011 Census) and is, consequently, also Sindhi cinema's biggest market.

If Malegaon specializes in making wholesale spoofs of Bollywood and Hollywood films, these Sindhi video films are replete with caricatures of individual stars, from Dada Kondke to Amitabh Bachchan. The actors playing the various roles are, quite evidently, not brimming with histrionic potential; most of them juggle day jobs with cinema, to which they devote time and energy for the sheer love of it, rather than to make money. The films are peppered with social messages that are unabashedly shrill and over the top. Some of the films to roll out of the Danwani 'studio' are *Do Paagal* (Two Crazies) and *Hu Kedo Pyaar?* (What Kind of Love Is This?)

All this is happening at a time when Sindhi commercial, big-screen cinema in India is not in the best of health. Homi Wadia is said to have made the first Sindhi film *Ekta* in 1942. *Abana* (1958), on the theme of the Partition, is considered a Sindhi classic. It featured Bollywood's popular yesteryear star Sadhana, then an unknown face, as a second female lead to actress Sheila Ramani. The 1984 romantic comedy *Hal Ta Bhaji Haloon* (Let Us Run Away), with a song by Lata Mangeshkar, was one of the last big hits. The last few films, like *Pyar Kare Dis: Feel the Power of Love* (2007) and *Faatho Aah Bhagwaan* (2013), were not able to recover their costs, despite attracting sizeable crowds. In fact, the mismatch between the high cost of investment and its subsequent recovery remains a big problem for the industry. Since the tickets are not competitively priced, even if a sizeable number of viewers watch it, the collections don't add up to much.

Sindhi is possibly the only regional Indian language in which people world over make films. While it remains a small video enterprise in India, the big screen and television productions are all being made in Pakistan, Danwani informs me. *Darya Paar, Babar Sher, Aakhri Feslo, Raawal* – he reels off the titles of some of the more dramatic ones. But producers for them are difficult to come by in India. With no state or region to call its own, the going has been getting tougher for Sindhi cinema. Neither subsidies nor governmental support has been forthcoming and with a scattered population of Sindhi speakers (in this country alone, the community is spread across six states and 100 cities, Danwani informs me) the distribution and screening of Sindhi feature films has become unviable. Ashok–Anil Multiplex is the only theatre in the Mumbai metropolitan region (in Ulhasnagar) that devotes multiple shows to Sindhi films. It is where Sindhi video-film production is also confined, despite cities like Mumbai and Ahmedabad being in the vicinity.

'Sindhis have spread all over the world. Like streams of water. *Doodh mein sharbat ki tarah mil gaye hain*. They have been absorbed like sugar in milk,' says Danwani.

Which is where his model of CD–DVD films comes in handy. Priced between ₹15 and ₹100, they have travelled to destinations where the Sindhi diaspora has a presence: the UK, the USA, South Africa, Dubai, Singapore… Now, a lot of them are also available on YouTube. And Danwani, who has no plans to hang up his boots, aims to keep at it.

Says he: 'As long as I am alive, I will do the best I can to keep [the] Sindhi language alive.'

He seems to be fighting a lone battle in preserving his language and culture. There might a few others, but they are neither as prolific nor as capable of matching his commitment or consistency. The next two productions from Danwani & Co. are set to roll soon. I have already received the invite for the mahurat and a box of *sev barfi* as well. It is clear that Danwani, at least, is relentless in his mission to propagate the Sindhi language and with it, the community's culture.

Fluctuating fortunes are all a part of the film game. While the bigger industries can survive the turbulence and remain stable, small video industries shut down almost as quickly as they are set up.

Not so long ago, Meerut had been an important centre for video feature films made on the surplus income of local farmers. The audience consisted of villagers, some of whom doubled as the films' producers and financiers. Films in *khadi boli* (Hindi dialect) were shot in banquet halls and farms, and had predominantly rural themes, as opposed to Bollywood that projected a larger-than-life, primarily urban and urbane world. Small-town India's alienation from Bollywood sensibilities was what such video films fed on. They filled the void, giving the local audience something they could identify with. Wealthy farmers in and around Meerut were keen on having their own films and started backing the makers.

The industry here reached its peak in 2004, when *Dhakad Chhora* (The Guy with an Attitude) blew into theatres like a storm. Made on a meagre budget of ₹2 lakh, it is rumoured to have netted a cool ₹2 crore. It was, in fact, such a stupendous hit that a sequel followed soon after, both the movies starring Uttar Kumar and Suman Negi, the *Jodi No.1* of Meerut films. Over the years, CD writers became cheaper, video piracy grew rampant and illegal copies of these video movies began to be circulated, thereby causing the distributors a loss. The decline in the making of such films was inevitable, with the result that the entire system has now almost collapsed in Meerut.

But what seems to be hovering on the verge of death here has taken root 175 km away in Dehradun. Garhwali video films are thriving in the capital of Uttarakhand. Unlike the satirical whimsy of Malegaon, however, or the resurgence of the grass-roots in Meerut, the Uttarakhandi film industry, like its Sindhi counterpart, among others, is primarily driven by a passion for the languages shared by members of the community and the determination to stem the tide of their diminishing relevance as a means of communication.

Anuj Joshi is Director No. 1 of the contemporary Garhwali video- and feature-film industry. As it is for Danwani, filmmaking for Joshi has been about identity issues. He makes films in the hope that they will succeed in preserving the Garhwali language and culture. And so firm has been his commitment that he gave up a flourishing career in Mumbai (he was the director of Ekta Kapoor–banner Balaji Telefilms' popular television serial *Kasauti Zindagi Kay*, 'making about ₹3–₹4 lakh a month') to live a life of fewer frills and – in terms of national recognition – near anonymity in Dehradun.

'Sadhu-type *aadmi hoon*; I almost lead the life of an ascetic. I am still a bachelor,' he confides, commenting on his modest, even austere lifestyle, as he dashes into my Doon hotel to meet me, before dashing out again. 'My demands from life are few.'

The son of a lecturer who was posted in rural Himachal Pradesh, 45-year-old Joshi spent much of his childhood quite unaware of what films were all about. But when he was in class VI, he watched his first film; and a storyteller was born within him. Joshi was mesmerized by films as a storytelling medium. From then on, he began participating actively in theatre, story writing and storytelling, and eventually left for Mumbai in 1994 to pursue his dream of making films.

'What was a hobby, to start with, became a passion,' he recalls.

He worked as an assistant director for films like Sanjay Leela Bhansali's 1999 blockbuster *Hum Dil De Chuke Sanam*, with Salman Khan, Aishwarya Rai and Ajay Devgn in the lead roles, and went on to become a big name in television, before leaving it all in 2002 to return to Dehradun.

'I never went to Bollywood for the glamour, anyhow,' he now says. 'I just wanted to learn the craft.'

It was on his return to his familiar milieu that he made his first Garhwali film, *Teri Saun*, released in 2003. He describes it as a pathbreaking film. *Teri Saun* is a fictional account of the movement in support of a separate state of Uttarakhand and the infamous 1994 Rampur–Tiranha police firing incident in Muzaffarnagar that led to the death of six activists, and the alleged rape and molestation of some women in the ensuing melee. The film makes a case for love, peace and the democratic means of struggle as opposed to violence. One of the activists promoting the movement, apart from Joshi and his family, produced and financed the film. A trilingual, it was also made in Hindi and in the other major Uttarakhand language – Kumaoni – and released in Uttarakhand alone. Since then, Joshi has directed innumerable Garhwali VCD–DVD films, from a 'romantic-family-horror' film like *Hantya* (2005) about a man discovering a spirit in the life of his new bride and the first Garhwali children's film *Gullu* (2010) to *Manswag* (Man-eater Leopard, 2012) on environmental issues. Joshi describes it as the *Life of Pi* of Garhwali cinema, since it deals with the man-versus-animal (tiger) conflict and the need for peaceful co-existence between the two species.

The first big-screen Garhwali feature film was *Jagwal* (The Long Wait), made in 1983. *Megha Aa* (Clouds Come), the first film to be released in Kumaoni, came much later in 1987. Since then, many more films have been made in Garhwali than in Kumaoni, but the success rate for both has been abysmally low. Even *Teri Saun* didn't rake in the moolah. The lone feature film from this region that hit the bull's eye was *Anjwaal* in Garhwali, released in 2012–2013. The absence of state patronage and the fact that most single screens have been shutting down have added to the woes, and are the reasons for the region's films thriving in the video format. Himalayan Films, a music company and the brainchild of prominent non-resident Indian (NRI) Ravindra Lakhera and renowned folk singer Narendra Negi, has been giving the region's cinematic efforts a further boost by selling video films online for Uttarakhandis living in India and abroad.

Anuj Joshi's 2011 film *Gundaru Ban Gaya Hero* (Gundaru Becomes a Hero) is an autobiographical film of sorts about the desire of a young boy to produce films in Garhwali. It sends out a message, loud and clear, that Garhwalis should not only take films made in their regional languages seriously, but should be ready to spend as much money on them as they do on religious causes and activities. According to him, it's neither the government nor politicians who can keep the rich language and culture alive, but the people themselves and society at large – with video films serving as an enabling tool.

It is a belief shared by a popular actress like Neetu Chandra, who produced *Mithila Makhaan*, the Maithili language National Award winner in 2016. Besides Bhojpuri, Maithili, Magahi and Angika are the other languages spoken in Bihar, her home state, and they are slowly dying.

'My idea is to restore the languages, scripts and the rich culture of the state. And the film is the best way forward,' she says.

Shot in the US, Canada, Nepal and India, the film is about how NRIs can come back to their roots and work wonders for the local community.

Sindhi and Garhwali films constitute a minuscule segment of Indian cinema, a mere speck in the country's vast cinema universe. But things can get even more microscopic here. Dialect cinema or sub-regional cinema is emerging to represent not just a linguistic identity, but also a geographical and cultural one. Bhili, Kunchi Kurve, Tulu, Badaga – films are being made in more tongues than one can imagine. 'After regional cinema, dialect cinema waits for its share of the spotlight,' writes Nandini Ramnath in the 17 April 2014 issue of *Livemint*.

The list includes films in dialects and languages that don't even have their own written scripts, such as *Lakniwalo Chwara* (Lambadi Boy), a 2012 Lambadi film about how the young and old regard their own Lambadi culture; *Byari*, a Byari (spoken in Karnataka and parts of Kerala) motion picture about social restrictions on women in Karnataka that won the National Award for Best Feature Film in 2011; *Faislo Manzoor Se* (Judgement is Accepted), a 2012 Bhili love quadrangle involving a dacoit and an Indian Administrative Service aspirant in Madhya Pradesh, and Vetrivelan's 2005 movie *Hosa Mungaru* (New Dawn/Early Spring Shower), made in Badaga, which is spoken largely in Tamil Nadu's Udagamandalam (Ooty, as it is popularly known). This discovery of obscure cultures and languages is one of the more interesting aspects of the National Awards, which are largely drowned in controversies, year after year. In 2016, films in Wancho, Bodo, Khasi, Maithili and Kurukh won a clutch of awards.

The growth in this sub-regional cinema has been aided, in large part, by digitization that helps bring down the costs of production, distribution and exhibition. It has also helped draw people living on the very margins closer to the mainstream, so that they can enjoy a share in the world of images.

It was a similar thought – of initiating a people's cinema movement on the very fringes – that has been driving Ranchi-based Meghnad. A social activist, Meghnad took to making documentaries in the late '80s on realizing that tribal issues, experiences and voices were not finding space in cinema and the media. He took a course in filmmaking at Sendit, Delhi, along with a few short-term courses at Pune's Film and Television Institute of India (FTII), and went on to assist filmmakers Tapan Bose and Suhasini Mulay. Since then, he and Biju Toppo, one of the first Adivasi filmmakers, who claims to have effectively used the camera to counter the misrepresentation of his community by the 'mainstream', have made several films on tribal and social issues: from land acquisition and sponge-iron industries to the use of compost manure, instead of chemical fertilizers, in farming; from alternative education for tribal-school dropouts and the narrow-gauge Lohardaga train to the National Rural Employment Guarantee Act; from water conservation in West Bengal's Purulia district to the people's movement against an aluminium factory in Koraput, Odisha.

In 1996, Meghnad set up Akhra in Ranchi. 'Akhra' is a word that originates from Mundari, the language of the Munda tribals, the second-largest ethnic group in Jharkhand after the Santhals and the Oraons. Traditionally, Akhra has always denoted an open space in the village, accessible to all, for community meetings and entertainment. Meghnad's Akhra is a group of committed people, mostly indigenous (tribal) youths, working in the field of culture, communication and the rights of indigenous peoples in India, in general, and in Jharkhand, in particular.

'It was felt that although Adivasi society had advanced in government services and in sports, there hadn't been enough presence in the intellectual fields; that is, literature, media and cinema,' Meghnad tells me.

'Despite being so rich in art and culture, Jharkhand doesn't have a single fine arts college. There is no good faculty in the mass communications department,' maintains Shriprakash, the state's most respected and awarded filmmaker.

So, it's in spaces like Akhra that students, teachers, filmmakers and artistes now gather for an adda. It has also fuelled a growing interest in cinema among young tribals. Seral Murmu graduated in editing from FTII, Samant Lakda in sound recording and Krishna Kumar Soren in cinematography. Similarly, Divya Hansda specialized in editing and Ram Krishna Soren studied direction at Kolkata's Satyajit Ray Film and Television Institute (SRFTI).

'Films on tribal society or any backward society can help them in the process of development,' Meghnad believes.

And who could be in a better position to make ones that ring true than someone from their own community?

In a development that was to be expected, Niranjan Kujur, a student of direction and screenplay writing at the SRFTI, made a 17-minute fictional short in 2012. Titled *Pahada* (Maths Tables), the film was in Kurukh, the lingo of the Oraon tribe. The first fictional film in the tribal language, it was made as an institute project and focusses on the impact of Naxalism on children's education in the hinterland. It shows how a tribal kid is unable to focus on learning Maths tables because of the sound of gunfire around him. We call Kujur moments after he receives the news that his second film in Kurukh has been selected for the International Documentary and Short Film Festival in Kerala. Called *Edpa Kana* (Going Home), the 26-minute film is about a tribal steel plant engineer, who finds himself caught between modernity and orthodoxy. It won a National Award for the best audiography in a film in the non-features section.

Niranjan Kujur was born in Lohardaga and grew up in Ranchi. Living in Hutar village near the state capital, he had always wanted to make a film in his mother tongue, Kurukh, and cast his own family members in his debut film. It was while studying at the Manipal Institute of Communication that he realized that making films was the one activity which engrossed him so thoroughly that he could forget to eat, drink or sleep. Having made this discovery, he decided to work with reputed Jharkhand filmmaker Shriprakash after graduation and then opted to study at SRFTI. While Kujur wants to work in Mumbai to start with, he is keen making more films in Kurukh and channelizing funds for them. All because he himself is not fluent in the language.

'I am trying hard to get back to it. Our whole generation has been brought up in Hindi and English, because it is a sign of having arrived,' he admits ruefully.

When his first film was screened at the International Film Festival of India (IFFI) in Panjim, no one even knew about the existence of Kurukh as a language. According to Kujur, cinema will help give the dialect the right push, platform and identity.

'Everyone knows Kerala from the films from the state, but no one knows the face of Jharkhand,' he observes.

There could, perhaps, be another reason as well for this state of affairs: Jharkhandi cinema speaks in many tongues – Santhali, Khortha, Ho, Mundari, Oraon, Sadri and Nagpuri. Around 15 Nagpuri films have been made since *Sona Ker Nagpur* (Nagpur Is Made of Gold) in 1998. Santhali films are more popular and 150 out of the 600 digital Santhali films in existence have been made in Jharkhand, with the rest having been made in Bengal. A notable Santhali film released in 2001 is *Chando Likhon* (The Script of God) by Lakhan Murmu, the first 35 mm film in the language. It is also one of the three Santhali films to have been made on celluloid and released commercially, the others being *Sagun Ena Sohag Dular* (The Victory of True Love), 2003, and *Jewee Jurie* (Life Partner), 2009. It is heartening to know that despite the baby steps that Jharkhandi cinema has been taking, women filmmakers are not far behind in the game. With *Mogod Dulaar* (Love Unexpressed), 2009, to her credit, Rani Mardi is the first woman filmmaker to have made a film in Santhali. However, constrained as it is by shoestring budgets and its reliance on digital technology, Jharkhandi cinema is still to find its feet and identity.

Shriprakash feels that the local industry is suffering, because the government has never extended adequate support to art and culture. There is neither a proper distribution network nor suitable exhibition spaces for films. Recently, two organizations, both based in Jamshedpur, have come up for the promotion of indigenous cinema. The All India Santhali Film Association (AISFA) has been organizing the Jharkhand Cine Awards and Film Festival, while the Pt Raghunath Academy of Santhali Cinema and Art (RASCA) is responsible for an event like the Jharkhand Filmfare Awards. Ironically, the biggest star of the Jharkhand film industry, or 'Jhollywood' as many refer to it, is Deepak Lohar, who trained at the National School of Drama, but has moved to Mumbai for better work opportunities.

'There is a lack of good technical people within Jharkhand,' says Shriprakash. 'The good ones invariably migrate to Mumbai or Kolkata or Chennai.'

Jharkhand cinema is actually an offshoot of the state's thriving music-video industry. In fact, its biggest hit – *Baha*, made in 2009 – has the music-album culture as its background and is set in Ranchi's Daily Market, famous for the production and sale of local pop-music cassettes. Made in both Nagpuri and Sadri, *Baha* is about a talented young Adivasi, who goes to Ranchi, the city of his dreams, to become a singer. He finds love and success, but also faces exploitation and bitterness, before returning to his village and his parents.

'*Baha* reflects the aspirations of today's young Adivasis, who are exposed to the music-album culture,' says Shriprakash.

Shriprakash had once shot wedding videos for a living. Later, he would go on to make award-winning documentaries on multiple issues like the impact of uranium mining on the locals (*Buddha Weeps in Jadugoda*, 1999), the coal mines of Jharkhand (*The Fire Within*, 2002) and the destruction of Adivasi homes by army firing ranges (*Kiski*

Raksha; In Whose Defence, 1994). He took to making fiction features, because he felt people were not ready to accept documentaries as a popular audio-visual medium. The local music industry, on the other hand, had caught their imagination. Shriprakash, however, finds the music industry exploitative.

'Tribal areas are rich in tradition, but it has been translated into a new form with the flow of new money and technology. The real people behind the music and songs get left behind,' he feels.

While the producers and music companies find success and money, the tribal musicians don't receive their due.

Indigenous compositions are plundered and experimented with, but their original creators go unacknowledged. Forget money, they are even denied due credit. Often producers, composers and singers pass them off unfairly as their own original creations. Which is where locals need to come in and seize the new video-film technology now available for use, Shriprakash maintains.

'It gives a window of self-expression to those who are not in the mainstream.'

Moreover, a platform like YouTube can help find them an audience across the globe. Shriprakash is planning to hold workshops to teach them the basics of technology for using smartphones to make and upload videos of their song-and-dance tradition.

If, on one level, local cinema in India is all about the survival of vanishing languages, identity and culture, on another, it's about linguistic rivalry.

At 54, it is not the youngest, but possibly the smallest commercial feature-film industry in India. Chhattisgarhi cinema, or 'Chhollywood', as it is popularly known, was born in 1965 with the release of the first film in a Chhattisgarhi dialect, *Kahi Debe Sandesh* (Convey the Message), written, directed and produced by Manu Nayak. In 2015, however, the Chhattisgarhi film industry was still trying to grow out of the shadows of its Big Brother – Bhojpuri cinema. Things haven't changed much since then.

Legend has it that *Kahi Debe Sandes*, a story of inter-caste love between a Brahmin girl and a Scheduled Caste boy was inspired by the success of the first Bhojpuri film, *Ganga Maiyya Tohe Piyari Chadhaibo* (Holy Ganges, I Shall Offer You the Auspicious Yellow Sari), released in 1963. The black-and-white film featured two songs by Mohammad Rafi, and others by Manna Dey, Mahendra Kapoor and Minu Purushottam. It was released on 16 April 1965 in Durg and Bhatapara, but because of the controversial theme and the protests it triggered, it was denied the commercial success it deserved and its release was stalled or delayed in many centres, including Raipur. Indira Gandhi, then minister for information and broadcasting, is said to have watched and, thereby, endorsed the film, after which the way ahead became much smoother. The next film, Niranjan Tiwari's *Ghar Dwar*, came out in 1971. Since neither of these movies fared well at the box office, no other Chhattisgarhi film was produced for nearly 30 years thereafter.

It was the creation of the separate state of Chhattisgarh that sparked the revival of this particular film industry.

Bastar-born Satish Jain, who has written the scripts of Bollywood actor Govinda's well-known films such as *Dulaara* (1994), *Pardesi Babu* (1998), *Rajaji* (1999) and *Hadh Kar Di Aapne* (2000), went back to Raipur to make the Chhattisgarhi film *Mor Chhaihan Bhuinya* (My Shadow and Earth). It was released on 27 October 2000. Three days later, then Prime Minister Atal Bihari Vajpayee announced the creation of the Chhattisgarh state. Riding on the general feeling of euphoria, the film went on to do extraordinary business, proving to be a bigger hit in the new-born state than Yash Raj Films' *Mohabbatein*, despite the Aditya Chopra–directed Bollywood film's multi-star cast that included the combined might of Big B and SRK. Produced at just ₹20 lakh, *Mor Chhaihan Bhuinya* grossed ₹2.5 crore. It ran for

27 weeks in Raipur's Babulal Theatre. The demand was such that in the two cinema halls of Razim and Nawapara qasbah, it was screened round-the-clock, with eight shows a day.

'I was the hero of the film,' Anuj Sharma tells me, making a point without dropping his casual manner.

The superstar of Chhattisgarhi cinema is also the first artiste from the industry to have been awarded the Padma Shri. The Bhatapara boy, and former Godrej marketing executive, is a very popular singer, anchor, stage artiste and radio jockey as well. He is also the only Chhattisgarhi star to have had eight releases in a single year. He has delivered four silver-jubilee hits – *Mor Chhaihan Bhuinya*, *Maya Dede Maya Lele* (2001), *Jhan Bhulo Maa Baap La* (2003) and *Mayaa* (2009) – the maximum for a lead actor in Chhattisgarhi films.

According to Sharma, the boom continued all the way through the early and mid-2000s. In 2005, Lata Mangeshkar sang for the Chhattisgarhi movie *Bhakla* (2006). It was followed by three super-hit films like *Mayaa* (2009), *Tura Rikshawala* (2011) and *Laila Tip Top Chhaila Angutha Chhap* (2012), all directed by Satish Jain. The arrival of digital technology helped give a bigger boost to the industry, as making and distributing films became easier and cheaper.

As of now, Sharma describes it as the smallest film industry in the world, what with just 35 centres of exhibition. Nagpur, home to a sizeable population of Chhattisgarhis, accounts for about 5 to 7 per cent of the total market for Chhattisgarhi films. They are also shown, occasionally, in places like Jammu and Jamshedpur, cities with plenty of Chhattisgarhi migrant labour.

The industry has grown in leaps and bounds.

'Earlier, we were totally dependent on Mumbai, Cuttack and Chennai for shoots and post-production. We didn't even have a spotboy of our own,' says Sharma.

Now, Chhattisgarhi cinema is self-sufficient and doesn't have to turn to Mumbai for anything. For not only does Raipur have its own editing and sound-recording studio, the industry has its own local cameramen, choreographers, editors and sound recordists too. And it has generated jobs for local actors.

Take Omkar Das Manikpuri, better known as Natha of *Peepli Live*. Resident of Ward No. 20 in Bhilai's Brindanagar, Omkar used to make ends meet by performing *Nacha*, the local folk theatre, and doing odd construction jobs. After getting into Naya Theatre, he was given the opportunity to act in classics like *Charandas Chor*, *Agra Bazaar* and *Kamdev ka Apna Basant Ritu ka Sapna* (The Love God's Own, a Springtime Dream). He had also been working on Chhattisgarhi folk albums. After getting noticed in *Peepli Live*, he has landed roles in local films.

There is, however, a darker side to this cinematic revival. Bastar and Dantewada in Chhattisgarh have acquired notoriety as Naxal dens and Naxalism is cited as one of the reasons for the decline in local film production over the last few years. Glaringly evident too is the fact that while even Bollywood has, in recent years, made films (however half-baked) like *Chakravyuh* that deal with the impact and ramifications of Naxalism, Chhattisgarh itself, the hotbed of Naxal activity, hasn't produced a single film on the contentious issue. Could the pervasive climate of fear be the inhibiting factor? Or is it an impetus for local filmmakers to seek oblivion in creating more of the usual escapist fare – family entertainers, romantic musicals and loud comedies – instead of diving deep into their own heart of darkness? A bit of both, perhaps.

Sub-regional cinema isn't merely about communities, languages and cultures thriving on the peripheries; it can help empower vulnerable individuals too.

When you think of Mathura, what comes to mind is its identity as the birthplace of Lord Krishna. Not many are aware that it is also the place that has given birth to a unique film and filmmaker, that too from the very margins of society. He has proved that a DSLR camera, a few thousand rupees and a die-hard attitude are all you need to make a film.

These were certainly enough for Mathura's Mohammad Gani when he made *Quaid* (Imprisoned) in 2014. An 80-minute feature film based on a short story by Gyan Prakash Vivek, it delves into the complex psyche of a child who is neglected, misunderstood and ill-treated both at home and school. That Gani has no formal training in filmmaking is a point worth noting. Forget training in the craft of cinema, he hasn't had any formal education beyond Class IV. In fact, it's been a long and arduous journey for him – from working as a daily wage-earning labourer to becoming a filmmaker – that could itself be the stuff of inspiring, compelling films, like *Slumdog Millionaire.*

'*Ajeeb si dastaan*, a strange story,' is how the filmmaker refers to his own life. His father, Naazar Ali, moved to Mathura from Etah district's Dorra village in search of work. He worked as a labourer in the construction of the Bhaagwat Temple in Krishna Janmabhoomi. The family began living in the shadow of the under-construction temple, and Gani and his siblings also pitched in, helping their father with the construction work, instead of going to school.

When they moved across the Yamuna River to a settlement for the underprivileged, Gani's father made him apprentice with a neighbouring tailor. At 15, while wielding scissors and needle on fabric, the teenager would dream of cutting and editing film clips.

'Film *banane ki prakriya zahan mein hamesha se rahi thi. Main cinema se judna chaahta tha*. Filmmaking was always at the back of my mind. I wanted to connect with cinema,' he says.

In 1990, Gani started his own tailoring business, and also learnt to read and write on his own. His special interest was photography. Chancing upon a write-up on cinematographer Baba Azmi, he came to know of the radical Indian People's Theatre Association (IPTA). Mathura had an IPTA branch and Gani was quick to become a member. That was when the Ram Mandir Andolan was at its peak. The young man acted in several IPTA plays that dealt with communal harmony. His interaction with intellectuals and progressive minds helped broaden his own horizons. He joined the Jan Sanskriti Manch (JSM), the cultural wing of the Left, and started Prerak, a theatre group for underprivileged children living in Mathura. Moving around with a projector in hand as part of The Group, JSM's film wing, he also screened films – most of them realistic and issue-based – in the town's different neighbourhoods. This would lead to debates and discussions, and create awareness among marginalized viewers.

Gani also bought a small plot of land with his savings and built a school for local children. It is now his primary source of income. The second big investment has been a camera. *Quaid* was made after the filmmaker experimented with a six-minute short, which had teachers and children from his own school pitching in as actors. It was shown across Mathura's different localities on makeshift screens, like walls or white bedsheets. Gani's next film will also be based on a literary work: Sushant Supriya's story *Mera Jurm Kya Hai*.

The filmmaker might consider himself an oddity in the world of cinema, but he isn't quite.

'Famous actor Mohan Agashe once told me that the next wave of Indian cinema will rise from the small towns and districts,' he says.

One such voice, like his own, to be heard from the very margins is that of 30-year-old Marathi filmmaker Bhaurao Karhade, a farmer from Ahmednagar district, Maharashtra. *Khwada* (Obstacle), his Marathi debut film, found a commercial release in October 2015 after premiering in January the same year at the Pune International Film Festival, where it won him the Best Director award. In fact, it was when *Khwada* was screened that Karhade's mother got to watch a film in a theatre for the first time in her life. The making of the film, which is based on the plight of the migrant shepherd community, has been as much a tale of hardships as the theme it deals with. It's about how Karhade rose from his underprivileged background, even selling off the five acres of family farmland in Ahmednagar's Gawadewadi village, where he had been cultivating wheat, millet, sorghum and onions till

2010, to start 'harvesting cinema' in Pune and make his debut film with an investment of ₹1.20 crore.

In his semi-literate family – his mother is unlettered, his father studied till class III and his elder brother dropped out of school after class IV – Karhade is that rare graduate. His love for cinema was fuelled by the hardcore Hindi commercial flicks he saw on Doordarshan: Sooraj Barjatya's *Maine Pyar Kiya*, Ramesh Sippy's *Sholay* and Indra Kumar's *Dil*.

'By the time I was in class X, I had made up my mind on becoming a filmmaker,' he tells us when we get to interact for an article in 2015.[12]

The family, however, wanted him to join the army or the police.

'They still can't understand filmmaking. For them, a director is someone who is a bank, company or society director.'

Initially, Karhade had turned to the FTII for training, but failed to clear the exam. So he went on to do a course in communication studies at the New Arts, Commerce and Science College in Ahmednagar. He made two short films after graduating in 2009: *Talab* (Addiction) and *Vanchit* (Deprived). It was in college that he was introduced to his cinematic Bible: Satyajit Ray's *Pather Panchali*, a film he has seen 32 times. He was also exposed to the international classics of his other gurus: Vittorio de Sica, Akira Kurosawa and Federico Fellini.

Karhade's debut film *Khwada* is rough, rustic and gutsy. His own rural upbringing helped him lend the theme a certain immediacy and authenticity. According to him, the inspiration for the film came to him, of all the places, at a railway station, where he had met some farmers from Aurangabad.

'Despite owning 35 acres of land, they had been forced to migrate because of the famine,' he says.

Set against the arid landscape of central Maharashtra, *Khwada* is about a family of shepherds who are forced to migrate in search of fodder for their flock, because the government has usurped their land. At the film's core is a prolonged legal battle: a shepherd's struggle to get his land back from the Forest Department. Karhade, who moved to Pune after selling his land, used to run a small hotel on the side called Ran Meva that that offered simple village fare to immigrants and blue-collar workers. During the last conversation I had with him, he had expressed the hope that he too would get back his five acres of farmland some day. I don't know if he got the land back however, in 2018 I got a call from him, inviting me for a screening of his second film, *Baban*. A rural tale like *Khwada*, but one of aspiration not despair, it unfortunately came a cropper at the box office.

Though unfolding on the margins of an urban Ahmedabad, the story of Dakxin Chhara, the first Indian feature filmmaker from the stigmatized Chhara denotified tribe, is also all about cinema of the *janta* (people), by the *janta* and for the *janta*.

Dakxin, whose debut feature film, *Sameer*, was released in 2017, has had to deal with the stigma of his father and his tribe being labelled criminals. He is the first generation of his family to have risen above the humiliation imposed by this fabricated perception, created and stoked over the years by the State and society alike. Chhara is one of the hundreds of tribes originally listed as 'criminal tribes', under the Criminal Tribes Act of 1871. The Criminal Tribes Act of 1952 repealed the notification and denotified these tribal communities. However, that hasn't entirely changed public opinion. Many members of these communities continue to be perceived as 'born' or habitual criminals. At the receiving end of State and police brutality, they are treated as outcasts, and forced to live in social isolation and economic penury.

Dakxin's own grandparents lived in Dhule, Maharashtra, in one of the open jail-like settlements created across the country to keep the supposedly 'offender' tribes in control. It was his father who moved to Ahmedabad in search of a livelihood and decide to educate his children, that too in English-medium institutions. Dakxin is a graduate in psychology, and has done his post-graduation in Theatre and Global Development from the University of Leeds on a Ford Foundation fellowship. However, despite having travelled far and wide, he continues to anchor himself in the Chharanagar settlement in Ahmedabad, to keep working with its residents.

His artistic roots lie in community-based theatre and he has been training underprivileged communities in theatre. Cinema is also an extension of that community-outreach initiative and shares the same concerns – identity politics, political and social issues, and an urgency in questioning the status quo.

Dakxin grew up watching Big B films, not on the big screen, but on television and video. A 1982 Gujarati film *Maa Vina Suno Sansar* was his first exposure to the world outside Chharanagar. And a VHS camera was all it took for him to learn filmmaking – on his own, by making mistakes and learning from them. In a nutshell, yet another means to self-fulfilment and empowerment.

In 2005, Dakxin made a documentary on the atrocities against a community of snake charmers and their fight for survival. It won an award and gave him just the right dose of confidence to enter filmmaking full-time. Since then, Dakxin has made 84 documentaries, all on various significant, contentious issues. He worked as an associate director with noted filmmaker Rakesh Sharma, best known for *Final Solution*, a film on the Gujarat riots of 2002.

Sameer took birth in his mind in 2008, when Dakxin set out to capture on camera the devastating scenes following the 21 bomb blasts in Ahmedabad. He may have specifically explored the anti-Muslim sentiment, the violence and terrorism, but the bigger picture has stayed the same for him.

'Be it the tribals or the Muslims, the face-off with State power and the concomitant cycle of oppression have been constant, shared realities,' he observes.

In Bhopal, the shared realities of a community took the shape of a unique crowd-funded and crowd-directed film called *Turup* (Checkmate), which was a festival favourite in India in 2017.

It's a rare film in which the credit roll names no individual director, for there is no single director; everyone is a director. The 70-minute Hindi feature film was made collectively over 2015–16 with local residents, most of them from working-class settlements in Bhopal, doubling up as crew and actors, often rehearsing for their parts late after work. Their homes are the locations; in the film, their own families can be seen milling about in the background.

Turup acknowledges the 'support and solidarity of friends and comrades'. It is an uncommon exercise in grass-roots cinema, based on volunteerism and the cooperative spirit. The basic script and screenplay came from Maheen Mirza, a FTII graduate and independent cinematographer, who works with various collectives and people's groups, and Rinchin, who writes and works with people's groups and movements in Madhya Pradesh and Chhattisgarh.

The process of making the film was a collaborative and evolving one, where ideas about the script, dialogues, shooting and even music were shared, discussed and debated, and elements added, deleted and changed before being finalized.

'Each person has contributed her/his own unique vision, skill and perspective to it, guiding and often manoeuvring it to reach its logical conclusion,' explains Mirza when I interact with her.[13]

Since the vision is a collective one, the directorial credit has also been shared and given to Ektara Collective.

All the collaborators worked for free. Funds for the production were raised through individual contributions. The idea was to make the film's ownership so broad-based that no single entity could influence its content or making. It also helped make the collaborators the channels of distribution.

'They see and then show the film around as something they are invested in. This builds a critical and diverse audience for cinema. In a country where the scope of watching independent cinema is limited, this becomes critical to help the film reach as many people as it can,' Mirza tells me.

This is not a first for Ektara. The Bhopal-based independent, autonomous, non-funded and informal group of individuals seeks to collaborate creatively with various communities to make films that are rooted in their own reality and individual experiences.

'For political thought formation, it is important to occupy cultural spaces. There is a need for creative expression and cultural engagement,' states Rinchin, who is also part of Ektara's core group.

'Most cinema is aspirational in nature; it doesn't seem to arrive from a familiar context, but from somewhere far away,' Mirza tells me.

'What if we made our own [cinema]?' is Rinchin's way of explaining the origins of Ektara's non-escapist model.[14]

The collective had made two short fiction films earlier: *Chanda ke Joote* (2011) and *Jaadui Machchi* (2013). *Turup* is Ektara's first full-length feature film.

Turup lends a whole new dimension to cinéma vérité. The film is grounded in the working-class lives of Bhopal's Chakki Chouraha area, where chess is an obsession; the moves are played on the streetside between chores – cooking, sweeping, mopping – or furtively, in time away from work. Against the backdrop of men challenging each other to matches, three intertwined stories take shape: of an old household help named Monika, who has always lived life on her own terms; of Neelima, a former journalist, trying hard to get a foothold back in the profession, even as she grapples with marital issues; and of a young janitor Lata, who is in love with Majid, a driver.

The cooperative spirit reflects in the essential simplicity and straightforwardness of the filmmaking. There are no elaborate, long-drawn sequences; in fact, the narrative moves from one short, terse scene to the next. The performances are artless, the language everyday, and the conversations commonplace.

The film lends veracity to the relationships, believability to the emotions and interactions, be it between an ideologically opposed couple, a pair of siblings or two lovers. There is nothing *filmi* about it.

Mirza explains how even the aesthetic emerges from the context: 'The way a scene is lit up, how people are illuminated. The idea was to make it real, rather than beautiful, or else, the believability would break.'

Religion, caste, class and gender debates play out against a growing fundamentalism. There is the Virat Hindu Sammelan looming large, slogans raised in support of *gau mata* and *sanatan dharma*, and WhatsApp messages against Muslims and interfaith marriage. Chess becomes the metaphorical playground for all these religious, business and political clashes. In a world where politics, religion and corporates are cosy bedfellows, the poor and marginalized become the pawns.

You can sense the underlying community spirit and also the points of friction, of hatred gradually raising its ugly head. Yet, there is also hope that all is not lost, that subversion can come from within, that barriers can be transcended from inside. For every person who stokes the communal flames, there is someone to douse it by pointing towards the real problems – inflation, poverty, unemployment. Even as the film reveals the challenges thrown at our syncretic culture, it also assures us that the warp and weft of life are still intact, holding on just fine. Conflict and the confluence of culture go hand in hand.

Eventually, it's the women who push the boundaries with everyday wisdom. Consider how Lata runs down the Hindu politicians: '*Paani tak nahi peete mere haath se aur mera kanyadaan karenge.* They won't even drink the water I offer them, but want to marry me off.' Or her comment on her doubly disadvantaged love – when her lover Majid claims she is better off than him, because she has religion on her side, she counters: 'Is there any place without caste?' You have Monika telling Neelima that it wasn't as though she couldn't get married, but that she chose not to. In one deft exchange, we see how much more self-aware she is than the educated journalist she works for.

Despite the lack of a principal director, the film doesn't lack direction. Not only is it clear-eyed about what it wants to say, but also how it wants to say it – with neither shrillness and stridency nor cynicism and bitterness. The music ties in beautifully with the spirit of the film. The guidance and support in musical arrangement came from the Kabir musicians of Dewas – Dev Narayan Saroliya, Kaluram Bamniya and Narayanji Delmia.

The music speaks of the eternal sound of the universe ('*anhad ka baaja*'); of how the formless king is decorated with visible finery ('*Nirgun raja pe/Sirgun sej sajayi*'), of the elusive god ('*Maula maula lakh pukare/Maula haath na aaye*').

The resolution of all contemporary dilemmas is seen in the philosophical legacy of poet-saint Kabir – in synthesis and syncretism, and in Sufi spirituality – and that forms the bedrock of the soundtrack.

While grass-roots cinema has been taking shape in Bhopal, a tiny, independent film from a little village in Assam has made the whole world its home. *Village Rockstars*, Rima Das' simple and quiet ode to a young girl's dream of owning a guitar and forming a band, came from nowhere, travelling to more than 80 festivals worldwide and winning over 40 awards. It was India's nominee this year, for the Foreign Language Film Oscar, a first for a film from the North East.

A self-taught filmmaker, Das shot the film entirely on her own. A one-woman army, she wrote, directed, edited and also took on the roles of the cinematographer, production designer, 'spotboy and driver'. She co-produced the film with her mother, with cousin Mallika Das helping with location sound. The locale was Chhaygaon – the village in Assam where Rima was born, and it's where lead actor Bhanita Das (who plays the free-spirited and rebellious Dhunu) and the rest of the cast belong to.

Her new film *Bulbul Can Sing*, that premiered at the Toronto International Film Festival and won the Best Film award at the Jio Mami 20th Mumbai Film Festival with Star in 2018, was also screened at Berlinale 2019. It follows the cinematic technique, language and vision of *Village Rockstars*.

Das describes *Village Rockstars* as a tribute to the people and the place she comes from. True to them, the film is rooted in the daily rhythms of Chhaygaon. There is a stillness to the frames in the way the camera lingers, both on the landscape and on people's faces.

There is something beautifully organic, unadorned and pure about Das's self-taught filmmaking. The most striking aspect is evident in how she has subverted gendered expectations in *Bulbul Can Sing* as well. Her heroines are not your typical girls-next-door. Her refreshing portrayal of adolescent friendships transcends man–woman divides.

Das is never hard-hitting. In her own gentle and indirect way, however, she manages to shine a light on the hardships and harshness, the deprivations and disasters underlying the seemingly idyllic rural life. There is matter-of-fact acceptance of its vicissitudes; no wallowing in its tragedies, lacks or inadequacies.

The money Das made from corporate and wedding films partly financed her first two films, while the award money for *Village Rockstars* has gone into making *Bulbul Can Sing*. Her camera is her biggest support and companion, 'more than a boyfriend,' she says.[15] With one foot in Mumbai's Malad, another in Assam and now travelling the world, it's been a peripatetic life lately for this filmmaker. But she wouldn't have it any other way.

Das is the latest addition to the list of filmmakers who have contributed significantly to the rise of north-eastern cinema. Over the last five years or so, much seems to have been happening there: New filmmakers are making their presence felt. Fresh and independent voices are being heard, interesting themes and stories are making it to centre stage, a variety of dialects – Sherdukpen, Wancho and Kokborok, among others – is coming to the forefront and a diversity of cinematic influences, both from across the world and within the region itself, is steadily gaining ground.

'The term "indie cinema" may be in vogue now, but it was always a part of us in the North East,' journalist-turned-filmmaker Utpal Borpujari had once told me.

The advent of digital filmmaking, along with its easy accessibility, has opened newer indie windows for aspiring filmmakers in the North East. There has been a growing pool of young, idiosyncratic, self-taught talent. Mapuia Chawngthu from Mizoram, who made *Khawnlung Run* (The Raid of Khawnlung) in 2012, has taught Hindi in a government school and made innumerable music videos, while directing films in his spare time. Belonging to a family of artistes, Prashant Rasaily, a musician, composer and self-taught filmmaker, who picked up the basics of camera work and editing on his own, made the Sikkimese film *Kathaa Stories* that was released the same year.

Local Kung Fu (2013), *Kothanodi* (2015), *Bokul* (2015), *Loktak Lairembee* (Lady of the Lake, 2016), and *Ralang Road* (2017) seem to be the crowd favourites. But there are more, from Arunachal Pradesh's first filmmaker Sange Dorjee Thongdok's 2013 debut feature *Crossing Bridges* to *III Smoking Barrels* (2017), Sanjib Dey's anthology of three shorts in a mash-up of several languages – English, Assamese, Hindi, Manipuri and Nagamese. In fact, these films are talking to us in an amazingly diverse range of tongues. Like Ningthouja Lancha's 2008 Manipuri film in Meitei *Mami Sami* (Blurred Shadow) that examines the army presence in Manipur or Jaicheng Dohutiya's *Haanduk* (The Hidden Corner) in Assamese and Moran that was released in 2016.

Most of these films present their makers' response to their roots and have been made with local people, often non-actors. Thondok's *Crossing Bridges* zooms in on a local dialect and a remote tribe, the Sherdukpen. The first person from his state to pass out of film school, Thondok decided to make his first film in his own dialect in his native village, Shergaon. The film's protagonist, Tashi, is a Mumbai-based web designer, who returns to his village after losing his job in the recession. While waiting for a response to his application for a new job, he slowly begins to reconnect with his lost identity and culture, something he had once derided.

Similarly the idea for *The Head Hunter*, Nilanjan Datta's first feature film, took root in the state where he grew up – Arunachal Pradesh.

'I used to see old tribal men in the marketplace in Itanagar,' the Assamese filmmaker recollects. 'The non-tribals used to detest them and make fun of their costumes.'

It is this civilizational clash that Datta chose as the theme for his film, which is the first in the Wancho tribal language and only the third one to come out of Arunachal Pradesh. The Wancho tribe lives in the Patkai hills of the state's Longding district. The film, which helps bring this largely unknown language and culture into focus, won the Best Film award in the Wancho language at the National Film Awards of 2015.

The Head Hunter is one of the several films from the North East that are anthropological and ethnographic in nature. *Yarwng* (Roots) in Kokborok, which brought the first National Award to Tripura back in 2010, is another example. Made by a Malayali priest from Kottayam, Father Joseph Pulinthanath, who has been living in the North East for more than three decades, the film is about the inhabitants of the once-prosperous Raima valley of Tripura, who were forced to leave when the valley was submerged as a result of the construction of a dam on the Gumti River in 1976.

The Head Hunter has a similar theme. It speaks of how the road to development can cause a tribal to lose his way home; about how intrusions in the name of progress displace tribals.

'Development is necessary, but at what cost? Do we uproot them from their ethnicities and then modernize them?' asks Datta.

The conflict portrayed in the film is between an old tribal and an educated young government officer.

The Head Hunter captures the daily rhythms and rituals of the Wanchos. There have been many misconceptions about them which Datta says he wanted to clear. The tribe of headhunters has been erroneously perceived by most as wild, violent and dangerous, even though the practice of human headhunting was abolished in

1991 through the efforts of the government and the missionaries of the region. Datta attempts to bring out their humane side and their relationship with nature. He calls it a film about the present encountering a lost past.

Datta found a lot of the Wancho youngsters he would cast in his film working in the beauty parlours and spas at Mumbai's international airport. Two of those girls, Nina Wangsu and Akom Arangham, helped as language instructors for the film. The young lead, Mrigendra Narayan Konwar, is an Assamese actor trained at the National School of Drama. The old Wancho man, Nokshaa Saham, is not an actor; he was chosen from among the tribal villagers who auditioned for the role.

Presenting a sharp contrast to *The Head Hunter* is Mukul Haloi's maiden feature-length documentary, *Tales from our Childhood*. As against the lyricism of the form, the subject that Haloi – a graduate in film direction from FTII, Pune – deals with is far from musical and mild: growing up in '90s Assam, surrounded by turmoil and violence when the United Liberation Front of Assam (ULFA) was heading an armed rebellion for independence from India, and the might of the State clashed with the fervour of local revolutionaries demanding their right to self-determination. It was a war from which none can claim to have emerged a clear winner, a conflict that hasn't been fully contained yet.

Haloi, who shot and edited the film, travels back to those years of insurgency through recollection and reflection, through vignettes that linger in memory: a childhood friend dons a uniform borrowed from a dead ULFA rebel's family; another shares the entries from her old diary; a group of friends rehearses a play from the times of the unrest; the filmmaker's mother talks of the family's own close encounters with fear and uncertainty, of the complicity of the villagers in the struggle, either as participants or as supporters. Through it all, Haloi's camera is a perennial fly on the wall.

The memories are dominated by violence, death and disappearances. The stories are about blackouts and dreaded midnight knocks on the door, about curfews and explosions, bombs and bullets, ambushes, brutal crackdowns and 'encounters'. They are chilling and stark, all the more so because of the matter-of-fact manner in which they are recounted. These stories are also suffused with an overwhelming sense of bleakness and loss. The narrative acquires a distinct shape through the fragmented nature of memories – the randomness with which they surface, observing no particular order, the absence of a linear connection.

Originally from Nalbari in Assam, Haloi shot the film between December 2016 and September 2017 in his own village as well as in Digboi, Dibrugarh and Guwahati. The landscape is pastoral, verdant and tranquil, but harbours unspeakable tension and an underlying fear.

There is something distinctly disquieting in Haloi's quiet imagery, a sense of urgency even in the unhurried pace.

He has not dredged up memories to seek resolutions or a closure, he says. The cessation of hostilities, the seeming normalcy of the present feels more ominous than a clear signal of peace.

Then there is a larger confusion a friend speaks of. 'Whose blood was shed for our good?' he asks. 'Both the army and [the] ULFA have killed innocents, and we have never been able to understand who the enemy was.'

Haobam Paban Kumar's *Loktak Lairembee* (Lady of the Lake) is also about raising questions – regarding the ecological issues faced by the floating biomass, or *phumdi*s, the precarious life of the fishing community on Loktak Lake and the flip side of the government's developmental activities. It portrays the State's apathy and ruthlessness, the people's resistance to State oppression, and the fears and anxieties that reach a flashpoint, and the conflicts that can be unleashed in the mind of a sensitive individual. The film has already travelled to several festivals – in Kolkata, Pune, Bengaluru, Dubai, New York and Berlin.

Loktak Lairembee was shot entirely on Loktak Lake. The largest freshwater lake in the North East, it has a unique ecosystem where people live in floating huts built on a floating biomass, comprising islands called *phumdis*. The filmmaker also roped in the local fisherfolk for the various roles, including that of the lead pair, played by real-life couple Ningthoujam Sanatomba and Sagolsam Thambasang. Kumar often didn't give them any dialogues; he simply explained the situation, and let them react and respond to it on camera.

The daily rhythms of life flow naturally on screen; the camera glides along, as smooth and gentle as the boat on the lake, while capturing the lives of the fisherfolk. But beneath the calm lurks a deep turmoil that seems to leap off the screen in the form of a monster of a dredging machine or a gun.

Filmmaker Bhaskar Hazarika's debut film *Kothanodi* (River of Fables) is in a league of its own. While rooted in Assam, it is all about reinventing local fables. There is a contemporary edginess to the film, even though its setting is classical.

The folk tales that form the crux of this Assamese film were compiled into a book in 1911 by Rasaraj Laxminath Bezbaroa. Titled *Buri Ai'r Sadhu*, or 'Grandma's Tales', this compendium of 20-odd stories has been a bestseller in Assam for generations.

The film's most remarkable feature is the radically different way in which it portrays motherhood, an otherwise much-revered concept both in Indian cinema and in reality. Hazarika drew the dramatic essence of four stories from the compendium, and stitched them together into a single narrative about four mothers struggling with their own demons. A crowd-funded film, it has been shot partly on Majuli Island and along the banks of the Brahmaputra river near Bhaskar's own hometown, Dergaon.

Opening up an entirely different window to the North East is Kenny Basumatary, who has also been making films on minuscule sums of money, and roping in his own family members and friends to play the roles. His first film, *Local Kung Fu*, was a comic, hyper-energetic action flick – more in the zone of a Jackie Chan or an Isaac Florentine – on the street fights and gang wars of Guwahati. In *Local Kung Fu 2*, he went wilder, mixing his own unique brand of martial arts and a wicked sense of the absurd with the Shakespeare classic *The Comedy of Errors*, about the hilarious mix-up between two pairs of identical twins.

Pradip Kurbah's *Onaatah* (Of the Earth), while based in the North East, has contemporaneity and relevance written all over it. Although it won the National Award for the Best Khasi Language Film in 2016 and was screened at select film festivals, it failed to grab headlines despite the rare sensitivity with which it depicted the emotive issue of violence and violation, that have been at the centre of debates post Nirbhaya and #MeToo. Relating the story of Onaatah, a young woman coming to terms with rape, the film gently tries to lend a new direction to the narrative, steering clear of what often comes with such themes – a propensity for voyeurism, and the worst cinematic clichés of revenge and retribution.

Onaatah is not about the external brutality the protagonist has to endure, but the process of internal healing she goes through. For one, the male participation here is refreshing in that it doesn't come across as righteous or patronizing; it is more a reflection of care and concern. Onaatah receives life-affirming advice from three men in her life: her father, who takes pains to explain to her that her life has not been ruined forever – it is only going through a momentary rough patch – and she should begin trusting people again; the visually impaired village elder, Bah Dondor, who cherishes the sun, the flowing water, the smell of fried fish and the puff of his beedi, offers Onaatah the lesson that life shouldn't come to a standstill for her, and that she should carry on being resilient in the face of adversity; and Duh, the village idiot, who loves her, and tells her that she has the right to love and be loved. It's he who finally convinces her that she is not a 'victim'.

Rima Das opened the door to the world for North East cinema with *Village Rockstars*. Dominic Sangma has opened a small window. Sangma passed out of SRFTI, Kolkata, in 2014. That very year, his diploma film *Rong'kuchak* (Echoes) was screened at the student film festival held at the Beijing Film Academy, where Xu Jianshang was studying. She took an instant liking to his work and the seeds for a unique collaboration were sown. Jianshang and Sangma would come together to co-produce his first feature film *Ma.Ama*, a small Garo-language film from Meghalaya.

An intensely personal story, it is Sangma's enquiry into his own mother's death, ostensibly due to the effects of black magic, when he was barely two. The film is not so much about the superstitions behind her death as it is about coming to terms with loss.

The entire Sangma family, including the director himself, along with his father, his siblings and his stepmother, plays itself in the film. The rhythm follows the slow pace of life in his village, Nongthymmai, where most of the film was shot.

Without any personal memories of her to sustain him, Sangma's mother had been an imagined figure in his head. The key person who could have connected the dots for him was his father. But he avoided talking about her for a long time following her demise.

On one level, the film is about a son coming to terms with the memories of his dead mother; on another, it is about the evolving relationship between a father and son, who had initially been distant, unable to bridge the divide between them. But the questions that Sangma raised about his mother would evantually draw him closer to his father. It was as much a redemptive, healing process for the older man as a catharsis for his son. All these elements have gone into the making of a film that, despite being rooted in Meghalaya, can tug at the heartstrings of every viewer, regardless of their ethnicity.

Soldiers of Cinema

ONE OF THE IMPORTANT turn-of-the-century developments has been the democratization of cinema. The steady spread of cine literacy, the strong influence of moving images, combined with easier access to technology and emerging online exhibition platforms, has meant that anyone who dreams of making a film now has the potential to turn it into a reality and find an audience for it, even at the grass-roots level. Filmmaking can become a mode of self-expression, a way of telling a story or highlighting an issue one feels strongly about. In a nutshell, an empowering tool, the voice of the voiceless.

Hyperlocal cinema that strives to preserve and promote local languages, traditions and cultures is being taken to the next level by indigenous communities, for whom it is a means of asserting their identity, protecting their interests and ensuring their survival. Indeed, it is a weapon they can wield to ensure due recognition of their legitimate rights and respect for their concerns by an establishment often infamous for its indifference to the social, economic and political challenges they are facing.

Take the residents of the small coastal fishing village of Nolia Sahi, near Konark in Odisha, who view filmmakers with deep suspicion. There is a reason for their distrust. It seems that not so long ago, one Subash Das had spent time with them, lived in their midst and apparently empathized with them over their troubles and concerns. He then went on to do something that would amount to a shocking betrayal of the trust they had placed in him: make a film that presented them in an unflattering light and was clearly weighted in favour of their corporate adversary, the South Korean steel multinational Pohang Iron and Steel Company (POSCO). No wonder the fisherfolk now deride him as a POSCO agent.

'He said that we have crab mentality; don't want to let go, don't like the idea of moving ahead and progressing,' they tell the anonymous, sympathetic filmmaker (present as a voiceover) in a video diary called *Nolia Sahi*, the duration of which is a little over nine minutes.

The short log, made in 2009, is a comment on their resistance to POSCO's efforts at building a port in the village for shipping steel. It also attempts to debunk the fallacy of advancement propagated by corporates, the state and the central government. Nolia Sahi that has, for long, been dismissed as a wasteland is actually pollution-free and houses 152 well-to-do families, says one resident who foresees the 'modern' future they are being promised as a bleak one that will bring about displacement, replace fishery and farming with manual labour in the steel plants, and force people to move out of their modest natural habitats into small, suffocating, box-like units. The development gurus might proclaim POSCO to be essential for Nolia Sahi, but more important than everything else, declare the villagers, are the rivers, paddy fields, vegetable gardens and betel vines.

The microcosm of Nolia Sahi represents a larger struggle in the state for preserving the environment, the indigenous lifestyle and local culture. The resultant turmoil keeps boiling over. The basic story remains much the same; while a tribe or a village may be replaced by another, their predicament is a shared one.

Films have begun to play a unique role in this struggle by helping indigenous people showcase their cause and raise their voice against the injustices regularly meted out to them. It also compels the privileged to break out of their insulated cocoon and take a hard look at the world which is far removed from their own – a world the disempowered inhabit.

The Human Zoo, for example, zooms in on the Adivasi Mela organized by the state government in Bhubaneswar on Republic Day. The urban population that throngs the fair regards the Dongria Kondh tribals of Niyamgiri in their colourful clothes, ornaments and accessories as though they were some unique species of animals in a zoo. By staring unabashedly at them and clicking their pictures incessantly, they show a complete lack of respect for them as fellow humans. What such outsiders fail to grasp is the important truth that these tribal people demonstrate – with their simple lifestyle and culture, they live in harmony with nature and are great sustainers and protectors of the environment.

The 8,000-strong community has its homes spread across more than a hundred villages in south-west Odisha's Niyamgiri hill range. Its members are the champions of trees in the densely forested hills and of rivers, streams and wildlife in the jungles. The highest mountain in the area, the 1,300 metre-high Niyam Donger, is regarded as a sacred grove, and Niyam Raja, the lord of natural resources, as its presiding deity. Every year, the Adivasis celebrate Niyam Raja during a festival held on the summit of the mountain. They believe in adapting themselves to their surroundings, rather than in exploiting the environment for their own use and convenience. Consequently, they sustain themselves on the resources offered by the Niyamgiri forests – the grains, pulses, plants and medicinal herbs – and practise horticulture and shifting agriculture.

This natural way of life is now under threat. The Dongria Kondhs have been strenuously resisting efforts by the exploitative Vedanta Resources-led bauxite mining lobby to undermine their pristine environment and eco-friendly ways. And it is through their battle against the global mining giant that these tribals have succeeded in drawing the world's attention to Niyamgiri's ecology and biodiversity, and the serious threat the area faces from the consequences of bauxite mining.

There are many more such films that throw light on local Adivasi movements and conflict points in Odisha. There's one that looks at fly-ash pollution in the 'industrial paradise' of Kalinganagar, and holds corporates and the State Pollution Control Board responsible for the disappearing ground water, the dust and smoke befouling the air and the effluents contaminating the water. The local Idital style of Saora Adivasi art is used for the illustrations in the animated short *Shot Dead for Development* (2007). The music is drawn from that of the Koya and Bonda Adivasi groups. The film trains the spotlight on those tribals who lost their lives to police gunfire since 2001 during Kalinganagar and Kashipur's anti-mining protests. *Niyamgiri: The Mountain of Law* (2008) draws up a list of all those individuals who have been abducted, jailed, tortured and murdered for espousing their environment-related cause.

All the aforementioned films are works by Surya Shankar Dash, an activist–filmmaker, who has been documenting various people's movements against industrialization and mining in Odisha since he left a much-coveted job in advertising in 2004. Not satisfied with that alone, Dash has also been helping tribals make their own films by teaching them the basics of using the camera.

'There is constantly an outsider's gaze on them; the community needs to tell its own stories,' he asserts.

From their own standpoint as insiders, his words imply. There are hundreds of such shorts, in addition to six of them which are of more than half an hour in length. All feature the tribals and villagers themselves as stakeholders.

Most of the tribals Dash has worked with hadn't even been exposed to a film-viewing experience before; teaching them to make a film might, therefore, have seemed a daunting task. But they took to it quite naturally, learning and relating to the language with apparent ease.

'It broke the literacy barrier. But we didn't impose any specific film grammar on them,' Dash remembers, attributing their affinity for the medium to the natural bond the tribals have with audio-visual culture. 'Their songs, dances, rituals and culture are so cinematic,' the filmmaker goes on, adding that the new generation seems even more drawn to the idea of using films to further their cause.

However, it's not about aesthetics; cinema at the grass roots in Odisha is a mode of activism and resistance. The camera is wielded as a weapon to help the disempowered fight for justice. The immediacy of context makes it a more real and felt experience, and is effective in creating and increasing awareness. This has resulted in an intensive, acutely focussed documentation of issues.

'These are not generalized films,' Dash is careful to point out.

When they first started on it some time in 2009, the film experimentation panned out in different ways in various places. The well-to-do farmers of Kalinganagar were quick to invest in used or new mini handycams. There were, however, places devoid of electricity and roads, where even projecting films on a solar-powered 10-inch screen was an uphill task. Dash and his group donated handycams (six of them over five years) and also built a pool of cameras that the tribals could dip into when required. Only editing had to be carried out with professional help and support from outside the tribal community.

Now with the availability of cheap, handy smartphones, almost everyone is equipped with a camera. Filming is no longer a big deal. Technology has been a mode of subversion in other ways too. Earlier, it was difficult to send out raw footage for editing or even to bring back the finished film for screening, because there was always the chance of its contents being misconstrued as subversive and, therefore, anti-establishment, thereby risking punitive action. These had to be smuggled out and brought back clandestinely. Now, all it takes is a WhatsApp message to do the needful.

Having taken the first step towards creativity with a cause and conscience, Dash's group now aims to help build a strong coalition, with indigenous filmmakers engaged in similar work, not just in India, but in South East Asia, Australia and New Zealand. Earlier, in January 2018, Dash attended the first-ever Indigenous International

Film Festival (IIFF) in Ubud, Bali, along with Dalit filmmaker Soumya Ranjan Mallik and Dinja Jakasika, a woman sarpanch from Niyamgiri.

'She has been the first from her community to get a passport and travel abroad,' Dash tells me.

Viewing films made by indigenous communities from across the world was inspiring and overwhelming for them.

'The experience made them realize that they are not the only ones fighting against the dominant discourse, and reassured them of [the strength and legitimacy of] their own resistance against the models of development constantly pitched at them,' says Dash.

Organized by Ranu Welum (Living Water) Foundation, Borneo's dynamic collective of filmmakers from 25 indigenous communities, in partnership with Handcrafted Films, If Not Us Then Who and Indonesia Nature Film Society (INFIS), the festival inspired Dash to hold a similar event in Odisha.

India's first international indigenous film festival took place in February 2019 in Odisha. An initiative of Video Republic, Dash's activist film collective that has been campaigning for local tribal movements in the state and against dispossession of indigenous people, the three-stop event kicked off in Bhubaneshwar on 19–20 February, moving on to Puri between 21–23 February, before travelling to various indigenous communities of coastal Odisha and south Odisha from 24 to 25 February. It showcased films, short films, music videos and documentaries made by people native to the region or by non-indigenous filmmakers in collaboration with local tribal communities.

The idea has been to shine a light on and celebrate the diverse native tribes and cultures, bringing into focus their concerns and the challenges they are struggling to overcome. The annual festival aims to serve as a platform for indigenous communities from around the world to engage in dialogue, share their views, collaborate on projects and use cinema as a mode of united resistance against exploitative forces. No wonder it was not sponsored or supported by any corporate, government or non-government organization.

'Odisha is known for its large indigenous population, diverse indigenous culture and widespread indigenous resistance against mining companies and other [entities engaged in] destructive practices,' says Dash in an interview I conduct for *The Hindu* (published on 30 November 2018 as 'India's first indigenous film festival soon'), months before the festival takes place. 'It is in [against] this backdrop that we aim to build an event of international indigenous congregation to learn and share from indigenous people from across the globe.'

According to him, indigenous communities across the world are teetering on the edge of survival. 'They will either survive or get wiped out,' Dash observes. 'The issues and struggles are not just parallel, but the same everywhere, highlighting the need for solidarity, to get[be] united... The future of mankind rests solely on the wisdom and knowledge of the indigenous people.'

The international participants this year included filmmaker Emmanuela Shinta from Indonesia's Dayak community. Last I spoke to him, Dash was planning to invite tribes from across India – Santhal, Ho, Munda from the east and North East, and tribes from central India, Chhattisgarh and Jharkhand – and also from Bali, Sarawak and Borneo. They have a shared sense of history and language, of geography and topography, of ecology and environment, and also of issues like bauxite mining.

'The strong connection of the indigenous communities was broken during the colonial period,' Dash tells me.

Now cinema can help restore the link.

In 2014, while making *Spring Thunder*, a film on the many problems besetting the villages and forests in the interiors of India, Mumbai-based writer-cinematographer-filmmaker Sriram Dalton was hit by a lack of manpower and resources. For the sake of authenticity, he was shooting in Netarhat, in his home state of Jharkhand, but had no filmmaking talent around him to fall back on. He had to make do with a team of 40 to 45 people, all non-film professionals and, primarily, farmers and mechanics.

The difficulties he faced then set him thinking and eventually prompted him to open a film institute in Netarhat. The institute, however, would be a unique one, with neither a building nor a roof to call its own. All it would have was the blue sky above. In 2016, when Maharashtra was dealing with one of its worst droughts, Dalton organized an open-air, 10-day filmmaking workshop there. With 200 participants coming from all over India, including 40 tribal women, it focussed on the issue of water scarcity. As a result, 13 original films emerged on the subject. The following year, the filmmaker went back to Netarhat to zoom in on the issue of deforestation; seven films came out of the workshop held in 2017.

In 2018, Dalton decided to not only concentrate on the subject of *zameen* (land), but also give an entirely new spin to his 'open-air, travel-oriented, film classroom without boundaries'. To gain insights into the ground beneath his feet, as it were, he decided to take a leaf out of Mahatma Gandhi's life: in the middle of June 2018, he took off on a padyatra. The original plan for this unique self-initiated walking tour was for Dalton to make his way from Mumbai to Boodha Pahad (infamous as a Naxal zone) in Jharkhand, covering a distance of about 2,000 km. While the beginning and end of the journey remain the same, the filmmaker, when we catch up with him in Malegaon, is now aiming higher. He plans to traverse 5,000 km on foot in three to four months, passing through eight states: Maharashtra, MP, Telangana, Odisha, Chhattisgarh, UP, Bihar and Jharkhand – all for a first-hand experience of the many land-related problems plaguing the country.

'*Zameen ko samajhne ke liye paidal chalna zaroori hai.* To get a feel of the land, it's essential to make the journey on foot,' he insists.

While covering between 35 and 40 kilometres every day, Dalton is busy researching his subject, talking to people, involving communities in ecological issues and screening his personal package of 22-odd short films. He is also shooting scenes along the way. He will make a film (which he has already titled *Megalith*) out of the reams of footage he has been accumulating. He also invited people keen to study filmmaking to join him in the initiative and learn the craft from him as he travels. The idea was to sensitize artistes and filmmakers to ecological and environmental issues, so that they could deal with it creatively in their work.

He hasn't, however, left the issues of water and forest behind him yet. Called Mahaprakritiparv, his journey's motto is Free Water India and zooms in on the entire triumvirate of issues: *jal, jangal, zameen* (water, forest, land).

We catch up with a distracted, disheartened Dalton in Malegaon on the afternoon of Eid. He had wanted to address the residents immediately after the morning namaaz and draw their attention to his mission, but was rounded up by cops and made to wait at the police station for three hours. The wait had stretched on from morning to afternoon. It is evident that in the communal cauldron that is Malegaon, everything is looked upon with suspicion, including something like his missiom that has far-reaching consequences for the betterment of community life.

'Just last night, we had participated in the Hindu–Muslim Ekta Manch programme under the aegis of the Narmada Bachao Andolan,' Dalton tells me, unable to comprehend why his group was picked up by the police.

With his 'precautionary' detention complete, he places his red-and-white banners in a corner of Mahatma Phule Chowk to set the stage for his '*Chauk-chaurahe pe baat-cheet* – engagement with the crowd at crossings and junctions'. He is like a street performer; people stop in their tracks, vehicles slow down for their passengers to gape at him. There is a gold-coloured handcart (designed by artiste Bashir Sheikh) right in the middle, with a stone sculpture symbolizing the three elements. Made by Nashik-based artist Neelesh Dheere, the sculpture weighs 80 kg and Dalton has been pushing it along all through his padyatra. This is what catches people's eyes and draws the crowds. Some have even placed coins beside it, assuming it is a representation of god, Dalton tells me. Along with it, the cart also symbolically houses a blooming plant and a bag to carry water in.

'Water, forests and land are fundamental rights in human life. Why should you pay money for water? It's mental slavery to have to do that,' the filmmaker tells the crowd that has gathered.

'Throughout the journey from Mumbai, the only things that caught my eye were barren hills,' he tells us. 'There would be a temple on top of a hillock, but no trees.'

He blames this state of affairs on social apathy and laxity on the part of an increasingly urbanized world.

'Society has reached an alarming stage when it comes to natural resources,' he says regretfully.

He feels it is nature alone that can help us strike a balance in a world where life is being reduced to a series of systemic failures.

'And ecology is safe only in the hands of the tribals,' he adds.

Dalton is dismayed that in an ecologically rich region like Boodha Pahad, the natural habitat of the tribals, it is they who are identified and targeted by the State as Naxalites. All the more reason, he feels, for them to be equipped with a basic understanding of cinema, so that they can tell their own stories.

'Since no one else is willing to tell them,' he explains.

Dalton's own mission is self-funded, with friends pitching in with contributions. Seven people from various parts of the country have joined him on his padyatra and more are expected to catch up with him as he travels further, covering different states. He sleeps wherever he finds space, eats whatever is available. On the way, philanthropic individuals and organizations also offer him food and shelter.

Meanwhile, while we return to Mumbai after giving him company for one leg of his journey, Dalton has already moved ahead. Leaving

Malegaon behind him, he has travelled past Jhodge and Kandhane, and onwards to Dhulia. The three or four live video updates every day on social media continue to keep him connected with the world.

'I might be an artiste on the margins, but I think globally,' he declares, soldiering on. '*Mera* cinema *meri muhim hai*. My cinema is my campaign.'

The Unsung Kollywood

A WORLD FAR REMOVED FROM India's remote tribal habitats that have given birth to the stark, cause-oriented films of the disempowered, the bustling city of Coimbatore is home to the kind of cinema that can justifiably be described as a sensory experience. With its swashbuckling, larger-than-life stars, revered more as demi-gods than actors, its many studios and once-opulent movie theatres, the city's dreams on celluloid were, in their heyday, all about entertainment for entertainment's sake, presented on a lavish scale. But somewhere down the line, time has taken its toll and what remain are defunct studios, dilapidated cinema halls, individuals still surviving on past glory and memories of what might have been. The remnants of those dreams, haunting, wistful and steeped in nostalgia, still linger, however, tantalizing the imagination.

The once-upon-a-time feeling hits me soon after I arrive in Coimbatore, eager for my first film-going experience at Delite theatre. I discover that there is an unwritten ritual involved in watching a film here. And it has to do with food, to start with, and more so in my case, because I have a long film ahead of me. I am advised by Sai Prasad Narendran, my young guide to the city, to fortify myself sufficiently for the next four hours. So just off Variety Hall Road, we head for the famous snacks kiosk outside Krishna Bhawan Hotel and help ourselves to fresh and scrumptious brinjal, plantain and banana *bajjis*. Just the way a lot of middle-class families, prior to watching movies at Delite, would – once upon a time.

Arrive at Delite and you are bound to start clicking pictures feverishly. This, despite the fact that at first glance, there's nothing so remarkable about it. It's a shabby building, once painted in shades of pistachio and khaki, with the walls inside painted a bright blue, standing on a grungy, yet bustling road full of furniture stores, and cycle and auto-parts shops, with the Town Hall at a distance. It is simply too nondescript to be noticed. Even its blue name plate is hard to spot in the surrounding visual din. But then there's an entire panel of apsara-like statues of voluptuous women adorning the theatre's outer façade. Too delightfully kitschy and gaudy for any eye or camera to ignore, it leaps out from its shabby environs, demanding attention. Quite like the eye-popping hoardings of Zee TV that loom large over Coimbatore and announce the telecast of James Bond movies in Tamil, featuring, as if to drive home the point, a *veshti*-clad Pierce Brosnan. Clearly, the idea is to endear the local populace and lure it into watching programmes on the channel.

Even harder for any film buff to ignore is the fact that Delite, at 104, is south India's oldest functional cinema hall. It was known as Variety Hall back in 1914 when it was built, and the road on which it stands was named after it. In the centenary year of the theatre, I've gone there to watch the 1958-classic *Nadodi Mannan* (The Vagabond King), featuring Maruthur Gopala Ramachandran (or MGR, as he is universally known). In this particular theatre, it is like adding another layer of history to what promises to be a nostalgic experience, anyway.

The entry into Delite's compound is something of an anti-climax; it makes you confront a world of ugly indigence, instead of the vibrant fantasies that cinema is supposed to be about. No middle-class families can be spotted here any more. The worn-out theatre is peopled with threadbare individuals, as unkempt and filthy as the building itself. It's an audience of the penniless, rather than the privileged, who seem to have cobbled together ₹7 for a 'third-class' ticket to MGR. There are three other classes of tickets, for ₹20, ₹25 and ₹30. The uncared-for balcony is no longer functional, what with thinning crowds and the growing cost of maintenance.

Dusty wooden chairs creak in protest as people stretch out their legs and place their feet atop the seat in front. Huge ceiling fans whir in unison, pigeons flutter near the ceiling, stray dogs loiter around and the stench of alcohol, bidis and sweat hangs heavy in the air. There are loud claps, cheers and catcalls as MGR appears on the screen. Movies and booze – that's what seems to make these lives go around.

At 220 minutes, *Nadodi Mannan* is MGR's longest film (its CBFC-certified length is 19.82 km). The first film that the actor also directed and produced (under the banner Em Gee Yar Pictures), it is in black and white as well as in colour. Based on the novel *The Prisoner of Zenda*, the play *If I Were King* and the film *Viva Zapata*, it has MGR in the double role of King Marthandan and revolutionary Veerangan. The film is about palace intrigues, poisonings and abductions. It's also about emotions, comedy, action, thrill and adventure. Above all, it is about politics. The film has recently been restored, digitized and re-released, I am told.

It becomes obvious, soon enough, that the crowd watching the film is familiar with each and every moment in the script. Members of the audience keep walking in and out, but are all there together to cheer in one voice during the crucial scenes. Barely 10 per cent of the hall is occupied, but the noises of approval for MGR are as loud as they can get, almost stereophonic, Dolby Digital, surround-sound quality.

'He is not an actor or a star; he is our god,' Sai whispers to me.

We are not watching a film, I realize, but participating in a spiritual communion.

But the film has more to offer than is initially apparent. It cuts painfully close to the lives of its underprivileged audience. The loudest roar of approval erupts when MGR speaks about the pathetic state of the poor and the oppressed. As the revolutionary Veerangan, he makes a case for democracy, the rule of the people, as opposed to the oppressive rule that monarchy imposes. The roars grow louder when, as the replacement king, Veerangan introduces a series of 'people-oriented' reforms. As an aside, Sai tells me that MGR never lost a single election. I can totally understand why.

After the film is over and we are seated in the manager's office, we spot a rare picture of Indira Gandhi with K.L. Johar, whose family now owns Delite. But to know more about the historic theatre, we have to head to the outskirts of Coimbatore, to Kalapatty where Paul Winfred, the grandson of the founder of Delite, Samikannu Vincent, lives. Winfred seems to be the only one from the large family who is still deeply connected to Delite. The others have moved on with their humdrum lives, caring little for the cine history and nostalgia that they are a part of.

It's easy to spot Winfred's house. There's a plaque outside, commemorating his grandfather Samikannu (18 April 1883–22 April 1942) as a pioneer of south India's motion-picture industry. Originally from Tiruchirapalli (also called Trichy), Vincent, a draftsman-clerk in the South Indian Railway, was one of south India's earliest travelling exhibitors, showing short films in makeshift tents in Madras (now Chennai). The plaque was a part of his grandfather's statue, which was erected by his family in Variety Hall Palace, but was removed when the theatre changed hands in 1985 and the Johars, a Punjabi business family, took over; it's currently owned by Pravesh Pratap Johar.

'The statue is now at my uncle's house in Ramanathapuram,' Winfred tells me.

'*Nulla Dies Sine Linea*. No day without something done' – the motto of Samikannu Vincent is imprinted on all the memorabilia: old photographs, film cards, brochures. Adorning the bright yellow walls of Winfred's living room are a picture of Vincent, a huge Belgian mirror and a 1914 wall clock from the Variety cinema hall. The 1.5-tonne mirror has a teak frame. There are also artistic elephant-face stands, teak chairs and a laundry basket in rosewood. Winfred serves us Vincent Crush from the soda company on Trichy Road, which was also set up by his grandfather. There are memories and more memories to share. Winfred reminisces about his grandfather's fleet of cars that included a Studebaker, a Morris Minor, a Ford, a Chevrolet and an Austin. He recalls that every Friday, Vincent would feed an elephant from the Perur Temple in the Variety Hall Palace's backyard.

Winfred, I realize, is clinging to a glory that has long, faded. In fact, Samikannu Vincent is barely remembered either in the annals of cinema or in the memoirs of Coimbatore. Nor is there a memorial to him in the city. But his story is fascinating, nonetheless. In 1905, while working in the railways, Vincent met a Frenchman who happened to be in the South with his touring-cinema equipment. When he had to return to France in a hurry, he sold his stuff to the Indian for ₹2,000.

Vincent screened his first film *The Life of Christ* in Trichy. He then travelled with his touring talkies across Asia to places as far away as Lahore and Peshawar, Afghanistan, Burma (now Myanmar) and Ceylon (now Sri Lanka). He set up Variety in 1914, and other theatres in Erode, Ernakulam and Chennai. Vincent opened 12 theatres in Coimbatore itself. The Rainbow screened English films. The Light House is now known as Kennedy Theatre. Edison's and Carnatic screened Tamil movies. In addition, there were Palace, Evacuee, Vincent Forces Cinema and Rex. Variety Hall Talkies screened a number of Hindi movies starring Dilip Kumar, which were big hits. Also screened at the theatre were Shakti Samanta's hugely successful Rajesh Khanna–Sharmila Tagore–starrer *Aradhana* (1969), *Yaadon ki Baraat* (1973), regarded by many as the Hindi film industry's first 'masala' film, featuring Dharmendra, Zeenat Aman and Neetu Singh, among others, and Basu Chatterjee's award-winning *Rajnigandha* (1974) that took a realistic look at urban middle-class life in an era when potboilers were ruling the roost, Shyam Benegal's debut film *Ankur* (1974), which was actress Shabana Azmi's first film to be released and was deemed a commercial and critical success. *Sholay* and *Enter the Dragon*, the 1973 martial arts action film that featured Bruce Lee in his final appearance before his premature death, had the longest run here for non-Tamil films.

Back then, the audience sat on the sand floor. Chairs were kept out only for important dignitaries. Gradually, benches were added. Upper and lower stalls were created. A balcony came up with an arrangement of chairs, which would subsequently be replaced by plush sofas. During the era of silent cinema, a man addressing the audience through a megaphone would provide a commentary on the story of the film being projected on the screen. The cinema hall was also used as a dance hall and a theatre for staging plays and holding musical performances.

Winfred was born in 1932 in Vincent Villa, a mansion (now demolished) that was located next to the theatre. It housed the entire joint family of 30. In those days, it was referred to as the 'Buckingham Palace of Coimbatore'. The vast establishment had been a joint property owned by Samikannu Vincent's five sons and two daughters, the eldest of whom happened to be Winfred's mother. A bitter family feud erupted in typical *filmi* style when the property was pledged to the Johars, and Paul Winfred is reported to have even filed a case against his own mother.

Delite is one of the few old single screens that still survive in Coimbatore. There's also the neighbouring Naaz, showing Vijay's *Thuppakki* (Gun), a 2012 Tamil action thriller, which was remade in Hindi as *Holiday* (2014), with Akshay Kumar in the lead. Other cinema halls have mutated into tea factories, shopping complexes and malls. Delite itself is in bad shape; the crowds are thin, revenues are low and upkeep is poor, but it is being run for the sake of the historical value attached to it. Meanwhile, Winfred says that people from the film industry have plans to declare 18 April, the birth anniversary of

Samikannu Vincent, as Cinema Day. They are keen to initiate an award in his name. Hopefully, it will happen soon.

Delite is not Samikannu Vincent's only legacy. He played a bigger role in Coimbatore's glorious cinematic past. Variously known as the fastest growing Tier 2 city, the 'Manchester of the South' and the fourth-largest metro of the South, Coimbatore is identified more for its industries, educational institutes, textiles and IT sector. But few know that it used to be an important hub of film production in the South in the early 1900s. It was the 'Kollywood' of days gone by, representing a slice of history which most in the South would be familiar with, but very few in the North are aware of.

'They produced some milestone movies till Chennai took over in the late fifties,' says film historian Theodore Baskaran.

Samikannu Vincent was one of the founders of Central Studios (1935–56), often referred to as the 'Prabhat Studio of the South'. Located in Uppilipalayam, near Singanallur on Trichy Road, the studio boasted of the BNC Mitchell Camera, which cost ₹5 lakh in those days. Then there was Pakshiraja Studio (1945–72) – set up by S.M. Sriramulu – on Puliyakulam Road, and Modern Theatre (1935–82) in nearby Salem, a major textile and steel centre in Tamil Nadu.

'It was run by the revolutionary T.R. Sundaram, who got the most modern of systems from Germany. He was an astute businessman and there was no one to match his scale of operation,' says K. Hariharan.

M. Karunanidhi wrote films in Coimbatore. MGR and Shivaji Ganesan shot several films here. M.K. Thyagaraja Bhagavathar's *Sivakavi* (1943) was made here. Ellis R. Dungan, the American who made several significant Tamil films from 1936 to 1950 (without knowing the language), marked his debut as a director in 1936 with *Sathi Leelavathi*, MGR's first film, operated from Salem and Coimbatore. The significant films shot in Salem were Dungan's 1950

Manthiri Kumari (The Minister's Daughter), with MGR in the lead, and *Alibabavum 40 Thirudargalum* (Alibaba and the 40 Thieves, 1956), the first Tamil colour film that became the actor's gateway to stardom. Shivaji Ganesan's *Maragatham* (Emerald), 1959, and *Kalyaniyin Kanavan* (Kalyani's Husband), released in 1963, were made in Coimbatore. In 1954, Pakshiraja was among the first to shoot a multilingual: *Malaikkallan* (Thief of the Hills), starring MGR, which was remade as *Azaad* (1955) in Hindi, with Dilip Kumar and Meena Kumari (the film being shot in Coimbatore itself over three months in as many schedules of 20 days each), *Thaskaraveeran* (Heroic Thief), 1957, in Malayalam, *Bettada Kalla* (Mountain Robber), 1957, in Kannada and *Surasena* (1957) in Sinhalese. In fact, these studios eventually became centres of 'Indian' film production, rather than of south Indian cinema alone.

'Even Sinhalese films were made there,' Hariharan informs me.

Gradually, bigger, better studios started coming up in Chennai – Prasad, Gemini and AVM, among others. In the course of time, they would overtake those in Coimbatore and Salem. Chennai eventually became the headquarters of all cinema from the South. Each of the four states built its own independent film-development corporations, drew out indigenous talent to set up studios and labs, and offered huge subsidies for filmmaking. With such developments, Coimbatore's clout as a centre of filmmaking in the South was completely eroded, though another reason is offered as to why cinema is supposed to have abandoned this city. Says Baskaran: 'The powerful Naidu community leaders in Coimbatore thought cinema was a bad influence on the youngsters.'

Now Rajalakshmi Mills stands where Central Studios once was. We are denied entry and told that there is nothing of the studios left inside. All that remain are workshops and textile-manufacturing units. The nine-acre Modern on Salem's Yercaud Road has been razed to build a residential complex. Promises have been made that the rare arches and studio houses will be preserved in an area close by. Pakshiraja is now a marriage hall: Vignesh Mahal Kalyana Mandapam. But it still bears a stamp of the past. Odd posters and dismantled sets lie stacked in a corner. An old car that had once been used in the studio's films has been given shelter in a shed. And still visible under a tree near the entrance is the eye-catching blue statue of the studio insignia: an eagle perched atop a globe holding a snake in its claws. A reminder of the technicolour dreams that Coimbatore once dreamt, which now throb with life in Kodambakkam.

Coimbatore may have had to play second fiddle to Chennai when it comes to being the cinema capital of Tamil Nadu, but I am told by trade experts that, along with Chennai and Chengalpattu, Coimbatore still remains one of the significant '3 Cs' – 'A' centres that new-age Tamil cinema, with its offbeat stories and sophisticated narratives, techniques and styles, has been increasingly catering to. The 'B' and 'C' centres of Salem, north and south Arcot, rural Tiruchirappalli and Madurai are where the massy films are supposed to thrive. Madurai, in fact, has been unique in creating a rough and rustic genre of cinema all its own. Between them stood a film industry that was a force to reckon with, not just in Tamil Nadu, but in the entire country and the world at large.

Cinema Paradiso

GIRINDRANATH JHA WOULD BE among those rare individuals who seem to have found their true calling. It's evident in the pride with which he declares to us that he is a farmer. Seven years ago, in 2012, this former journalist at the India Abroad News Service (IANS) and the Jagran group, and a research fellow at Sarai-CSDS (Centre for the Study of Developing Societies), decided to bid farewell to New Delhi and head back home to plant *kadamb* trees and grow rice, wheat and maize in his village, Chanka, that lies in Bihar's Purnia district, one of the country's 250 most backward ones, according to the Ministry of Panchayati Raj, 2006.

The region, however, has not only been an unexpected breeding ground for literary talent, but has been brought marvellously alive in the works of Padma Shri Phanishwar Nath Renu, one of India's most seminal writers in Hindi. Born in 1921 in Araria district (then Purnia), he is best known for giving the *anchalik katha*, or regional story, a prominent place in Hindi literature and drawing the voice of rural India into the mainstream through works like *Maila Aanchal*, published in 1954, and 'Maare Gaye Gulfam', a short story that was first published in 1958 in a Patna magazine called *Aparampara*. The story, which would come out a year later as part of an anthology called *Thumri*, was adapted for the screen in 1966 by Basu Bhattacharya as *Teesri Kasam*, starring Raj Kapoor and Waheeda Rehman.

That, however, would not be the district's sole connect with Indian cinema. Jha, former journalist and researcher, may have decided to return home to work in the fields, but his love for good cinema that he had grown and cultivated over years spent in the capital remained within him. So, in between sowing seeds, irrigating the land and harvesting the crop, he found a way to share this passion with the local children. Downloading significant public-service ads, cartoons and film clips, he would show them to the children on his laptop. It was better for them to watch films, he felt, than idle away their leisure hours in needless pranks and mischief. He named this small personal effort 'Gaon-Cinema (Village-Cinema)' and was soon known by both young and old as the man who switched on his laptop the minute someone mentioned the word 'film'.

'Good films can help educate children and make them aware. Cinema can be like a proxy guardian, especially for rural kids,' he maintains.

Unfortunately, the only films the village seemed to have easy access to were not even bad Bollywood flicks, but subpar Bhojpuri movies, often watched on mobiles after smartphones became accessible in rural India. Before that happened, it was a matter of watching the odd movie on television or catching one during a visit to Purnia town.

Despite such limited exposure to films or, perhaps, because of it, there were many takers for Jha's thoughtful selection of films. Besides *Chhota Bheem* and *Lagaan*, the most popular of his set of 'laptop' films turned out to be Ashutosh Gowariker's *Swades*. That this Shah Rukh Khan–starrer struck a chord with the locals in Chanka isn't surprising, for it was about one NRI's effort to make his village self-sufficient in generating its own electricity. Twenty-five kilometres from Purnia town, Chanka is a backward tribal village with just a primary school to boast of. Forget cinema halls, even electricity and metalled roads are pipe dreams here.

'The whole world has changed, but not Chanka,' says Jha.

Even today, homes here are dependent on batteries or a pooled generator for power. It is these power points that keep the villagers' personal television sets running, their alternative access – in addition to their mobiles – to movies and the world outside.

In November 2014, Gaon-Cinema spread its wings and expanded its scope when Jha helped organize Cinema Haat, a film festival for rural children, in association with UNICEF to mark 25 years of the adoption of the UN Convention on the Rights of the Child, including the right to entertainment. The festival took films produced by the Children's Film Society of India to Patna, Gaya, Vaishali and Purnia town, as well as to small villages around it, like Damdaha and, of course, Chanka. It was the first time that a film festival had travelled to Bihar's villages. And it was made possible with the help of that ubiquitous lifeline – the generator.

Apart from exposing rural youngsters to good children's films, the idea behind the festival was also to recreate the urban cinema hall-going experience, complete with individual seat tickets, popcorn, snacks and a cold drink for each of the kids.

'We wanted to show them how films are watched in big cities,' Jha explains, recalling how the 2,000 children who attended 'went delirious with joy'.

A joy experienced for the first time, but hopefully, not the last. At a larger level the festival helped bring the world's attention to Chanka. It made Jha focus on a sustained attempt at bridging the urban–rural divide. He invites city folks, specially artistes, to experience village life as part of the Chanka Residency programme. Cinema does have its positive side-effects.

Dhenuki village in Bihar's Saran district is around 370 km from Chanka, but has much in common with it: lack of electricity yet, despite this major impediment, an exposure to good cinema. It all started in 2012 when Suraj Prasad and Anuj Malhotra, two youngsters working with various film clubs and festivals, founded one of their own: Lightcube. One of the primary aims of this film society is to take the projector and, in turn, good films beyond the confines of the metros and the mainstream to alternative spaces, including far-flung corners of the country, and screen them for the local audience.

'Films are for everyone, not just a privileged few,' say Anuj and Suraj, voicing the main thought that drives their project.

The activities of their film society had officially begun with the first Dhenuki Cinema Project, a series of film screenings organized over one night in Suraj's village, Dhenuki. The idea for it was sparked during a conversation he had with Anuj. Suraj was telling him about the many villages without electricity and how he wished that a number of films they had had the good fortune of watching in the city could be shown there too. He kept citing his own village Dhenuki as one such underdeveloped place. It prompted Anuj to suggest they initiate the project there to begin with.

It proved to be the perfect launching ground for their endeavour. Dhenuki, near Chhapra, is a village still unexposed to the Internet. There is no cinema hall in or around it, the closest one being about 10 km away in Mashrakh. The women of Dhenuki had never seen a film. The exceptions, like a lady from Tinsukhia, in Assam, were those who had watched films in their parents' homes before being married into families living in this village. They still missed those years when they enjoyed the cinema-viewing experience.

Suraj had to use the local resources at hand – bed sheets stitched together to serve as a movie screen, a locally sourced projector and a diesel genset to screen films for the residents of the village. And it would all take place in the courtyard of the mukhiya's house, with the host himself watching a film on the big screen after a gap of 25 years. A 70-strong audience gathered to watch a film that marked Hrishikesh Mukherjee's directorial debut in 1957: *Musafir*, remarkable in more ways than one, for not only had Dilip Kumar acted in it, but had even sung a song for it. Among the viewers was an 85-year-old man who had never seen a film in his entire life. A serious, sombre, tragic and rather slow film, *Musafir* didn't go down too well with many in the audience. For a village that sleeps early, however, Dhenuki wanted more when the film got over at 11 p.m. Giving in to their demands, Suraj then screened Kamal Haasan's *Pushpak*, a silent comedy that they were able to connect with instantly. The audience stayed on to watch it until the end and dispersed only at 1.30 a.m.

'Despite not being exposed to the nuances of cinema, they responded to the small moments,' Suraj remembers.

It was also a happy community experience, an occasion for the entire village to get together, enjoy the moving image and share an experience.

With successful pilot projects in Bihar, Chhattisgarh, Assam and Nagaland, The Dhenuki Cinema Project has now grown into a well-known, cinema-based outreach and education programme. As part of its affairs, the society enlists various volunteers and cine-activists to visit villages and smaller towns in different parts of the country to organize film screenings. The broader purpose of this mobile screening exercise is to create an opportunity for conversation in these villages, to enable residents to introspect on their individual roles in building the larger mythology of the region to which they belong.

Cine-activists travel to the village and stay there for three months, initiating the film club, which screens films at different locations within the village. They then hand over the equipment and the functioning of the film club to the local population, which attempts to make the club sustainable in the subsequent six-month period, before initiating the building of a multipurpose resource centre in the village, with its residents as participants and stake-holders.

A similar cinema-outreach project has been blooming in the interiors of Kerala. In 2014–15, Kazhcha Film Forum, a film lovers' and filmmakers' collective, started 'Cinema Vandi' (a cinema van equipped with projection equipment) that is literally all about movies in motion. It travels to villages and towns, and screens films wherever invited – film societies, clubs, colleges. An alternate distribution channel for independent movies, Cinema Vandi conducted its first tour across Kerala over 3 months, successfully screening Sanal Kumar Sasidharan's *Oraalppokkam* in over 110 locations. It later toured to screen feature films such as *Karie* directed by Shanavas Naranippuzha, *Shavam* directed by Don Palathara and Sasidharan's *Ozhivudivasathe Kali*. Initiatives like 1018mb have been helping organize on-demand screenings – of not indie movies alone, but popular classics as well. Most significantly, newer community spaces are emerging, where intimate group screenings can be organized.

As in Chanka and Dhenuki, there is no cinema hall in 'Little Lhasa' either, I am informed, when I travel to McLeodganj towards the end of 2015. The closest one is in Pathankot, about 90 km away. They tell me that there used to be a Himalaya Talkies in Dharamshala, which has now been turned, quite predictably, into a mall. A multiplex is coming up there soon and, subsequently, as I put pen to paper, I learn that Gold Cinema in Maximus Mall, Kotwali Bazaar, is functional and screening films. But the majority of the residents in McLeodganj, the headquarters of the Tibetan Government in Exile, still watch films on television and DVDs.

Then there is Cinemaa 1 on Jogiwara Road.

No landmark this. It's easy to miss Cinemaa 1, unless your keen eye manages to spot the signage and your curiosity is sufficiently piqued to peer inside. Tucked behind a row of shops, it's a hall that has been converted into an informal viewing room by throwing together some 30-odd chairs – 28, to be precise – with a screen and home-theatre projection system to boot. Red carpets, blue wallpaper and blue-and-red chairs – the colours are in perfect synchronicity. A *Pirates of the Caribbean* poster stares at you from the wall and the familiar musty smell that permeates the interiors of buildings in cold mountain regions invades your nostrils. There used to be many such hole-in-the-wall video parlours in McLeodganj; in fact, about six or seven on the same road as Cinemaa 1. However, unlike this sole survivor, they were all illegally run and had to eventually shut shop when the government came looking for licences.

The owner of Cinemaa 1 is the ever-smiling Yaqub Ahmad Shalla. His father is from Kashmir, his mother from UP, and he himself was born and brought up in Nashik, Maharashtra. Now he runs a Kashmir handicrafts and crystals shop in the heart of McLeodganj, just outside Himachal Tourism's popular Hotel Bhagsu. Why McLeodganj, of all the places? Quite by chance, it seems. Shalla had landed here in 1999, when his plans to settle down in Switzerland were thwarted by the country's refusal to grant him a visa. The laidback, but politically energetic town appealed to him enough for him to stay on. Always a film fanatic, Shalla would travel all the way to Delhi, back then, for his fill of films, especially the English ones. And in 2008, he set up Cinemaa 1 to satisfy his own appetite for cinema.

'I bought the home-theatre system, the amplifier, all the way from Hong Kong in 2007 and had to pay 60 per cent of the cost as customs duty,' he remembers.

Apart from this investment of ₹4 lakh, it would take him another year to get the licence.

The collection of movies at Cinemaa 1 is eclectic and they get screened four times a day: at 12 noon, 2.30 p.m., 5.30 p.m. and 8 p.m. But the tickets to the shows don't come that cheap, after all; the prices are comparable to that of a Delhi or Mumbai multiplex. If the viewers for a particular show are few in number, the cost of a ticket could be as much as ₹300, but if there is a group of about 20 people for a show, the price of a ticket drops to between ₹150 and ₹200. However, the returns from Cinemaa 1 are still not enough. Shalla depends on the handicrafts shop for a steady income. Cinemaa 1 is more of a hobby and an indulgence.

Posters strewn across town list the movies on view, from *The Darjeeling Limited* (2007) to *The Best Exotic Marigold Hotel* (2011), from *Silver Linings Playbook* to *Life of Pi* (both released in 2012), from *Elysium* to *Trance* (both 2013 releases). These are all Hollywood films catering to the tourists who are in town to visit the Dalai Lama Temple.

'Quite often, they leave behind interesting films from their own collections,' says Shalla.

Given the 'Free Tibet' cause and the interest in Buddhism, two films are played constantly on a loop: 1997 releases *Seven Years in Tibet* and *Kundun.*

When we visit him at the end of 2015, Shalla is desperately missing his Israeli patrons, who typically come visiting after their compulsory military conscription.

'They were all recalled after the trouble in Gaza,' he explains.

He remembers the good old days when around 80 or 90 of them would come down to Dharamshala and stay for a year or two. Now the visas they are granted don't allow them to stay in India for more than six months.

'*Veer Zaara*, with Hebrew subtitles, was very popular amongst them,' Shalla confides. 'We used to play it very often in our hall.'

Perhaps, it's the only Bollywood movie in demand in this Tibet away from Tibet.

Travel across India and you'll find Cinema Paradisos as unique as Cinemaa 1. From rickety buses equipped with video players to live-streaming and downloading on mobiles, mofussil India is watching films in more quirky ways than one. I remember travelling to Udaipur on a bus from Delhi. An almost 12-hour unforeseen delay due to a traffic jam on the Delhi–Jaipur highway was made bearable by the round-the-clock screening of films and the concomitant discovery of some hitherto unknown gems like Pankaj Parashar's insane laugh riot *Peecha Karo* (1986), starring Amjad Khan and Farooque Shaikh. Thirst, hunger and heat were quelled, the frustration of passengers kept in check with the distraction, a soother of sorts, offered by films. The only ones unhappy with the entertainment provided were the few in search of peace and quiet, unattainable with the speakers in the bus blaring.

The intercity buses in Maharashtra might be in bad shape themselves, but almost all come with video players attached, whether you are travelling to Malegaon or Satara from Mumbai. But that arrangement for entertainment may not last in the long run, what with passengers having their personal cinema packed into their mobiles, preferring to watch their favourites by themselves instead of catching any random flick in the company of fellow travellers. Travelling to Pune in 2016 to meet filmmaker Nagraj Manjule, I saw two schoolgirls at a highway pit stop watching a bootlegged print of his then recently released *Sairat* (later remade in Hindi as *Dhadak*, starring Ishaan Khattar and debutante Jahnvi Kapoor, daughter of the late Sridevi) on their mobiles. They had loved the film when they watched it in the theatres, but wanted to catch it again, they told me, adding that some of their friends who had watched it on their mobiles had actually seen it again on the big screen. From communal to personal or personal to communal, the film-viewing dynamic is ever-changing and never-changing, and, in the case of a film like *Sairat*, curiously increasing the hype and hysteria around the film, even while treading on the dangerous illegal terrain that the downloading world is often all about.

You can't be blamed for assuming during an experience at Sunset Drive-In in Ahmedabad that this big-city attraction has little connect with cinema viewing in mofussil India. This unique open-air cinema offers, after all, the perks of urban entertainment, beginning with the largest screen in Asia. You can park your car, order some grub from the food court and watch a film under the stars. Having opened in 1973 with the Amitabh Bachchan–Jaya Bhaduri–starrer *Abhimaan*, the cinema can accommodate more than 6,000 people and about 650 cars at a time. The only other drive-in of this kind is again in a big city – the Prarthana Drive-In in Chennai – and another is coming up in the Mumbai megapolis. 'While some people may prefer Netflix to chill, there is this marvellous open theatre in the city that is worth abandoning your couch for!' is the selling line of Sunset Drive-In to draw customers out of the isolationist experience of cinema consumption. The idea is to combine cinema with the notion of an outing or picnic, and for ₹60 per person and ₹90 per car, that's not a bad deal at all for the city slickers.

Most of all, it's about nostalgia and memory.

'In the 1970s, when television was not common and cinema halls were limited, makeshift film screens were often set up by the government in various localities in cities, small towns and villages alike, and people used to watch films from the comfort of their homes and neighbourhoods,' says local resident Tejas Patni.

Most of these films back then were family-oriented, with strong social and educational messages attached; at Sunset Drive-In today, the usual mainstream releases of the day are played.

No, there really doesn't seem to be anything remotely small-town about drive-in theatres. But if you're wondering whether its inception was inspired by Western trends, you will be surprised to discover that the unusual concept of community viewing isn't necessarily a phenomenon imported from foreign shores. It can actually be traced back to the culture of touring talkies in rural India, especially in the hinterland of Maharashtra, a tradition that has been appropriated in cities for its uniqueness and exotic value.

Simply put, touring talkies are all about itinerant movies (prints and projectors), travelling in trucks to remote villages where tents are pitched and makeshift screens put up to bring alive the magic of moving images to farmers, workers and labourers, who would, otherwise, have little or no access to them. This roaming, wandering cinema is particularly popular during harvest-related festivities and religious festivals and fairs.

In India, touring talkies are reported to have been started in 1904 by Monik Sethina. Curiously, almost nothing is known about him. He might not have existed at all, but for a mention, a mere entry in the archives of Indian film history. Although sporadically present in West Bengal and south India, the organized form of this mode of cinema can be found only in Maharashtra, where you have actual companies with employees – driver, projectionist, gatekeeper, ticket seller – running the show. Meticulously researched and documented by scholar Shirley Abraham and photographer Amit Madheshiya for over eight years, this endangered tradition and business is the subject of their documentary *Cinema Travellers* that premiered at the Cannes Film Festival in 2016. According to 'Nomads of cinema', a report by Sankhayan Ghosh in the 27 April 2016 issue of *The Hindu*, Mumbai, what enticed the filmmakers into exploring the phenomenon is the discovery that travelling cinemas are a 70-year-old tradition, an organized industry that has been quietly thriving on the margins of Indian cinema. It has also been the inspiration for Dev Benegal's 2009 film *Road, Movie* and Gajendra Ahire's 2013 Marathi release *Touring Talkies*.

'It flows like a simple story with three characters: a benevolent showman, a shrewd exhibitor and a maverick projector mechanic,' Madheshiya is quoted as saying in *The Hindu* report.[16]

The characters referred to are representative of the stories of people who run these cinemas.

Anup Jagdale of Vajod village in Satara district owns one such touring talkies called, quite simply, Anup Touring Talkies. His father Ashok, a farmer, set up the family business in 1963.

'He bought a second-hand 1930s Japan-made projector and started screening films in villages in two-three districts of western Maharashtra,' Jagdale informs me, when I spoke to him in 2016.

He himself moves around with the projector in the Satara district, the season being from December to April.

'In my father's time, it used to run longer, for about eight months. My father would get tired of screening films, but people never got tired of watching them,' he remembers.

Indeed, they would not. For tent cinemas brought entertainment right next door to the homes and fields of poor villagers.

'Even today, many of them have to travel a hundred kilometres to the nearest cinema hall,' says Jagdale.

Back then, they lined up not just to watch the films, but to also see the cinema reels being carried on an elephant's back during rallies before the screening.

Today, the colourful posters and kitschy cutouts of stars are as much an attraction. While fairs are being held, film shows can run back-to-back from afternoon until the next morning, with people sitting cross-legged on the ground, staring at the screen, wide-eyed with wonder.

When Jagdale is on the move, three trucks carry all his equipment, prints and projectors. Typically, it's a 10-day affair at every stop – a day to set up things, eight days of screenings, and one more day for dismantling the equipment and packing it up for the next leg of the tour. The films screened travel through several villages, and are largely mainstream Hindi and Marathi ones, escapist fantasies that offer communities a shared break from the drudgeries of their day-to-day existence.

Jagdale never screens these films in big cities, but he did hold an exclusive session in Worli's Jamboree Maidan for Ahire's film. On that occasion, however, the tent was different. It had proper seating, carpets and even air-conditioning. Two years ago, in the month of February, Jagdale had also organized a seven-day film festival in Sangli.

But when we speak to him, he is pessimistic about the larger picture.

'I wonder if this tradition will last[even] for another two-three years or not,' he observes. 'I am somehow persisting with it; but like a film, tent cinema is also in its climax, breathing its last.'

According to him, there were 1,000 such tent cinemas in Maharashtra in 1970, but now only 10 of them survive. Of these, three are in western Maharashtra, and the rest are in the Marathwada and Vidarbha regions.

Television, DVDs and mobiles are apparently luring the core audience away. Costs are mounting and the government is apathetic. There are neither subsidies nor tax incentives to keep such shows going.

'Marathi films, *tamasha* get tax relief, but we have to pay entertainment tax,' says Jagdale.

Their business is not eligible for bank loans, and insurance companies are unwilling to insure their equipment. The expenses for a whole season (roughly from October to April the following year) exceed ₹1 lakh. This includes the cost of the reel, travel and other overheads. Add to this the commercial power rates they have to pay, and the 'exorbitant rent' that Jagdale claims he has to pay local governing bodies for setting up their tent.

Every year, the government promises effective measures to ease their burden, but never follows through. To keep up with the times, Jagdale has, on his own, invested in digital technology to access the latest films for his viewers, before they land up on their television screens. He travelled with the 2013 Aamir Khan–Abhishek Bachchan-starrer *Dhoom 3* and was hoping to take *PK* (2014), featuring Aamir Khan and Anushka Sharma, to the interiors. Despite the problems he's facing, he wants to hold on to his trucks and tents, prints and projector – somehow.

'If we give up now,' he says, explaining his stand, 'we will lose a part of our culture and we won't be able to revive it ever again.'

With the spectre of drought always looming large over Maharashtra, and the miseries of farmers omnipresent and too widespread to be alleviated by the occasional *filmi* fantasy, the end might be nearer than one imagines. But, as is the case for most of us, a sad ending is not what Jagdale looks forward to. Neither in movies, nor in life.

Jagdale's trump card – digitization – has been the tool for survival for the many languishing single screens across Indian towns, big or small. Like the Kohinoor and New Kohinoor cinema halls in Jodhpur.

It's a short, though treacherous, walk through the rain from my hotel to New Kohinoor down the busy Chaupasni Road. Potholes along the way and pools of rainwater showing no signs of evaporating lead to the grimy, nondescript theatre. Standing in front of its façade, it is impossible to believe that it could be living Bollywood's new dream-turned-reality of a technology called e-cinema.

New Kohinoor is a twin theatre, with a double shot of single screens – upper and lower – both of which opened in 2000 with the Salman Khan–Karisma Kapoor–starrer *Dulhan Hum Le Jaayenge* and Hrithik Roshan's blockbuster debut film *Kaho Na... Pyaar Hai* respectively. Creaking chairs, patties, cream roll, 'machine-*wali*' coffee in the canteen, viewers generously spewing betel juice, along with wolf-whistles – it's like thousands of other charming Indian Cinema Paradisos, but one where a film is shown, without the film.

New Kohinoor went digital in 2005. In its handkerchief-sized projection rooms, the giant 35 mm Christie and Cinecitta projectors look like relics from a bygone era.

'Showpiece *hain ye. Lohe ke bhaav bhi nahin bikenge.* They won't even sell at the price of iron,' rues head operator Mohammad Afzal.

Their carbon arc lamps don't shoot light through film strips to create the illusion of movement. Instead, small laptops store images as files and pop them on to the screens. The new technology has the blessings of Allah, with a Mecca–Medina photo and the sign of '786' showering blessings from their perch high on the wall.

In the last few years, many such cinemas have got a new lease of life by retro-fitting/ upgrading their shows with digital projectors. For the downbeat trade in Bollywood's so-called 'B' and 'C' centres, it has almost been like the last kiss of life. The laptop has revived Eastmancolor dreams – at least, for a while.

And how has it managed that? By helping save costs. Discs come cheaper than prints. Also, you no longer need to transport 50 kg of film reels in canisters. Instead, the movie is stored in a high-capacity disc drive, about double the size of a cigarette pack, which is couriered to the hall where the film can be downloaded to the server. It can be downloaded through a dish as well. The digitally encrypted signal comes with an access password – to keep pirates at bay. The technology has reinvented the conventional distribution-exhibition model in India, much to the joy of film fans in smaller cities. Traditionally, after doing the rounds in metros and big cities, the same prints would be passed on to the 'B' and 'C-grade' centres, and reach them after a gap of five or six weeks. With the use of discs, films have been arriving much more promptly in small towns, enabling faster recovery of money.

Afzal looks happy with the change it has brought about in his role as a projectionist. Does he fear that the new technology will render him obsolete?

'No, it's more about adapting to new technology,' he replies. '*Aur mehnat bhi to kam ho gayi hai*. There is much less to do now.'

No painstaking, time-consuming rolling and rerolling of reels, and assembling and loading the film on a plater. No splicing, gluing or taping it. No change of reels after every 20 minutes. All Afzal has to do now is click on the mouse and keep a watch. Besides, he also has an AC in his projection room now, all because the server and sound system demand a temperature-controlled environment.

'*Ek* machine *ne insaan ko garmi se rahat dila di*. A machine has brought us humans relief from the heat,' he smiles.

Screen Dreams in Limbo

SRINAGAR-BASED JOURNALIST ASIF Qureshi remembers his final farewell to a cinema hall.

'It was 30 November 1989,' he says. 'I remember the date, because all cinema halls had closed down on 1 December 1989 under militant diktats.'

It was the results day at school; the day to collect the annual report card. But, instead of doing so, Qureshi and his friends had gone to watch Vidhu Vinod Chopra's 1989 Madhuri Dixit–Anil Kapoor–Jackie Shroff–starrer *Parinda* at Broadway, the last time he would ever watch a film in a cinema hall.

Though he did manage to catch *Parinda*, he had to give Aamir Khan's critically acclaimed and commercially successful debut film *Qayamat Se Qayamat Tak* (1988) a miss, something he still regrets. His uncle, who was working in the state government's Excise Department, had been posted at Shah Cinema. But all the shows of *QSQT* were sold out. Tickets were simply not available, even at black-market prices.

'My uncle kept refusing to get us passes and, eventually, when he relented, the closure of cinema halls had already been ordered,' Qureshi remembers.

Nowadays, like everyone else in Kashmir, he watches films on DTH or pirated DVDs, and managed to see *Haider* (2014), thanks to a pirated print downloaded on a USB drive.

From *Kashmir ki Kali* in 1964 to *Noorie* (1979), *Henna* (1991),

Roja (1992) and *Dil Se* (1998), from *Mission Kashmir* (2000) and *Jab Tak Hai Jaan* (2012) to *Haider* and *Fitoor* (2015), Kashmir has been the favourite location and backdrop for Bollywood films. Years ago, before Switzerland took over, it was *the* go-to place for film shoots. One song filmed in Kashmir was almost mandatory back then. Bollywood's favourite location was also its most passionate consumer of films.

'It was a religion in the Valley,' declares filmmaker Rajesh Jala, who grew up in Kashmir.

'The kind of enthusiasm that was there for films in Kashmir, perhaps, exists only in the South now,' says filmmaker-actor Aamir Bashir.

No irony, then, that it was a film, albeit a foreign one, that lit the spark of resistance.

'Anthony Quinn's *Lion of the Desert* ran for many weeks,' Bashir remembers. '[The] Audience reacted to its portrayal of the Libyan resistance. That's when the sloganeering against Sheikh Abdullah started building up.'

Quinn played the Libyan leader Omar Mukhtar fighting the Italian army under Mussolini. Many Kashmiri youth were inspired by his portrayal to rebel against the Indian government. One of them was Yasin Malik, chairman of Kashmir's pro-freedom separatist outfit Jammu and Kashmir Liberation Front (JKLF), who remembered watching the film as a student at Srinagar's Regal Cinema in 1985.

'When we came out after watching the movie, there were protests against Sheikh Muhammad Abdullah, who was until then the undisputed political and spiritual leader of Kashmir,' said Malik, according to a report by *KashmirNewz*, dated 15 September 2009. 'Those days, his posters could be spotted on every other shop in Kashmir. After that it was not to be.'

In fact, those very posters of Sheikh Abdullah and his propaganda were set aflame, and there were widespread protests against the government that, in turn, forced cinema halls to stop screening the film that had been running to a full house in its very first week.

Cinema doesn't fire the imagination of the young any more in Kashmir. It can't. Now cinema is the stuff of painful nostalgia. There was a time when Srinagar had nine cinema halls – Firdaus, Shiraz, Khayyam, Regal, Broadway, Palladium, Neelam, Naaz and Shah. There was one more in the cantonment known as Militia (often pronounced 'Malaysia'). All of them had to shut shop in 1989 when the separatists ordered their closure on the grounds that they were providing entertainment, an activity deemed 'un-Islamic'. In 1996, Broadway and Regal opened for a brief period, and so did Neelam, a little later. But grenade attacks forced them all to close down for good. In fact, a grenade lobbed at viewers returning from a show of Sunny Deol-starrer *Pyaar Koi Khel Nahin* (1999) at Regal killed one person and injured dozens.

The closure of the cinema halls wasn't merely about a receptive audience being denied a form of entertainment. It also led to unemployment, to thousands losing their means of livelihood. In *Cinema in Kashmir*, Rajesh Jala's documentary for DD Kashmir, Amit Amlaa, owner of Broadway, talks of 70 to 80 members of his workforce becoming jobless overnight. There were ancillary businesses linked to cinema halls – tea stalls, restaurants – that also had to suffer considerable financial losses.

The cinema halls are in ruins now. Some, like Neelam, were transformed into military bunkers, complete with concertina wires. Others, like Palladium in Lal Chowk, were totally gutted in a crossfire between militants and security forces. Yet another, like Khayyam, was resurrected in a new avatar – the Khyber Medical Institute.

You hear many cinema stories from the past: about the huge crowds that used to throng the halls despite inclement weather, about the black-marketeering of tickets for popular films (the art is long dead in the new system that prevails), about everyone walking safely back home after a show finished at 1 a.m. Dharmendra, Amitabh Bachchan and later, Mithun Chakraborty, were the favourite stars. *Coolie* was a landmark film, and the scene where Big B was accidentally injured during the shoot would be played with a placard offering viewers information about his injury. Invariably, the response to the scene was deafening applause. Another crowd favourite was the famous dialogue from the same film: '*Tere haath mein maut ka saamaan toh mere seene mein Khuda ka naam*. You may have weapons of destruction in your hand, but I have god's name lodged in my heart.'

Qureshi remembers the posters that used to spring up right before Eid: 'Neelam cinema *ki taraf se tamaam ahli Islam ko Eid ki khushi par* sex, action *aur maar-dhaad se bharpoor tohfa*. Neelam cinema presents, on the occasion of Eid, a gift replete with sex, action, fights and fisticuffs.'

It was a common hoarding found across Srinagar; only the name of the respective cinema halls kept changing from locality to locality.

In the intervening 30 years since 1989, a whole generation of youngsters has grown up in Kashmir without knowing what a cinema hall is like, seeing posters of films on their walls or experiencing the special thrill and pleasure of watching films inside one. Yet, even 30 years after the closure, their impact of these cinema halls has not been entirely wiped out. Most of the areas, squares and roads in Srinagar are still named after them: Firdaus Stop (a bus stop), Shiraz Chowk (a crossing), Khayyam Chowk, Regal Chowk, Broadway (another bus stop), Palladium Galli...

Cinema is dead in Kashmir. Long live cinema.

Fringe Festivals

BACK IN 2010, WHILE on an assignment for *Outlook* magazine, I had a conversation on cinema with young viewers at the Haryana International Film Festival (HIFF), which was being held in the business-driven town of Yamunanagar.[17]

'We have never seen realistic, songless films before,' confessed Radhika Sharma, a wide-eyed mass communications student from Jalandhar's Doaba College.

The word 'never', in fact, popped up again and again in my chats with college students from Jalandhar, Kurukshetra, Sonepat, Khanpur and Rajpura.

'We've never seen films from south India before,' Robin Gupta acknowledged during my film-related conversation with him.

'In fact, we never knew so many films were made in languages other than Hindi and English,' Jaspreet Singh piped in.

These students had travelled from various towns just to attend HIFF and participate in the accompanying film appreciation (FA) programme organized by journalist Ajit Rai in association with Yamunanagar's DAV College for Girls.

Their excitement at discovering cinema, other than Bollywood, was infectious, their sheepish acknowledgement that it wasn't easy viewing, disarming.

'The first day was a little boring,' Suman Varma candidly admitted. 'We are not used to watching three or four serious films a day.'

'I was scared that I might not be able to last the entire duration,' confessed Sonia Hooda.

But that fear was overcome soon enough. The self-conscious giggles and sniggers at the scenes of sex and nudity in Udayan Prasad's British film *My Son, the Fanatic* were surprisingly few and far between. Journalist Vinod Bhardwaj, who presented Cristian Mungiu's hard-hitting Romanian film *4 Months, 3 Weeks, 2 Days* (about two students trying to arrange an illegal abortion), was pleasantly surprised by the women's 'open' response, an interesting counterpoint to the obvious discomfiture of the men, in an area infamous for female foeticides. Filmmaker Seema Kapoor was overwhelmed by the response to her film *Haat, the Weekly Bazaar* on the Rajasthani custom of Natha Pratha, which dictates that if a woman wants to part company with her husband, her father or anyone else supporting her, she has to pay a compensation.

'They understood everything I wanted to say and noticed the minutest of details,' she observed in wonder.

At the finale of the seven-day festival, the students were reeling off the names of their favourite films: *City Lights, Seventh Seal, Bicycle Thieves, The Hero* and *Pather Panchali*. Just as animated was their talk of shot-taking, scripting, 'interpreting' the 'hidden meaning' and 'symbolism' in various films.

The youngsters in Yamunanagar looked no different from their big-city counterparts. They wore the same skinny jeans and fake Abercrombie T-shirts. But it was heartening to discover that their television-fuelled aspirations went beyond looking hip. You could also sense a hunger in them to see, hear, read, experience and absorb more than their restricted environment offered. The three-year-old HIFF had been able to feed that curiosity, whet their appetite for expanding their world. In a region patronizingly lauded for 'brawn', rather than 'brain', where, so goes the joke, the 'only culture is agriculture', the festival provided a much-needed window to high art.

The shifting dynamics of small towns are difficult to pin down, especially by urbanites like us who carry along set assumptions. The fact is, not everything about the social milieu there can be easily defined in black and white. Radical ideas can co-exist with hardcore conservatism. Not a single person I met in Yamunanagar, for instance, was disapproving of, let alone hostile to, the films being shown there, however out of their comfort zone they may have been. None of the students spoke of their families being suspicious of what they were being exposed to. Perhaps, the youngsters are watching these films clandestinely, I thought. Or had the newfangled ideas driving such cinema projects already reached homes and families through television, that strange purveyor of the modern as well as the archaic?

'Haryana has been in the news for khap panchayats and honour killings. Such events help to change the image of the state,' said journalist and programme organizer Rai.

For actor Om Puri, who has now passed away, the festival made one thing clear: 'It's ridiculous to assume that small-town audiences are not ready for serious cinema. We have to give them an opportunity.'

A thought that still holds true, even though the original HIFF itself has gone defunct since the last festival held in 2012. Meanwhile, it has been replaced by a short-film festival, also called HIFF, held in Hisar, under the stewardship of film and theatre actor Yashpal Sharma.

A change of hands at the managerial level, and a, lack of sustained funding and patronage were the obvious culprits for its sudden demise, I am told. It's the bane of a lot of film festivals mushrooming in small towns and mofussil areas, fuelled by the initial enthusiasm, aspiration and continued support of the audience, but unable to keep pace with the demand without a viable economic model to sustain them in the long run.

When I probe deeper, however, questioning people with inside knowledge of organizing festivals, I get some complicated, off-the-record answers as to why for every new film festival starting in a small town, there are two others shutting shop. It's not for the lack of an audience, certainly. Nor has it anything to do with the way residents of mofussil areas watch films. It is the absence of commitment on the part of fly-by-night operators.

'Some of them are not in it for passion for cinema, but in the business of making a quick buck and name by riding on a good cause,' I am told.

However, such is not the case for Cinema of Resistance, 'a revolution of people's films', as documentary filmmaker Subrat Kumar Sahu calls it. The autonomous festival that focusses on non-mainstream, political, issue-based cinema has only grown over the years and spread its wings across India, with committed organizers, dedicated filmmakers and a keen audience for constant support. The unspoken motto is: smaller, further, wider.

So you have Sergei Eisenstein, the legendary Soviet filmmaker best known for the classic silent film *Battleship Potempkin*, who made his way to eastern UP for the first time in 2006. It was the year that The Group, the film wing of Jan Sanskriti Manch, the CPI-(ML)'s cultural arm, organized the first Cinema of Resistance (CoR) festival in association with the Gorakhpur Film Society, the Peoples' Forum and the Peoples' Union for Human Rights (PUHR). The venue was Gorakhpur, the birthplace of filmmaker Anurag Kashyap, actors Saurabh Shukla and Jimmy Shergill, and a town otherwise well known as the site of the Chauri Chaura *hatyakand* (carnage) that had taken place on 5 February 1922, a turning points in India's freedom struggle. The home of Gita Press, the largest publisher of Hindu religious texts, Gorakhpur also enjoys a certain notoriety for the blatant smuggling activities that flourish along the neighbouring Indo-Nepal international border.

It is, moreover, the home of Yogi Adityanath, *mahant* of the Gorakhnath Temple, founder of the Hindu Yuva Vahini, BJP MP from Gorakhpur since 1998 and now chief minister of Uttar Pradesh. The man behind *ghar wapsi*, he is also alleged to have incited the 2007 Gorakhpur riots. CoR, therefore, has been existing as a significant left-wing cultural island in this right-wing communal cauldron. Has there ever been any political pressure, I ask.

'Never direct,' replies Manoj Singh, founder-member of the Gorakhpur Film Society.

Indirectly, of course, it has meant the denial of the university hall – the original venue – for film screenings. The festival devoted to the cinema of protest still flourishes, despite Yogi Adityanath's position as CM and his pervasive influence, though it is not at the university that films are screened any more, but at the grubby Gokul Atithi Bhawan that also serves as a venue for private functions, including marriage receptions. The number of viewers has grown over the years, despite the rise of right-wing politics. The government too has not interfered in any significant way, preferring to ignore this subversive set, rather than deign to acknowledge it.

The idea of the festival was to make good, non-Bollywood cinema accessible to a place and people deprived of it, free of cost, and also to provide a platform for 'constructive, creative dissent' through cinema in the politically volatile, communally sensitive small towns. The initial response was overwhelming.

'We showed almost 20 films, including short films, animations, documentaries and full-length feature films,' recalls Sanjay Joshi, cinema activist and national convenor of CoR. 'After the screening of Anand Patwardhan's film *War and Peace*, we conducted a discussion on the film, anchored by a panel of four people. More than a hundred people participated in the discussion which lasted for 45 minutes. Around

4,000 people enjoyed the screenings in [at] the festival. At least 500 people from surrounding small towns participated in the festival.'

In the first year, they hand-picked well-known films, opening the gates to local filmmakers much later.

He still remembers the interesting responses from young viewers.

One of them, after watching Shyam Benegal's *Ankur*, wrote: 'Are such films also made? If yes, then why aren't they shown to us?'

When it comes to CoR, Gorakhpur is a divided town. The uncaring majority still goes for its dose of Bollywood and Bhojpuri films. A small audience, however, has stayed committed. On one level, the films and discussions at the festival may appear to be aimed at the already converted – those in the level-headed, progressive minority – rather than at the cacophonous, polarized majority. But the idea is to make these subdued voices grow louder to counter the dominant discourse. In a predominantly right-wing Gorakhpur, the festival is like a little cocoon of liberalism that brings together like-minded people, forging a crucial connect and hoping to bring more of them into its fold. Though the larger, communal Gorakhpur may give it short shrift, it aims to build a sorority of secular minds, one small step at a time.

In its first year, the festival was clubbed with the 75th year of Bhagat Singh's martyrdom. In 2007, it also went for the first time to Bhilai (5 May–6 May) besides being held for the second time in Gorakhpur. Subsequently, it has become a continuous journey for CoR.

The year 2017 was a unique and crucial for the festival. CoR has been a liberal, secular, syncretic and progressive cultural island in the Hindutva laboratory that Gorakhpur has come to be identified as. Will the festival keep scoring liberal points through cinema, despite Yogi Adityanath being at the helm of the state? It was the question on everyone's lips.

Joshi was confident in his reply: 'There has been no change in the curation,' he told me during telephonic chat for an article.[18]

The programming focussed that year on Dalit and tribal representation.

At last count in 2017, there were 15 chapters across Uttar Pradesh, Rajasthan, Bihar, Uttarakhand, Maharashtra, Andhra Pradesh and Delhi, with CoR all set to launch in Jharkhand too. Fifty-nine annual festivals, including many smaller screenings, had been organized. Participants included important names in cinema like M.S. Sathyu, Shaji N. Karun, Girish Kasaravalli, Saeed Mirza, Kundan Shah, Saba Dewan, Anand Patwardhan and Sanjay Kak, among others.

In 2017, CoR also brought John Abraham's Odessa Collective into focus. Abraham's initiative, set up in 1984, was aimed at empowering cinema and building a cine-literate audience by making common people the stakeholders in film production, distribution and exhibition – an ideal that CoR is following in its own way. It runs without governmental, institutional, corporate or NGO sponsorship, but with the active support and cooperation of civil society.

I had the opportunity of attending the 10-year celebrations in Gorakhpur in March 2015 for a piece in *Outlook*.[19] The festival was held to commemorate three radicals: Leftist artiste Chittoprasad, who took on colonialism and feudalism, as well as the classicism of the Bengal School; Marathi reformer and activist Govind Pansare, shot down by unknown assailants in Kolhapur; and Avijit Roy, the Bangladeshi activist, who lost his life for the cause of freedom of expression. Like the first year of the festival that was also Bhagat Singh's 75th death anniversary, its 10th year too coincided with the day he had attained martyrdom.

The prelude to the festival was, ironically, marked at the New Delhi railway station itself, teeming with farmers eager to board the Vaishali Express to return home after protesting against the Land Acquisition Bill in the capital. The inaugural film at the three-day event in Gorakhpur was called *Shramjeevi Express*, a documentary on a similar show of defiance by the silent, cheaply available workforce living in a dreary hellhole called Kapashera on the fringes of Delhi. Tarun Bhartiya's view of the workers' bleak lives in the urban jungle holds a mirror to the cruel oppression and disparities obscured by all the talk of 'Make in India' and '*achhe din*'.

Whether by design or because of financial constraints, the Gorakhpur film event I attended was appropriately devoid of frills – no red carpet, no fancy venue or high-tech screening facilities. No stars or celebrities either. No ACs, or even noisy fans. Films were shown on a makeshift screen at the Gokul Atithi Bhawan, with the audience swatting away mosquitoes and cursing the many interruptions brought about by the frequent power cuts. Discussions with the audience, however, were ISI mark – informed, incisive and in-depth.

Interestingly, Gorakhpur city has a Cinema Road, which runs from Golghar to Vijay Chowk. It had earned the nomenclature simply by virtue of the six single-screen theatres that once dotted it. While the street name has survived, only three of those theatres are still functioning.

'And we can't say till when,' says Manoj Singh. 'Till 1990, the town had 14 theatres, but only four of them survive now.'

Libraries too have been shutting down steadily and the town has no auditorium, save those at the university, which are expensive to hire. Art and culture have given way to malls and apartments, growth and development. Whatever cinema thrives locally is squarely mainstream fare. At the time of my visit, the town's walls were plastered with posters of the new Bhojpuri blockbuster *Patna Se Pakistan*, starring superstar Dinesh Lal Yadav, better known as Nirahua. It was running to a '*shaandaar teesra hafta*. A third terrific week.' The '*bhavya pradarshan* – grand presentation' of the sequel to Ravi Kishan's–megahit *Panditji Batayi Biyah Kab Hoi* was right round the corner.

However, at CoR, it was an alternative Bhojpuri voice that spoke out. Pawan Shrivastava's crowd-funded *Naya Pata*, capturing the pain and dilemmas of immigrants, struck a chord in the Poorvanchali among the audience, evident in the thunderous applause, loud whistles and catcalls. As did Bikramjit Singh's Bengali film *Achal* on the dreary lives of entertainers living on urban margins, brought to the fore by a man who plays statue on Kolkata's busy streets.

Clearly, it wasn't aesthetics so much as activism that was high on the agenda. The political undercurrent was undeniable in the choice of films and the issues addressed in them: caste, communalism, capitalism and censorship, not just governmental, but societal as well.

'We screened *Garam Hawa* just a month after the 2007 communal riots in Gorakhpur, got the liberals together and made a progressive point, without taking recourse to any speeches,' says Joshi.

In 2015, they screened Nakul Singh Sahni's politically volatile *Muzaffarnagar Baaki Hai* that probes the unholy nexus between politics, the economy and communalism in the Muzaffarnagar riots of 2013. For the closing ceremony, former IBN associate editor Pankaj Srivastava (reportedly fired from the channel for questioning the lack of coverage for the Aam Aadmi Party in the run-up to the Delhi elections) sang his own compositions on Varanasi and on 'Gujarat *ka Lala*', bringing the house down with energetic lines like '*Daanav saare roop dhar rahe devon ka, buddhu hai bhagwan hamari Kashi mein.* Even as demons are donning the garb of deities, it's God who's getting fooled in Varanasi' and '*Kya kya na gul khilaye hai Gujarat ka Lala, Obama ko pataye hai Gujarat ka Lala.* What wonders the child of Gujarat is working, like trying to ingratiate himself with [the then US president Barack] Obama.' At the 2009 festival in Gorakhpur, Arundhati Roy had spoken on American imperialism. In 2015, she created a stir by calling Mahatma Gandhi India's first 'corporate NGO'. Contrary to what one might have anticipated, the administration stayed quiet, either unaware of what was going on or, as some suspect, preferring to ignore it so as to not give it undue importance.

'We are not just about entertainment, but also about representing the region, intervening in the daily life of people in a positive way,' Joshi declares.

It's an observation that seems to have substance, if you consider that the 2013 film festival in Gorakhpur subsequently led to the making of a documentary on Japanese encephalitis, which was raging in the district at the time. It was shown in various affected areas to build awareness about the disease and helped in its eventual eradication.

In the buzz created by the Jio MAMI Mumbai Film Festival with Star, the IFFI (International Film Festival of India) and the IFFK (International Film Festival of Kerala), it's unlikely that you'd have heard much about the Cinema of Resistance or the HIFF, but that doesn't discount the formidable work they have done in taking cinema to the grass roots. Most significant film festivals in India have been confined to the big cities – Mumbai, Thiruvananthapuram, Panaji, Kolkata, Bengaluru and Chennai – and have, of late, been battling their own demons, mostly organizational, financial and sponsorship woes. The good news is that many alternative out-of-the-box festivals that are being held away from the mainstream, in places and spaces that are on the very fringes, geographically as well as in our minds, are coming up with new programming and financial initiatives.

CoR, for example, shuns patronage, whether from the government, NGOs, corporates or MNCs. Theirs is a small, self-sustaining model built on voluntary donations from the audience. They have successfully organized 40-odd film festivals without having to rely on a single sponsorship.

'The mode of funding is critical to the independence of a festival and the kind of films you get to show; our idea is that of seeking no sponsorship, which helps us take our own critical decisions,' says Sanjay Joshi. 'It's run with the active support and cooperation of the common man. It's not event management, but a cooperative movement.'

Donations are received in collection boxes placed outside the venue, while more funds are generated through the sale of books and films. The first festival was organized at a cost of ₹95,000, of which ₹80,000 was collected from the town; the rest was given by the core team. The festival itself has grown, with chapters in several small towns now.

The hunger for good films is as much a determinant in its success as the well-oiled way in which it is run by organized Jan Sanskrit Manch cadres. It is also, perhaps, the reason – other than the fact that the festival may be deemed too niche, too inconsequential to merit attention – why political rivals stay out of its way, instead of seizing the opportunity to turn it into a political issue. Most significantly, in a strange sort of way, the overt Hindu agenda and saffronization of the country's political and cultural landscape have lent CoR and the liberal, progressive, syncretic and secular values it stands for an added urgency, much like the importance given to a rare species that needs to be saved from extinction, come what may.

Just like the Cinema Of Resistance, Puri's Bring Your Own Film Festival (BYOFF) also aims to be a people's festival, rather than that of sponsors. A non-profit event put together by a bunch of creative people, especially young filmmakers from Odisha, it runs on the goodwill and steam of its participants, volunteers and audience – a mix of cinephiles and filmmakers. The last few years, however, have been trying, not so much for financial reasons as for the dilemmas created by a modern-day phenomenon – the rise and rise of digital technology.

Held every February since 2004 in tents pitched on the grounds of the Pink House Hotel, located in the so-called hippie, backpacker side of the temple town, BYOFF has often been referred to as 'the Woodstock of cinema'. The catchphrase is '*Bhadaas Dho*' which, in Puri slang, means the sound of a collision and an explosion respectively. Besides offering viewers an interesting, experimental clutch of films, it also promises to facilitate the coming together of other art forms – music, dance, arts, literature and photography. There's more on offer: good food, cheap alcohol, legal grass, the sea and sand. And a promise that for those five days in February when it is held, life will be a carnival on the beach.

It is an informal, bohemian event where anyone can register and screen his films, including home videos and works in progress. Films are shown under the night sky by the beach till the wee hours for whoever is keen to watch them in makeshift tents or out in the open. There are neither rules nor regulations, none of the hierarchies and bureaucracies of a conventional film festival. There are no juries or awards either. A film festival in its most informal and alternative format, it thrives on word of mouth, usually online and on social-media platforms.

The founders of BYOFF, filmmaker Susant Misra and his friends from Pune's FTII – Gurpal Singh, the late Swagat Sen and others – had hoped to eventually organize small BYOFFs across India so that they could take the 'indie' movement to the grass roots. But that was not to be. With the onslaught of digital technology, which has given indie filmmakers alternative avenues, such as YouTube, BYOFF seems to have lost its shine over the past few years.

The first edition saw the participation of 150 filmmakers, Misra tells me when I attend the first day of the festival in 2018. According to Surya Shankar Das, a member of BYOFF's core team, it was down to 40 films in 2017. There have been times they could not even cover their expenses.

'We were sure it would be "Die-Off" this year,' laughs Puri resident and ardent BYOFF supporter Satya, unable to resist punning on the acronym that represents their joint endeavour.

But the cult festival believes in fighting to stay relevant. Understandably, to compensate for the no-sponsorship policy, BYOFF, for its 2018 edition, sought crowd-funding and also raised the registration fee from ₹3,500 to ₹5,000, and the screening fee by 20 per cent.

It also attempted to reach out to the Dalit youth of the neighbourhood's fishing community – one of the ways the politically conscious festival tried to reinvent itself and stay relevant in its 15th year.

The organizing committee decided to involve underprivileged youth, not just as viewers, but also as participants in workshops.

'Even if we can inspire five of them, it will enrich cinema,' I remember Das telling me during our conversation.[20]

In a bid to reboot the festival and create opportunities for the exchange of indie filmmaking experiences globally, it was also opened up to international filmmakers in a big way, by waiving the hitherto mandatory requirement of their physical presence at the screenings. Thus films from Poland, Argentina, Germany, Hungary, Iran and Indonesia were part of the programme.

In addition, some filmmakers were making exclusive BYOFF content. Public installations and video art were on the wish list. Collaborative filmmaking during the festival was also on the cards. But BYOFF was clear that it would remain the free space that it has always been.

'Even the most inclusive spaces are exclusionary,' says Das, proud that BYOFF continues to be participatory and spontaneous.

Such unconventional and informal viewing is also a part of the Sonapani Film Festival, held at the Himalayan Village (run by the couple Ashish Arora and Deepa Pathak) near Mukteshwar in Kumaon's Nainital. The brainchild of Pune's FTII graduate Gurpal Singh (one of the founders of BYOFF), it is like a small adda, an intimate gathering of those who not only want to discover, absorb and understand films, but also obtain insights into the mind of a filmmaker or film technician. A trio of filmmakers share their works, concerns and experiences over three days with a small group of viewers. From filmmaker Sriram Raghavan to animation whiz Geetanjali Rao, many have participated in this event. The idea is to have intensive, in-depth discussions, and casual and compelling chats over wonderful food and several cups of tea against the backdrop of the stunning snow-capped Himalayas, of pine, rhododendron and oak tree forests, and of apple, apricot, plum and peach orchards. The in-residence festival is also about escaping the city for a few days. Without a television set in the room, it is all about being suspended in time, with only cinema and the hills for company. A biannual retreat into movies, it has become a regular pilgrimage for many a jaded city soul.

'Let a thousand filmmakers and cinephiles bloom' appears to be the motto for the Aurangabad International Film Festival.

Organized by Mumbai's Yashwantrao Chavan Pratishthan, in association with the Nath Group and the Mahatma Gandhi Mission, the five-day festival kicked off in January 2019 with *Cold War*, a black-and-white masterpiece on love, longing and music in the time of political turmoil directed by Poland-born, UK-based Pawel Pawlikowski that was a foreign film Oscar front runner. It closed with another Oscar front runner and Cannes 2018 Palme D'Or winner – Hirokazu Kore-eda's *Shoplifters*. Jia Zhangke's *Ash Is Purest White* (China) and Andrey Zvyagintsev's *Loveless* (Russia) were the other big attractions in the world-cinema section.

Besides taking the best of world cinema to the interiors of Maharashtra, promoting film literacy and a robust film-viewing culture, a major aim of the festival – in its sixth edition – was to encourage filmmaking in the Marathwada region.

A competition of short films, limited exclusively to upcoming filmmakers from the eight districts of the region, was set up. Of the 35 entries received, nine were in the competition for the top award worth ₹25,000; seven played in the non-competition segment.

A masterclass conducted by well-known filmmaker Umesh Kulkarni on making short films and a seminar on mobile-phone filmmaking – the pros and cons of emerging accessible filmmaking technology – were organized to reach out to young and aspiring filmmakers. The works of the 40 students from the film school in the Mahatma Gandhi Mission campus in Aurangabad were also shown at AIFF this year.

'There are three drama schools in Aurangabad. There is the

drama department of the Marathwada University [now known as Dr Babasaheb Ambedkar Marathwada University]. It is culturally a very rich city,' says festival director Ashok Rane, who took over the reins of AIFF in 2016. 'The intent has been to make it cinematically rich as well.'[21]

To that end, Rane himself has, since 2006, been independently conducting a week-long film-appreciation course in the drama department of Dr Babasaheb Ambedkar Marathwada University. A one-year certificate course in filmmaking was introduced in 2016.

The Yashwantrao Chavan Pratishthan itself holds a Chitrapat Chavadi (Film Adda) in the city once a month.

'Special efforts were taken [this year] to go to various educational institutions and cultural groups to conduct film-appreciation workshops prior to the festival; to let the audience know what AIFF has for them in [the] form of programming,' says Rane.

Originally started as a franchisee of the Pune International Film Festival (PIFF), AIFF is now one of Maharashtra's leading independent film festivals. Besides the big ticket, big-city film festivals in Mumbai and Pune, smaller festivals are being held in Lonavla, Nashik and Nagpur as well. However, Aurangabad and Kolhapur are regarded as the more serious grass-roots film initiatives in Maharashtra, with cinema outreach and education playing an integral role in their agenda.

Though presented in a more traditional format, the Dharamshala International Film Festival (DIFF), held in McLeodganj since 2012, exudes a similar feeling of intimacy, warmth and cheerfulness. Spread over three days and two venues – the Club House and the Tibetan Children's Village School in Dharamsala Cantt., with the regular venue, the Tibetan Institute of Performing Arts (TIPA), undergoing major renovations in 2018 – it offers a wider selection of films. But these are programmed in such a way as to give you enough space to breathe between films, and the time and leisure to absorb them. The discussions are enlightening and access to filmmakers is disarmingly hassle-free. But what stands out about the festival is its unique choice of films and how they are thematically aligned – most are about people on the margins, about protests and struggles.

'The idea is to pick films which reflect the state of our world today, and are relevant across borders and cultures... They are about political conflicts, the marginalized and on questions of identity,' explains filmmaker Ritu Sarin, who founded the festival and is its director, along with her filmmaker husband Tenzing Sonam.

Its motto is simple: 'Bringing independent cinema to the mountains.'

In 2013, for instance, you had a Marathi film like Nagraj Manjule's *Fandry* as a centrepiece. It is about a much-oppressed family of pig catchers living on the very margins of rural Maharashtra. They trap pigs for their daily meal, the very pigs which feed on human excreta. The film implicates many a privileged viewer in the humiliation of its young Dalit protagonist, Jabya, especially in the long, harrowing last sequence that ends in a jolting climax. It reproaches the audience and, in turn, arouses its collective remorse.

The post-film discussion zoomed in on how not asking a person his surname, dismissing caste talk with the complacent shrug of a shoulder is also a privilege of those who are already entitled.

'Most have no choice. Caste biases are too firmly entrenched to vanish with the personal correctness of a few. The stigma of caste remains,' Manjule observes.[22]

No wonder some viewers, despite having witnessed a devastatingly unequal and inhumane world in the film, still ask him about the 'lopsidedness' of caste-based reservations.

His argument is clear-eyed: 'Reservations are necessary till everyone reaches the same stage, when everyone can run the race from the same starting point. But Dalits are still more than 500 metres behind the rest.'

It's the focus on such significant social issues that seems to have become DIFF's calling card in the three years of its existence. The spirit goes well with the region's consistent politics, and its long-standing support for and seminal engagement with the Tibetan cause, where even small cafés have 'Tibet will be free' as their rather revolutionary Wi-Fi passwords. Most of the chosen films are driven not just by their aesthetics and craft, but by a distinct spirit of independence.

Amit Virmani's documentary *Menstrual Man* is one such example. It documents Arunachalam Muruganatham's fascinating journey as he seeks to find a way of producing affordable sanitary napkins for poor women, who would, otherwise, end up using unhygienic rags and husk during their periods. A school dropout and a man of limited means, Muruganantham shows the way to a successful social-entrepreneurship model that he himself calls the 'Butterfly' model, as opposed to the 'Parasite' model of profiteering. His efforts haven't just made basic hygiene accessible to the poor, but the various, easily assembled machines and production units that contribute to the manufacture of the pads have also given people a sustainable means of employment. The quirky film comes alive with Muruganatham's own self-deprecatory humour and the many jokes about his weird research methodology – involving an artificial uterus, a football for a bladder, goat blood and even the act of wearing the sanitary pad himself. The last even made his wife and mother assume that he was some kind of pervert. Virmani highlights these dramatic moments by using melodramatic clips from Bollywood films. But between the many laughs, *Menstrual Man*'s essential cause is never forgotten: not to scale up, but scale deep for the sanitary drive to reach the remotest corners of India.

Nishtha Jain's documentary *Gulabi Gang* is also driven by the rough sense of humour that is an attribute of its central character, Sampat Pal. She is the leader of the pink sari-clad gang of women that fights for justice for its own gender and for Dalits in Bundelkhand. Their battles could be inspired by issues as diverse as irregularities in the government's Below Poverty Line (BPL) schemes or the mysterious death of a young woman. Most of the vigilantes representing the Gulabi Gang are uneducated. Their feminism is unstudied, their subversion of well-entrenched patriarchy is spontaneous and their urge for bringing about a change in traditional mindsets is strong. Yet, the movement itself is weighed down by its own complexities, dichotomies and dilemmas. They come to the fore when the issue at hand cuts close to home. Consider an individual case of honour killing, for instance, where the family of one of the activists is involved. The woman concerned is seen supporting her kith and kin, rather than the movement, which favours justice for the victim and punishment for the guilty. But in her documentary, Jain aims for impartiality. She presents the situation without taking sides, without pronouncing judgement.

'It's good to maintain a distance,' she declares. 'There is a danger in romanticizing such a movement. I have tried to present a realistic picture than turn it into some kind of a hagiography.'[23]

And that's what makes the film so powerful.

At DIFF 2014, I discovered Avinash Arun's *Killa*, a poetic and meditative look at growing up in the interiors of Maharashtra, and dealing with death, deceit and displacement. It's a film about childhood, about innocence making way for teenage rebellion. The highlight of the festival, however, was 27-year-old Pushpa Rawat, an unassuming and modest Ghaziabad girl, who thought there might be a film in the story of her failed romance. In *Nirnay*, a disarming documentary, she trains the camera on her life, her family, her women friends, the young man she was unable to marry and his family. She ended up making friends with the girl her beau eventually married.

The most remarkable bit in the film involves the way she manages to pose distinctly awkward questions to the man, his parents and her own, drawing them out and receiving the responses they hadn't been ready to part with. She is persistent, repetitive, but not judgemental. Perhaps, it has something to do with her quiet voice, her gentle ways, her empathetic manner. There is a certain cussedness in her, but it never degenerates into confrontation, a kind of 'I shall have my way' attitude, without really allowing it to snowball into an argument. It is something her conservative, yet loving parents can't hold against her either.

While talking to me, Rawat confided that though she did have unlimited access to the people she interacted with for the film, she was careful to maintain her distance and exercise restraint. This helped her subjects open up, despite their abiding apprehensions, and also, albeit unwittingly, brought their gender biases into focus.

The fuss-free, candid viewpoint sharpens the dilemmas, confusion and discontent experienced by Rawat. It's a simple piece of filmmaking devoid of flourishes. But it conveys a sense of the repression women have to endure and an understanding of the resolve underlying their silent rebellion. As the filmmaker herself puts it, it's not about a momentary outburst of rage, but a persistent negotiation to carve for yourself your rightful place within the family, in society and in the world at large. The unknown Lata, Mithilesh, Geeta, Vinita and Pooja find a voice through Rawat, and an audience through her film and a festival.

Radio Cities

FOR AN ENTIRE GENERATION of Indians who grew up listening to the radio, instead of watching television or surfing the Internet, Ameen Sayani's voice – soft, suave and gentle – was the one to remember. Understandably, he was never a face for them; many of his fans wouldn't have recognized him by his benign, now bespectacled look. Rather, it was his characteristic way of addressing them – '*Bhaiyo aur beheno.* Brothers and sisters' – that would be enough to make them crowd around radios and transistors, and listen – not just to the songs he played, but also to the anecdotes and interviews he used to intersperse them with. Sayani had hosted the iconic *Binaca Geetmala*, the first-ever weekly countdown show of top Hindi film songs broadcast on Radio Ceylon, and later, on the Vividh Bharati service of All India Radio.

It was the participative nature of the show, the way it involved the viewers, which ensured its immense popularity. In the beginning, the programme did not rank film songs, but played seven contemporary ones in no particular order. Later, the songs would be ranked on the basis of sales of records in India and listeners' votes on Radio Ceylon. The process was further refined, with their popularity being gauged on the basis of record sales and the verdicts of record-store owners and *shrota sanghathans* (listeners clubs). The most eagerly anticipated shows were the year-end lists, compiled on the basis of points earned by songs through the year.

Born in 1932, Sayani is said to have produced and compered over

54,000 radio programmes and 19,000 spots and jingles, including popular shows like *S. Kumar ka Filmi Muqaddama*, *Saridon ke Saathi*, *Shalimar Superlac Jodi*, and many more. In the process of hosting these shows, especially *Binaca Geetmala*, he also formed a unique bond with listeners (more so, with the *shrota sanghathans*), who often wrote to him with requests for their favourite Hindi film songs to be played. His relationship with them would grow over a span of several years through the many letters they sent him.

One such familiar name for Sayani was Bachkamal from Bhatapara.

It is said that the radio announcer was once travelling from Raipur to Bilaspur, when he saw a board bearing the name 'Bhatapara'. He immediately asked the driver to stop the vehicle and enquired if it was 'Bachkamal's Bhatapara'. Bachkamal, who has been sending *farmaishi* postcards – postcards requesting certain Hindi film songs of his choice to be played – to AIR for 55 years, is Bhatapara's most famous resident. He is known to practically everyone in the region across age groups and even to regular radio listeners spread far and wide across the country. Consequently, when Sayani's driver confirmed that Bhatapara was, indeed, the place to which Bachkamal belonged, the radio announcer promptly asked him to take a detour to the town, just so he could meet the man in person and put a face to the name that he had, till then, only seen scribbled on innumerable letters.

An accountant in a private firm, 1952-born Bachkamal had first written to Radio Ceylon in 1960.

'I still remember I had put a 10-paise stamp and a three-paise "By Air Mail" slip on the letter,' he recalls over a phone call.

He got to hear his name announced on the programme a week later.

'I couldn't contain my happiness,' he confesses.

You can still recognize the thrill, pride and sense of achievement in his voice. He followed it up by sending *farmaishi* postcards to Vividh Bharati and to the Akashvani and FM stations in Delhi, Jabalpur, Indore, Bhopal, Raipur and Bilaspur, and has been sending them all these years without a break.

What compels him to write, I ask.

'*Bas, shauk tha. Ab unmaan ke taur par kar raha hoon.* It was just a hobby. Now I am following it like an obsession,' he says.

Besides Ameen Sayani, he has also met Manohar Mahajan, another well-recognized voice on Radio Ceylon, once popular for his characteristic opening line: '*Awaaz ki duniya ke doston ko* Manohar Mahajan *ka pyaar bhara aadab, namaskar*. Fond greetings from Manohar Mahajan to all the friends of the world of sound.'

Ordinary Joe Bachkamal was afflicted with polio when he was barely a year old. It has since affected both his legs and reduced his mobility. Besides the thrill of hearing his name, that too from a much-admired voice, radio has done for Bachkamal what several rounds of treatment and surgery could not. It has helped him soar, travel far and wide within the country – metaphorically speaking.

'People in distant, far-flung areas know me, come to Bhatapara to meet me,' he declares with obvious pride.

No wonder letter writing is such a strong commitment for him. On a Tuesday, which happens to be his day off, he writes between 100 and 150 of them at a go, posting them through the week. It's the joy that radio brings to what could have been a depressing life that makes his family – wife, son and younger sister – encourage Bachkamal's hobby.

'They have always been very cooperative,' he acknowledges.

Bachkamal is not the only one of his kind. There are many such diehard radio fans in Bhatapara who share his passion and belong to either of the two *shrota sanghathans* in the town, each comprising 20 to 30 members. It's like a cooperative of letter writers, whose members religiously post letters to radio stations.

'We pool in our efforts, because people have become too busy and have very little time to spare these days,' Bachkamal explains.

To this end, they have had special song-request cards and envelopes printed. The addresses for various AIR programmes and stations, a broad format of the letter (film, song, singer and so on), and their own names and addresses are printed on postcards or embossed on especially made rubber stamps. All they have to do is fill in the titles of the film and the song, the name of the singer and other relevant information, and send off the card.

One such *shrota* is a 56-year-old accountant at Ambuja Cements. Shiv Sharma has been writing in for the last 36 years. He started off with letter writing during his college days in the '80s and has also been involved in some programmes on AIR.

'In the middle of your responsibilities and while fulfilling your duties and obligations, listening to your favourite film songs on *Chhayageet* used to help get rid of the fatigue. Radio *se iss jeevan ki spardha halki ho jaati hai.* Radio eases life's burdens,' he feels.

In fact, if it weren't for Bachkamal, Shiv Sharma and the *shrota sangathan*s, there wouldn't be much else to write about Bhatapara – other than the fact, perhaps, that it has a famous *dhaan ki mandi* (rice market). The rice bowl of Chhattisgarh state, the small town with a population of barely 1 lakh also boasts of a reputed college of agricultural research. Located on the Howrah–Nagpur–Mumbai railway line, Bhatapara lies in Baloda Bazaar district, about 80 km from Raipur and 50 km from Bilaspur. The Bhilai steel plant is a mere 100 km away.

'A mall, three-four temples and a couple of talkies is [are] all we have,' says Bachkamal matter-of-factly.

Bhatapara is one of a clutch of obscure, off-the-map, run-of-the-mill Indian towns – most of them in the Hindi belt – whose identity, sense of pride and belonging are derived from their radio connection.

Known as much for its forests, natural resources, minerals and tribal culture as for Naxal insurgency–related violence, Chhattisgarh also has another little-known facet: it's a state of ardent radio listeners. According to a February 2018 report published in the newspaper *Nai Duniya*, Baloda Bazaar–Bhatapara and Durg are the two districts in Chhattisgarh with the largest concentration of radio listeners in the state.

There are, in fact, many such little towns inhabited by Ordinary Joes, whose happiness is derived from being heard on air by the whole wide world, by people they don't even know. Consider, for example, Sohagpur in Hoshangabad and Katni near Jabalpur, Madhya Pradesh, Maunath Bhanjan near Varanasi, UP, Karanja Lad in Maharashtra's Washim district and Chaibasa in the West Singhbhum district of Jharkhand – they are all populated by individuals who write passionately and regularly to AIR. The place most cited and written about of them all is India's own Timbuktu: Jhumri Telaiya in Jharkhand's Koderma district. Most of these places are bound to leave you confused about their geographical location. They bear names that you probably imagined existing only on Radio Ceylon or All India Radio's listeners' choice programmes like *Aap ki Pasand*, *Aap ki Farmaish* and *Manchaahe Geet*, rather than on Planet Earth. But they are real. And the radio is a living entity for many of their inhabitants, offering a channel of 'communication' that has added a certain zest to their otherwise humdrum existence.

Such deep, heartfelt affiliation for something as mundane as a radio service may seem bizarre to the television-addicted, Internet-savvy, gadget-obsessed kids of today, but not to their middle-class parents who grew up on Radio Ceylon and Vividh Bharati. For the latter, these names and places are the very stuff of nostalgia, a reminder of an almost extinct culture and way of life. They also represent a slice of that era when radio was the only medium for the masses to connect with cinema.

'Back then, the interviews [were]on radio and, most importantly, the constant playing of the film songs – these were possibly the only things outside of movie theatres for people to access Bollywood,' says theatre and film actor Manav Kaul, who grew up in the company of radio, has acted in Sushant Singh Rajput–starrer *Kai Po Che!* (2013) and is best known for his role as the husband of the radio-jockey character Vidya Balan played in *Tumhari Sulu* (2017).

Writer-lyricist Varun Grover, who spent his early years in Dehradun, Lucknow and Varanasi, remembers his daily ritual of listening to *Chitralok* from 8.15 a.m. to 8.45 a.m., before heading to school. He was also an avid follower of Vividh Bharati's Sunday programmes, which were replete with cinema-based fare.

'I can't imagine the same level of craze for cinema, had there been no radio around. Radio was the ultimate promoter and keeper of cinema treasure,' he says.

Shashank Kumar, an IIM Calcutta graduate, spent his childhood during the '90s in Jharkhand's Pakur district, bordering West Bengal, where radio was one of life's essentials. His mornings started with *Sooraj ke Saath Saath*, a programme of old film songs on All India Radio's Urdu service, followed by a 15-minute show on Radio Ceylon. Then came the 8 a.m. news, capped by the new songs played on Vividh Bharati.

'Radio interviews, songs and anchor talks built cred around movies and movie stars,' says Kumar. 'Radio was a place for some authentic storytelling around songs, movies and movie makers, and it stoked the flames of curiosity regarding Bollywood.'

It was an experience that television seems to have appropriated. Or rather, diluted and robbed us of completely.

Senior journalist Ajay Brahmatmaj, who has lived in Champaran, Purnia and Darbhanga in Bihar, points out the variety of programming: the abridged stories of films, *Chhayageet* on the film stars and *Rangbhoomi*, which dealt with the entire film script. Vineet Kumar, author of *Mandi Mein Media*, who lived in Bihar Sharif, Nalanda, from 1982 to 1996, believes that radio showed him the many ways of enjoying a film: songs, dialogues, interviews and behind-the-scenes developments.

Says he: 'If I read cinema as a serious text today, it is all because of how radio brought it to me in my early years.'

My own introduction to a place as apparently insignificant to my life as, say, Bhatapara happens through someone who doesn't even live there: Prakash Ingole, a 55-year-old Nagpur-based officer in the Public Works Department of the Government of Maharashtra. He is another compulsive letter writer and requester of songs. Ingole sent his first postcard to Akashvani, Nagpur, in 1976 when he was living in Somthana village in Maharashtra's Jalna district and would join his fellow villagers in a small local shop to listen to the radio.

'The postcard cost 15 paise and I heard my name [announced] 15 days after having posted it,' Ingole recalls.

That was when he became hooked to the radio. He has been sending letters for 42 years and claims to have despatched 2 lakh of them when I last spoke to him in 2016. For most like him, it is the experience of hearing their name and the title of their chosen song announced over the radio – interpreted as a form of acknowledgement, even recognition – that keeps motivating them to continue writing such letters. For Ingole, letter writing has also helped nurture his other passion – building a database of Hindi film songs, especially the rare, not-so-commonly-heard ones.

Says he: 'We get to know of uncommon songs and their details by requesting for them.'

He also has a collection of about 1,000 song-request postcards collected from various listeners. Ingole's enthusiastic networking with active and committed letter writers like himself, and his travels far and wide to meet them have led to a camaraderie, a brotherhood forged over a shared, quirky passion.

'I am in touch with 90 per cent of them,' he proclaims, adding that 'most of the radio listeners in India are shopkeepers, especially the paan-shop owners who keep hearing songs while doing their business.'

In 2015, Ingole was travelling to Bhatapara to attend a wedding in the family of one of his many radio-programme 'devotee' friends, when an engineering student, who was his co-passenger, mentioned during a conversation that she knew of Bhatapara only through the radio, but had no idea exactly where it was located. This, despite being from Chhattisgarh herself.

Chances are that though she may well have heard of Barkakana on the radio, she wouldn't, in all likelihood, be familiar with its location either. Known as the vegetable basket of Jharkhand, Barkakana has been much in the news for a picturesque train route from Ranchi to Ramgarh, through the forests and hills, that has been in the pipeline for long. The narrow-gauge train project is part of the 200 km Ranchi–Hazaribagh–Koderma rail line, whose construction, suspended indefinitely for unexplained reasons, lies in a state of perennial postponement. Located in the Ramgarh district of Jharkhand, Barkakana is an area rich in coal mines, with a population of just about 16,000 to 17,000.

It is also home to 50-year-old Ifzal Taj. An office superintendent at the central store of Central Coalfields Limited, and also a homoeopath, Taj began sending song-request letters between 1975 and '76 to AIR in Ranchi and Patna.

'It used to be a part of the daily routine, along with[my] studies,' he remembers.

He continues to write about 25 to 30 letters daily and owns three old transistors – Bush, Murphy and Phillips – besides the FM in his car. All to keep himself perennially tuned in to Hindi film songs.

Jhumri Telaiya's Jagannath Prasad Sahu is just as committed to radio. The owner of a flour mill, Sahu also works at Central Hospital and has been sending letters for the last 43 years.

'*Kal hi aaya tha mera naam* radio *par*. They read out my name just yesterday on the radio,' he says. 'Some announcers have such a sweet voice and manner that I just feel like listening to them constantly.'

I gather from his words that such silent communion with a distant voice offers a proxy companionship of sorts, the gentle, sympathetic tone helping assuage the listener's inherent loneliness. Otherwise, Sahu's small town, situated between Jhumri village and the Telaiya reservoir and dam, hasn't got much to offer by way of distractions. Once a big mica-mining centre, its importance waned dramatically with the introduction of cheaper synthetic substitutes for the mineral and the collapse of the Soviet Union, which used to be India's largest foreign market for it. Today, it's the moist, creamy and delicious sweet *kalakand*, along with the famed radio connect, that this town of 85,000-odd residents is known for.

But even that strange distinction seems endangered now. Radio, as we have traditionally known it, has become outmoded. The new generation has many more options available for entertainment.

'Hardly any shortwave radios are available in shops any more,' Ingole says ruefully.

Besides, with their growing presence online and on television, music programmes are increasingly 'performance'-oriented audio-visual 'spectacles'; it is only on FM that they are actually heard, usually while driving from one place to another. As for postcards, they don't seem to matter any longer in these days of email and SMS. Jhumri Telaiya, Barkakana and Bhatapara and its radio freaks seem like anachronisms today, caught in a time warp.

Their old-world niceties are heart-warming, nonetheless. The network of *shrota sangathans* spread across India would put any social networking site, be it WhatsApp or Facebook, to shame. They share a phone book of the listed members, stay in touch through regular phone calls and meetings, and now through WhatsApp and Facebook groups as well. They look out for each other, attend each other's family weddings and also mourn a loss together. So it was Ingole who led me to Bachkamal and the others.

'We have been able to connect with people in far-off nooks and corners, all for the love of films, music and radio,' says Taj. 'If we travel to any place where there is a *shrota sangathan*, our stay, boarding, lodging, hospitality – everything gets taken care of.'

'Radio *se hamara samajik daayra badha hai*. Radio has helped expand our social circle,' is Ingole's take on the matter.

The *sangathans* are now going beyond short- and medium-wave radio programmes to write more actively for FM – all to stay relevant and in tune with the times.

'FM has increased the craze for radio,' says Bachkamal.

Radio is a belief system and faith they steadily hold on to. All they know is that radio cannot die; they won't let it die while they are still alive.

Ingole's last comment on the matter seems final and conclusive – at least as far as he is concerned: 'PM Narendra Modi *bhi to apne* Mann Ki Baat radio *par hi toh kah rahe hain*. Even PM Narendra Modi's show *Mann Ki Baat* is on the radio.'

That, admittedly, is an indisputable point.

Museums of Tunes

SOME JOURNEYS COME WITH an overwhelming feeling of uncertainty. You don't know what lies ahead.

I get off the Bhopal bus at the Indore stop and, in a matter of minutes, am picked up and whisked away in a white van with a bold banner proclaiming: 'Chaurasiya Tamboli Mahapanchayat Evam Parichay Sammelan'. The community, its big assembly and matchmaking congregation (which is what the banner refers to), is not something I am particularly interested in. The journey to Pigdambar village in Rau, 14 km from Indore, on the highway to Mhow, is being undertaken to explore a unique museum that lies deep within in its dusty lanes. I am hoping that it will be well worth the effort and time expended on it. If it weren't for the museum or IIM Indore, there would be nothing about Pidgambar to make it stand apart from any other small town in north India.

Set up and run by Suman Chaurasiya, the owner of a small tea shop, Lata Deenanath Mangeshkar Gramophone Record Sangrahalaya is dedicated, as is evident from its name, to his idol 'Didi' – Indore-born 'Nightingale of India' Lata Mangeshkar, who had spent some of her growing-up years here, moved prime ministers and other illustrious dignitaries with her performances in her heyday and is still a revered name in the country, particularly in Bollywood, for lending her evergreen voice as a playback singer to its most idolized female stars over the decades. Housed on the first floor of Chaurasiya's own humble, spartan home, the museum, spread over 1,600 square feet, is not one of those spotlessly clean, sanitized, air-conditioned spaces we associate with typical exhibition areas. It doesn't look like it's built to be an exhibition space and the precious collection on display is as exposed to the elements and the vagaries of weather – heat, dust and moisture – as the residents of the house themselves.

Time, however, does stand still within, as it does in most museums. Peer out of the window and you will see fields all around, stretching into the distance. Inside, posters, photos, old radios and gramophone players lie around in casual display; they are not arranged in any organized manner the way precious artefacts – which these genuinely are – would be. I detect no thematic representation or chronological order in the way the exhibits are set up. Rare old gramophone records are tightly stacked on the many shelves along the walls. But despite its seeming ordinariness, this is a priceless collection indeed. With the advances in technology, the digitization of music and the march of MP3, the gramophone has become extinct. The exhibits in this Indore-based museum, then, are treasures worth a fortune for anyone in search of rare, old melodies in the analogue format. Almost 90 per cent of the collection consists of Hindi film songs and artistes of yore, and the focus, as is evident in the name of the museum itself, is on Lata 'Didi'.

Importantly, it's all about one man's initiative and commitment. No institute or government has pitched in to help Chaurasiya in his effort to preserve and archive Indian music.

Each and every one of the gramophone records is carefully catalogued in Chaurasiya's head. He knows exactly which one to pull out from which shelf. That's no mean feat, considering his collection comprises 28,000 records and more than 1 lakh songs, some of them also from Pakistan, Bangladesh and even the West.

His memory is razor-sharp, perhaps, because he has built up the collection so painstakingly with his own hard-earned savings, sourcing the records from far and wide – from Mumbai's Chor Bazaar to the streetside shops near Delhi's Red Fort. Ahmedabad, Vadodara, Kanpur,

Varanasi – he has travelled to all these cities to get his fix of rare records and music. He even claims to have 'rescued' some records from their owners who were selling them off as scrap, because they could no longer spare the space to store them at home.

The oldest record in Chaurasiya's collection, a random unidentified one, dates back to 24 November 1902 and was priced at a single US dollar in America at that time. He also has records of rare political speeches; notably, one by Mahatma Gandhi. And as is to be expected of an ardent admirer of the singer, almost every song ever sung by Lata Mangeshkar.

'Her first ever recorded song is the most precious,' he says.

Lata sang '*Naachu yaa gade, khelu saari mani haus bhaari*', when she was all of 13, for the Marathi film *Kiti Hasaal*. It was later dropped from the film. Chaurasiya even has the songs she has rendered in Sinhalese, Burmese and Malay – all original compositions.

It was at the time of India's war with neighbouring Pakistan in 1965 that Suman Chaurasiya became a Lata Mangeshkar *bhakt*.

'Those days, the radio played songs, nothing else, with brief, hourly news bulletins, leaving us no choice but to listen to music all day.'

He has met his 'Didi' several times and proudly shows off a letter of appreciation, lovingly framed, from her on the opening of the museum.

He still loves the old songs, music directors like Roshan and Anil Biswas, writers like Sahir Ludhianvi, Bharat Vyas, Naqsh Lyallpuri, Yogesh and Shailendra. Speaking of Mangeshkar's '*Man dole*', '*Thandi hawayein*', '*Mohe panghat pe*', '*Jyoti kalash chhalke*', he goes into raptures over the quiver in her voice.

'Melody ruled till the '70s in Hindi cinema. The '80s and '90s marked a shift,' he says.

A shift for the worse, evidently. He doesn't much care for the lyrics of today either, describing them as mere rhyme, rather than poetry.

Apart from the upkeep and maintenance of his collection, Chaurasiya has also published five books, including that of R.S. Yadav (better known by his pen name Ajatshatru) – *Baba Teri Son Chiraiyya*, a collection of appreciative essays on 80 of Lata Mangeshkar's songs brought out in 2008 to mark the singer's 80th birthday. Another volume, called *Lata aur Safar ke Saathi*, features every singer she sang with. *Sadiyon Mein ek... Asha* deals with the works of Asha Bhonsle and *Beete Kal ke Sitare* is on music that dates back to the period between 1913 and 1950. Currently, Chaurasiya is entirely focussed on digitizing his collection so rare film music is preserved for future generations.

Soon after meeting Chaurasiya, I head off to catch up with Zafar Ansari to have a look at his antique collection. Ansari's isn't, however, some *chor bazaar* kind of knick-knack shop. He is a serious collector of old film memorabilia and a walking encyclopaedia on early Indian cinema. His collection, precious enough for a museum to be proud of housing, includes articles as diverse as *Mughal-e-Azam*'s lobby card (one of those small, thick, postcard-size posters of early films that were handed out to viewers in the theatre lobby, both as promotional material and as a souvenir) in Tamil (especially made, perhaps, for Tamil-speaking viewers in Madhya Pradesh) and the *khanjar* (small dagger) used as a crucial prop in Sohrab Modi's 1953 classic *Jhansi ki Rani*. There's a rare family portrait of the Mangeshkar family taken in Indore by Lala Deen Dayal and the work of photographer Ramachandra Pratap Rao from whom Dadasaheb Phalke is said to have learnt trick photography for *Raja Harishchandra*. Ansari has 4,000 faded lobby cards – of *Pukar*, *Sikandar*, *Jogan*, *Chalti ka Naam Gaadi*, *Mother India*, *Kohinoor*, *Nadiya ke Paar*, among others – and 1,000 copies of old magazines like *Picturegoer* and *FilmIndia*, right from the first copy of *Filmfare* to little known mags like *FilmLand*. There are also 8,000 synopsis booklets, along with silent-era cameras and gramophones. Ansari's prized possession, however, is the Magic Lantern from 1890, 'the optical toy that was a precursor to cinema,' as he puts it and the movie slides used in it. Developed in the 17th century, it is broadly described as an image projector that uses sheets of glass, a lens and a bright light source painted on to project pictures or photographs. Then there are the ads of the English movies that were released in Mumbai in the '50s and '60s.

An inclination towards silent-cinema memorabilia is very pronounced.

'You can't talk of cinema without taking that era into account. The objects from that time are rare and there is a thrill in collecting them,' Ansari explains.

An independent civil engineer, he runs a private model-making studio in Indore for architects. There is deep passion in him for architecture, museum research and Indore history. Ansari's engagement with these film-related artefacts seems to have a simple enough explanation.

'It's a medium that every common man feels connected with,' he says.

His collection has only grown over the two decades that he has been at it.

'I can fill two galleries of the National Museum of Indian Cinema in Mumbai just with my collection,' he says proudly.

His wife, children and friends are encouraging and appreciative of this long journey, but to be a collector is ultimately a lone crusade.

'It takes years of hard work. You can't get the material together in one day,' Ansari points out.

The film goodies are still housed in boxes and bags from which he takes them out lovingly to show aficionados. He admits that he needs to organize the archive systematically and intends to make the cinema collection a part of the larger mission in his life: to build a private museum on the history of Indore.

He is averse to giving away his riches to any other museum or collection, be it government-run or privately owned.

'No one understands the pleasure, pain and passion in building a collection. The organizations can't empathize with its deeper value and significance [for the collector],' he says.

At the end of 2019, Ansari is keen to hold an exhibition on Dilip Kumar, whose films like *Aan* (1952) and *Dil Diya Dard Liya* (1966) were shot in and around Indore. He claims to have the lobby cards of almost all of the thespian's films.

There have been other film celebrities associated with Indore and he gives us all the details, right down to Lata Mangeshkar's love for *dal bafna*, a delicacy from the Malwa region. Popular comedian of yore Johnny Walker was from Indore; Kishore Kumar studied in Indore Christian College. But the most significant connect has been Lata Mangeshkar, who was born in Indore's Sikh Mohalla in 1929.

Says Ansari: 'A Raymond's showroom now stands in place of her aunt's house, where she was born.'

More than 600 km away in Jodhpur, 54-year-old Girdharilal Vishwakarma is involved in something similar to Suman Chaurasiya's passion. His focus of interest is the rare 78 rpm record, which existed before LPs became all the rage, and featured just one song on either side. His exceptional collection, unknown to the world, lies tucked away in a small room in his home in Alamsar village, located in Rajasthan's Barmer district near the India–Pakistan border.

When he moved to Jodhpur to look for a job, Vishwakarma couldn't afford to travel with his treasures.

'It's still difficult to find an inexpensive room to house it here,' he tells me.

Vishwakarma leads a dual life. A miniature artist, he works as a painter with an export firm. His entire day goes in the company of handicrafts, but evenings and nights (from 6 p.m. to 11 p.m.) are spent in his small, cluttered, nondescript room, where he devotes himself to old Hindi film music, diligently documenting, sorting, logging, classifying and cataloguing them on his computer. The computer is the most significant object occupying Vishwakarma's workspace and is carefully covered with plastic sheets to protect it from dust and sand. In a bush shirt and trousers, the bespectacled Vishwakarma looks more like a regular office-goer than a passionate film-music buff, who grew up listening to the radio. When we meet him in Jodhpur, he has already digitized some 8,000 rpms. His database of 10,000 songs that were released between 1932 and 1953 is also complete, filed with all the relevant details: about the film, its year of release, the singer, the music director, the lyricist and the lyrics. All this information has been painstakingly gathered from books, encyclopaedias and old film booklets.

'I keep building on the base, keep adding information as I get it,' he says.

There is no larger aim for undertaking this laborious, time-consuming exercise beyond a passion for music, which he seems to have been born with. The ever-smiling Vishwakarma is seeking no material returns for his efforts either.

'I used to take copious notes on the songs I heard on Vividh Bharati,' he says, adding, 'the idea is to take facts to people, to the next generation that won't have any source of information to fall back on.'

One can understand his concern and commitment, because he has a lot of '*durlabh gaane aur jaankari* – rare songs and information' that he is willing to share with anyone with a genuine interest in them. He has put together MP3 CDs of his own collection of rare songs that includes those of music composers Khemchand Prakash and Ghulam Haider.

One of his singular achievements was to be able to trace the only film song rendered by a little-known singer called Usha Bhatia for the 1951 film *Maldaar*. He put it up on his own home page on YouTube, where he shares his music. Bhatia's son picked it up from there.

'He called to tell me that she herself heard that song after 60 years,' he informs me. 'They had given up on it as a lost song.'

With Vishwakarma, many such lost songs may well get a new lease of life.

Chaurasiya and Vishwakarma are similar in the intensity of their passion, which has made the other aspects of their lives almost pale into insignificance. For both, the family is very much around, assertive and supportive, but also equally good-natured about playing second fiddle to the men's first love – film songs.

The two are not alone in their efforts keep rare old music playing. There are several such collections and databases growing in Indian homes beyond the realm of museums and official archives. I catch up with two of them in Jaipur.

Were it not for films and music, there wouldn't be much to distinguish 60-year-old Arun Aggarwal's sprawling home from among the other well-to-do ones in Jaipur. Except that the many almirahs and cupboards here are not packed with clothes, but are spilling over with music and films, assiduously compiled and catalogued by Aggarwal himself. Coming from a family that has served as military suppliers and been involved in the marble business, Aggarwal grew up watching films, at times, on the sly (since they were not an approved pastime in conservative families of the day and frowned upon as a distraction that hindered studies), and listening to *Binaca Geetmala* and *Geeton Bhari Kahani* on the radio. The love for records was born when a Garrard Record Changer came home. It was one of the objects taken over by the Indian Army after the 1971 war and later bought by the Aggarwal family. An HMV Fiesta record player came as a gift at Aggarwal's wedding in 1980.

'Fuelled by the gift, my love for records became an obsession then,' he says.

Today, he has an enviable collection of 1,500 LPs, 700 EPs and several cassettes, and a 5,000 GB hard disk of recorded radio programmes (like *Bioscope ki Baatein*) as well as DVDS, VCDs, books and magazines. He has built up his own song collections, based on specific subjects and words in film songs and also on individual artistes.

Aggarwal is a member of SurYatra, a serious, committed Jaipur-based group of music aficionados that organizes meet-ups, discussions and exchanges, as well as interactions with artistes like the late Ravi, Jagjit Singh, Naushad and Juthika Roy. The fandom for them might be immense, but not irrational. The discussion on their music is informed and scholarly.

'It hasn't been about taking their pictures or autographs, but about getting insights from them about the creation of music, what went behind it, getting to know more about particular songs and compositions,' Aggarwal clarifies.

The group is the brainchild of journalist M.D. Soni, among others, and according to him, 'It's run with passion [rather], than [with the intention of] seeking publicity for itself, and has a handful of committed members.'

Aggarwal, of course, is one of them.

'Movies *aur masti mein rehta hoon*. I live without a care, with movies for company. I want my whole house to be filled with music,' he declares.

But he does worry about what might happen to the collection once he is gone. His family members, evidently, don't share his passion, caught up as they are in the day-to-day business of life. He constantly broods over the possibility of them discarding the collection or selling off the mementos dirt cheap.

'*Chaat-pakodi ke bhaav na bike kahin*. Let's hope it [the collection] doesn't get sold off somewhere for peanuts,' he says.

Like Aggarwal, Prakash Jain doesn't quite know what to do to preserve his radio collection after he is gone. It was his love for film songs that fuelled interest in the gadget that brought them home to him. Now several radios lie stacked in a rented godown a few kilometres from his home. Random pieces from that collection lie scattered around his home. An old Phillips from 1955 is perched on a window ledge in one of the bedrooms. A Grundig from 1960, proudly displayed in his room, is still operational and he is tinkering with the skeleton of an antique one. Besides, there is an entire album of pictures to share with me, pictures of models that are safely locked away.

A sound/audio engineer with his own electronics business, Jain has always been a music buff, especially inclined towards old film songs as well as ghazals, thumris and bhajans, with Lata Mangeshkar, Shobha Gurtu, Mehdi Hassan, Ghulam Ali, Begum Akhtar and Jagjit Singh being his favourites. The collection of rare radios started when he saw a scrap dealer breaking open a radio to extract its metal parts. He bought the gadget from him for ₹75, marking the beginning of an acquisition overdrive. Today, he has 160 different models – Phillips Holland, Grundig, Pye Cambridge, HGEC, Empire and many more antique, unknown ones. A hundred and forty of them still work, claims Jain. It's the signals that are getting distorted.

'Only FM seems to work,' he tells me.

He is, nevertheless, worried about their health. The possibility of termites eating away the beautiful wooden cabinets is his biggest concern. A reason why he wishes to give his private collection away to a good institute that will take care of it.

'*Haddiyan boodhi ho rahi hain*. The bones are aging,' he sighs, acknowledging the inevitable decay that comes with the passing of years.

His own, as well as those of his beloved radios.

The last we heard, the National Film Archives of India was keen to acquire it. I hope Jain's collection gets a safe home in its vaults.

The one to connect them all – Hindi film music aficionados, collectors and archivers in India – is the modest Harmandir Singh 'Hamraz' of Kanpur, the ultimate point person and authority on Hindi film music. With intensive research and hard work behind him, he has, single-handedly and without any hype and hoopla, put together voluminous books titled *Hindi Film Geet Kosh*, a priceless, five-volume compilation of data on Hindi film songs, right from the first talkie *Alam Ara*. The 65-year-old gentle Sikh, who retired from his job with the State Bank of India, remembers how he had to pass up promising opportunities for advancement in his career with the bank to concentrate on his project.

'I could not afford to go on transfers awarded with promotions,' he says.

His monumental journey to put together the most authoritative work on Hindi film music is, by itself, worth a film.

In the early '60s, songs being played while marriage processions were taken out through the streets used to attract him. His mother, the late Surinder Kaur, was a popular folk singer known for her rendition of Punjabi songs and the Punjabi Shabad, as well as for reciting the Guru Granth Sahib. While studying, he would listen to songs on the radio – the only other source of music available, besides gramophone records. Vividh Bharati, Radio Ceylon and the Urdu Service of AIR, Delhi, were the main radio stations. In the late '60s, he also started visiting Chor Bazaar or Parade Bazaar in Kanpur, where old gramophone records were sold for one, two or three rupees, depending on their condition. Hamraz purchased a few, but could not afford a gramophone player. Television would enter his world much later and for many years, *Chitrahaar* was the only weekly programme on this medium featuring Hindi film songs.

In the early days, Radio Ceylon would broadcast its *Vakya Geetanjali* programme every Sunday night. The announcer would articulate a meaningful sentence consisting of seven or eight words and ask listeners to send in the titles of Hindi film songs beginning with each word. It was Hamraz's desire to participate in the various programmes of Radio Ceylon, particularly, the *Vakya Geetanjali*, that prompted him to note down the relevant details of all the film songs he liked on a regular basis. Henceforth, he would jot down the opening lines and all the credits of every film song he ever listened to. To save space in the exercise books he used for the purpose, he abbreviated the names of singers, lyricists and music directors. For Lata Mangeshkar, he wrote 'L'; for Majrooh Sultanpuri, 'MS'; for Naushad, 'N', and so on. For example, a song with credits would appear as: L (SB, N); in other words, the title of the film in which that particular song had featured and the song's opening line, followed by the names of the singer, the song writer and the music director.

This served as the very basic foundation of his tome on music.

On many occasions, when Hamraz was involved in the process of noting down the opening lines of film songs (with their attendant details), he would miss out on some of the credits. Sometimes, he would fail to catch the title of a film or the singer's name. Later on, if he happened to like a song, he would be impatient to fill in those crucial gaps in information. Around 1967, when he was still in school, he strongly felt the need for a book which could provide him correct and complete information about all the film songs he had ever listened to. Since none existed, he decided that he would try to compile such information himself.

In the early '70s, Kapil Dev Sharma, a music lover and engineer from Kota, Rajasthan, spoke to Hamraz about the book he had in his possession: *Indian Filmography*, compiled by Mumbai's famous film historian Firoze Rangoonwalla. Published in 1970, it contained the titles of Hindi feature films (both silent ones and talkies) up to 1969 and also included the names of their respective directors, music directors and artistes. It turned out to be a boon, a foundation for Hamraz's own work.

Beginning from the silent era, say, the early '20s, and right up to the period covering 2004 and 2005, every producer was bound to publish a booklet for each film that he produced, containing the story synopsis, cast and credits, and full text of the songs featured in them. But it did not include the names of the singers, music composers, lyricists and so on. In addition to tracing such booklets, Hamraz had to consult the catalogues of gramophone record-manufacturing companies, like HMV, for the names of the singers and related information. He also lifted a great deal of information directly from gramophone discs, and old film magazines like *FilmIndia* were equally useful for his purpose. Many music lovers too came forward. Numerous film personalities were contacted in Bombay (now Mumbai) and other cities to source information related to the films they had acted in. In a nutshell, the information was scattered and Hamraz had to put in a great deal of painstaking effort to compile it, using every means possible. In the process, he visited many cities, including Indore, Bhopal, Bombay, Bhusawal, Calcutta (now Kolkata), Delhi, Baroda (now Vadodara), Ahmedabad and Rajkot. He visited the National Film Archives India, Poona (now Pune), several times in his quest. He is known to have pursued one particular source over 13 years to extract a piece of information, which he eventually obtained free of charge.

Having joined the SBI in July 1972, Hamraz had no worries about earning a living and could devote all his time after office hours to collecting the information he needed. He availed of his Leave Fare Concession – what is today a Leave Travel Allowance (LTA) – to visit many cities and, for over a decade, continued compiling information on Hindi film songs that had been released between 1931 and 1970. By mid-1978, he had checked the compilation sheets and found that films from the golden era – those released between 1951 and 1960 – could be taken up first to constitute a volume for eventual publication.

It was B.N. Chatterjee of Bhopal (currently living in Nagpur) who helped Hamraz prepare the manuscript containing the details of 1,063 Hindi films that would subsequently be published as *Hindi Film Geet Kosh*, Vol. III (1951–60). Hamraz contacted two old, established publishers of Kanpur: Sahitya Niketan and Sahitya Ratnalaya, located in the city's Shivala area. A certain Mr Kapoor to whom he showed his manuscript gave it a cursory glance before asking him two questions: who he was and what this was all about? Hamraz, who was hardly 28 years old at the time, was so annoyed by this kind of response that he resolved not to contact a publisher ever again.

Henceforth, he only approached his well-wishers, who contributed as much as they could to further his goal – sometimes, ₹250 or ₹500 and, occasionally, even ₹1,000. Hamraz promised to repay the money, without interest, but only through the income he earned from sales. The printing-press owner who took on the responsibility for the book was also assured that he would be paid the balance amount after the sale of copies went through. Adding his own savings from the bonus and overtime he had earned as a bank employee to the contributions from music lovers, Hamraz managed to raise ₹25,000 and brought out 1,000 copies of the book in January 1980. Advance booking of copies was offered at a price of ₹25 and ₹35 respectively for the paperback and hardbound editions, though the printed price for the same was fixed at ₹35 and ₹45. Sales were initially rather sluggish and it took nearly four years to sell the entire stock. Hamraz was unable to come out with the second edition of this volume that had demanded maximum effort. Instead, he started providing music aficionados with photocopies of the book, charging them the nominal sum he had to spend for getting each copy photocopied, and continued to do so for 17 long years. He is said to have distributed 2,000 such photocopies in all – until the publication of the book's second and revised edition in April 1997.

Due to a lack of funds, the alphabetic song index could not be included in the book's first edition. In addition, a great deal of hitherto missing information had been collected from various sources after its publication, prompting Hamraz to come out with a second edition with a fresh dust jacket. This would set the pattern for subsequent editions published in 1984, '86, '88 and '91. Due to the first edition's missing index, one particular music lover, Subhash Khatri, an advocate from Bikaner, would even serve Hamraz a legal notice, stipulating that the latter should either prepare the index for the published edition or include it in the second edition, failing which he should be prepared to face Khatri in the consumer court.

Thereafter, the other volumes were published at regular intervals. Volume II (1941–50) was published and released in Mumbai on 25 February 1984, followed by Volume IV (1961–70), published and released in Delhi on 7 July 1986, Volume I (1931–40) on 8 October 1988 in Mumbai and Volume V (1971–80) on 31 March 1991, again in Mumbai. A thousand copies of each of the volumes were thus published. Release functions were arranged and attended by veteran film personalities and music lovers visiting from across India and abroad.

In the early '80s, a top executive from Batliboi visited Hamraz at home and actually threatened not to budge from his place until he had been provided with a copy of Volume III. It prompted Hamraz to come out with a photocopy, a solution he had hit upon earlier. He followed up the idea again and had photocopies made of the other volumes as well whenever original stock was sold out, and they were provided at a minimal cost to those who sought them. Barring the second edition of Volume III, photocopy editions of all the other four volumes are still available against payment.

In 1993, Hamraz decided to digitize the data published in five volumes, for the period from 1931 to 1980. The entire second edition of Volume III was prepared using Ventura (a DTP software, hardly used in those days by others, as it is very difficult to operate). Thus, not only did he play the role of a music lover, compiler, publisher and bookseller, but of a printer compositor as well. This had become a one-man show.

To cater to the needs of music lovers, television channels, radio stations, gramophone record and CD/DVD manufacturing companies, Hamraz has been trying, since 1999, to engage a number of professionals to digitize his book. Unfortunately, no one has been able to meet his expectations so far. According to him, potential recruits are not diligent or careful enough with the information, hence are, unreliable. At present, all the data has been stored in a computer, but much needs to be done before it can be made available to users through the Internet. A lack of funds is the main hurdle standing in the way of the project's completion. Ideally, this project, involving the compilation and digitization of data on all Indian films, should have been undertaken by NFAI in Pune.

'But archiving in India is in a lamentable state,' Hamraz says despondently. 'It is much too late and we have already lost, perhaps, more than 50 per cent of our film heritage. Yet, due to new storage devices like computers, DVDs, etc., we can archive the remaining treasure, before it is also lost for ever. NFAI is the only institution which should come forward, but being a government body, nothing concrete has come out till date, as far as the compilation of data is concerned.'

I gather the main hindrance is bureaucratese, along with the many layers of permissions that submitted material must go through successfully before it is deemed eligible for archiving.

Meanwhile, work on future volumes of *Geet Kosh* is under way. Looking at the increasing number of Hindi films being produced every year, beginning with Volume VI, all subsequent volumes would cover a period of five years each.

Music Directors of Hindi Films is another project Hamraz has been working on for the last 10 years. In addition to the list featuring every music director who was associated with a film, it would contain a brief sketch of their lives, their photos and the awards they had won, among other related information.

'I am 63 now,' Hamraz tells us the last time we speak to him. 'It took me more than four decades to put together the Hindi film song data for the period 1931 to 1980. During the rest of [my] life, I intend to update it to the present. If god wills it.'

In this day and age of disposable, use-and-throw culture, music and movies too are being regarded as experiences available for instant consumption, rather than those of lasting value and long-term engagement. The quest for a deeper knowledge or understanding of them is rare, especially in times of Google and Wikipedia, where a quick Internet search circumvents the need for intensive research, especially as the reliability of the information unearthed seems just a minor concern. In such a world, Hamraz is one of a kind, painstakingly compiling the most intricate details about his chosen area of interest and ensuring that the information he puts out is accurate enough to bear scrutiny. Here is a true soldier, marching on for Hindi film songs to find their rightful place in our collective – and increasingly depleting – knowledge pool.

Of Return Tickets and Long-distance Affairs

BACHCHAN CLOTH HOUSE, GULZAR and Sons – the two shop names you spy on the way to Nishat Talkies in Shahjahanpur are enough to make you suspect that the town's heart beats frantically for Hindi cinema. Kuldeep Bhagi's did as well.

'I was born in a cinema hall,' he smiles. 'I grew up with its audience.'

Bhagi is, of course, speaking metaphorically. His family owned the iconic Nishat cinema hall that once used to be Shahjahanpur's entertainment centre. No wonder the road on which it stands continues to bear its name, even though the hall itself is no longer functional.

Sharply attired in a red T-shirt and white trousers, quite like a Bollywood hero of the '70s, Bhagi meets us in the compound of Nishat, now a mere relic of its glorious past. The crumbling walls, the chipped façade, an almost illegible notice on a weather-beaten board from the past, stating that ticket prices will not be refunded in case of a power failure post-interval, and a deserted, desolate complex make it difficult for you to imagine that films like Feroz Khan's *Qurbani* (1980), Manoj Kumar's *Kranti* (1981), Dilip Kumar–Sanjay Dutt–starrer *Vidhaata* (1982), or *Jaan ki Baazi* (1985), featuring Sanjay Dutt yet again, could have once played to a packed house here, that Rajesh Khanna could have delivered six to seven consecutive hits, running for over 25 weeks each, at this very movie theatre. Its only connect with civilization now seems to be an odd dish antenna perched precariously on one of the ledges.

Shahjahanpur was once teeming with cinema halls: Durga, Majestic, Chitra, Amba. And, of course, Nishat. The stories still linger: of how the entire front façade used to be plastered with posters; how people would take long morning walks just to see the posters for forthcoming films; how an elephant or bullock cart would roam the streets, displaying publicity material from a film; how the execution-by-hanging scene from Manoj Kumar's *Shaheed* (1965) was played out like a live street show.

'*Ab woh deewanapan nahin hai filmon ke liye*. Now that madness for movies is no longer there,' Bhagi confesses.

He still lives in the shadow of a ghostly Nishat. A small side gate set in the cinema hall's boundary wall leads to a flight of stairs that climbs up to a section of the building he calls home, where he resides with the many memories of his brief fling with the movies. Sixty-seven-year-old Bhagi was among the first from this small UP town to have ventured into Hindi cinema, long before the other famous actor who hails from the same town – Rajpal Yadav – did so. Shahjahanpur is just 80 km away from its more famous cousin Bareilly that has had a more publicized Bollywood bond; not only is it film star Priyanka Chopra's hometown, it has served as the backdrop for the '*Jhumka gira re*' song from *Mera Saaya* (1966), featuring the late yesteryear star Sadhana in a double role, and more recently, for the popular 2017 romantic comedy *Bareilly ki Barfi*, starring Ayushmann Khurrana, Rajkummar Rao and Kriti Sanon. Few would know, however, that besides Bhagi and Yadav, Shahjahanpur has yet another cinema connect from the past; eminent art director Desh Mukherjee of *Purab Aur Paschim* (1970), *Deewar* (1975) and *Kranti* fame, also grew up watching films at Nishat.

It couldn't have been easy to dream of cinema in this land of sugarcane and sugar mills, of paper, fertilizer and ordnance factories, with the carpet-weaving industry being an integral part of it. But his family's association with filmdom smoothed the path for Bhagi to get there. A student from the 1971–73 batch of the acting course at Pune's FTII, he was taught by the legendary guru Roshan Tarneja. In fact, Tarneja, along with Durga Khote, were the judges for Bhagi's audition and selection to the much-in-demand course. His illustrious batchmates were Shabana Azmi, Rita Bhaduri, Kanwaljeet Singh and Shailendra Singh, who studied acting at FTII, acted in a few films that didn't quite set the box office on fire, like *Do Jasoos* (1975), *Janta Hawaldar* (1979), *Nauker* (1979) and *Agreement* (1980), but earned greater recognition as a playback singer, particularly following his sensational break with the song '*Main shayar to nahin*' for Raj Kapoor's *Bobby*. He subsequently became Rishi Kapoor's singing voice in films like *Khel Khel Mein* (1975) and *Zamane ko Dikhana Hai* (1981). It is clear from the pictures on Bhagi's Facebook wall that he is still close to the two Singhs – Kanwaljeet and Shailendra

'Raza Murad, Romesh Sharma, Mahendra Sandhu were my seniors. Mithun Chakraborty and Ranjeeta were in the following batches,' he recalls.

His wife-to-be, Lakshmi, was also his batchmate at FTII. The two married soon after the course got over and Lakshmi never acted in a film.

Those were his wonder years and it is clear that FTII has left a lasting impression on him.

'Pune was the education hub; it was beautiful and green, sheer heaven,' he recalls.

They were taught how to deal with the camera, an instrument sensitive to the subtlest of expressions.

'We were taught yoga, meditation for concentration and for bringing out an emotion from deep within. There were classes for movement,' he says.

He goes on to talk about filmmaker Ritwik Ghatak and the iconic Wisdom Tree in the FTII campus, where he used to hold his film addas, viewing films day and night, discussing them threadbare, learning everything from sound and photography to direction.

The Mumbai years that followed – he would spend five of them in the 'Maya Nagri' – have left Bhagi less effusive about life. Within six months of his arrival, he was taken on board by Basu Bhattacharya, but his contract with the director did not permit him to sign another film till his stint with him was over. That film is Kuldeep Bhagi's sole imprint on the history of Indian cinema; the IMDB entry lists him as the hero of Basu Bhattacharya's *Tumhara Kalloo*.

'It's a film in the genre of *Bhuvan Shome, Saara Aakash*. The no make-up, limited-gesture film; and it was shot in Vasai,' he tells me.

The 1975 film was the one and only time Bhagi faced the camera, before returning to Shahjahanpur, never to set foot in Bollywood again. His return ticket was bought sometime between 1978 and 1979.

'I looked a bit like Sanjay Khan back then,' he says.

He reminds me more of that actor's younger brother, Akbar Khan. Like *Tumhara Kalloo*'s protagonist, Bhagi also comes from a wealthy, small-town family. But there's more to the film's story. Kalloo is an illiterate man who falls in love with Lakshmi, an educated girl. What happens when she writes him a letter and expects a response forms the core of the film. India's official entry to the Berlin and Moscow film festivals, *Tumhara Kalloo* was released in Mumbai and Kolkata, but not in UP, and certainly not in Bhagi's own hometown.

What brought him back home? He is not particularly forthcoming with his response, though I get the impression that what prompted his return was a combination of factors: the necessity of managing the family property back home, the futility of the struggles Bollywood had put him through, the hint of a brief dalliance with Indira Bredemeyer, the Miss India runner-up of 1975. But most of all, he attributes his return to a lack of ambition.

'I had no aims and targets in life, no limo that I needed to buy. I was comfortable with what I had,' he recalls.

The tussles involved in trying to establish a career in films can dishearten many, but it can be equally heartbreaking to fade into anonymity after taking a shot at stardom. Bhagi, however, seems unruffled as he feeds his kitchen's famed keema parathas to his close friends, many of whom would probably not recognize him at all if they were to watch *Tumhara Kalloo* on YouTube. Other than Nishat Talkies, nothing in Bhagi's milieu screams cinema. For now, an actor and a film lie lost to the world in the chaos and crowd, heat and dust of Shahjahanpur.

It was sometime in the '70s that film star Vinod Khanna became Swami Vinod Bharti and quit Bollywood at the very peak of his career. Few would know that his *sanyas* also irrevocably changed the life of an aspiring actor from Jalandhar called Gautam Kapoor.

Kapoor, who assisted Gulzar for nine years and on six films, including *Kitaab* (1977), starring Bengal's Uttam Kumar opposite Vidya Sinha, *Kinara* (also released in 1977), with Hema Malini and Jeetendra in the lead, *Meera* (1979), with Hema Malini in a stellar role, and Sanjeev Kumar–starrer *Angoor* (1982), was set to star opposite Rekha in a Yash Johar production called *Hamesha*, with Vinod Khanna and Hema Malini as the lead pair. It was a film that died a sudden death with Khanna's departure. So did Kapoor's career as an actor.

Now the owner of Jalandhar's Radisson Hotel, Kapoor, who is 70 odd years, is brimming with stories and gossip about the film industry as it used to be back then.

Movies had been a part of Kapoor's growing up years in Jalandhar. As founder-president of the East Punjab Motion Pictures Association, his grandfather, Sitaram Kapoor, was responsible for bringing the film industry to the Punjab town, for making it the hub of film distribution for Punjab, Haryana, Jammu and Kashmir and Himachal Pradesh. The Kapoor family financed many films made under the Navketan banner, as well as those of producers Tito and Tony, and owned Hari

Palace and Jyoti cinema halls. Distantly related to Bollywood's famous Kapoor *khandaan*, Gautam Kapoor remembers the Kapoor patriarch Prithviraj coming often to Jalandhar to perform in the town's theatre. He also recalls how Yash Chopra (with whom he studied till the age of five in Jalandhar), J. Om Prakash and Dev Anand would arrive in town with their films to celebrate 100 days of screening, apart from silver or golden jubilees.

'Since there were no great hotels in Jalandhar at that time, stars like Dharmendra and Rajesh Khanna would come home,' says Kapoor. 'They were all very humble and the parties were like family affairs.'

Dropping out of college, he decided to embrace showbiz and started off by working as a third assistant with producer Premji, who had been Dilip Kumar's secretary, on the Amitabh Bachchan–Shashi Kapoor–starrer *Imaan Dharam* (1977).

'There was no money or salary given to us,' he remembers. 'I used to survive on the ₹500 given to me every month by my father.'

Kapoor went on to become a production controller for Gulzar's *Meera*, went location hunting in Rajasthan for the film and has fond memories of working with the director who was a 'fellow Leo'.

'I used to live as a paying guest in a little room of [rented out by] Mrs Coelho in Turner Road,' he recalls. 'Our day meals used to all come from Gulzar Saab's home: *pakode* and fresh cucumber and tomato sandwiches. We used to look for excuses to go to his home in Pali Hill to tank ourselves up on some good food. If we were shooting in Mehboob [Studio], then lunch was always *vada-pav* and dinner was at Sardar ka Dhaba at Bandra station.'

The mention of the poet-lyricist-writer-filmmaker still sends Kapoor into raptures; Gulzar is the one man he remembers and respects the most. He remembers how he used to just up and leave Bombay (now Mumbai) to think and write. How he would lock himself up in a room in Bangalore (now Bengaluru) to let his thoughts flow through his pen.

'He is a true intellectual, a genius,' says Kapoor. 'His poetry is both traditional, as well as contemporary. He has great control over Urdu, but never gets heavy with his use of it and he connects brilliantly with people.'

As a filmmaker, he remembers Gulzar's *Maachis* as a stark and realistic portrait of militancy in Punjab, a socio-political phenomenon that had directly affected Kapoor's own extended family, and would kill thousands in the state and devastate countless families.

'He showed the intrinsic violence of the situation without showing a single fight or drop of blood,' Kapoor remembers.

What did he learn from the man?

'To chart one's own path; find one's own niche. He never followed what others were doing, was confident about himself.'

Moreover, Gulzar always gave newcomers a break. Among them were Romu Sippy, Meraj, N. Chandra, Shatrughan Sinha, Vinod Khanna, Asrani and Paintal.

'He has given so much talent to the industry,' Kapoor declares.

So why didn't a talent like him persevere in his film career the way the others he mentioned had?

Pat comes the answer: frustration.

'I was not getting the right break and I wanted results too fast.'

After opting out of showbiz, Kapoor initially missed it quite a bit. But once he made money and tasted success in his new career, it stopped bothering him.

'Bollywood celebrates the success of just a handful of people. There are also thousands who don't make it and are never written about,' he confides.

Kapoor no longer misses the glamour, but he is still nostalgic about a few individuals. Despite him having been away from Bollywood for long, the Gulzar connect still lingers. Once, while travelling from Shimla to Jalandhar, he heard a new song and identified it immediately as having been written by Gulzar. His daughter argued that it couldn't be, because the film was a south Indian production. Later, she would realize that her father had been right. The film was *Dil Se* and the song '*Jiya jale*'.

'I know the way he writes. No one else could have written "*Masle phoolon ki mehak mein titliyon ki kyariyaan*. In the fragrance of crushed flowers is the garden of butterflies."'

He had last called up Gulzar when *Jai Ho* won the Oscar, asking him why he hadn't gone to Los Angeles for the ceremony.

His answer was quintessentially Gulzar: '*Mere paas kaala* coat *nahin tha*. I didn't have a formal, black tuxedo.'

Meanwhile, nothing of Gautam Kapoor's film business remains. With the distribution business having been taken over by the big corporates, small individual distributors like the Kapoors have literally become extinct. The cinema halls owned by them have also undergone a transformation: Hari Palace is now a godown and Jyoti has metamorphosed into a mall.

The commute from Kankarbagh in Patna to Bollywood has not been easy for Rekha Jha. And it continues to be strewn with many ifs and buts. One of Asia's largest and most densely populated colonies, Kankarbagh has a star resident in Rekha, the singer of the popular *Gangs of Wasseypur* song '*O Womaniya*'. However, marriage, kids and domesticity have conspired to ensure that her tryst with Bollywood remains conditional, sporadic and somewhat remote.

In fact, it has been so with her singing career in general. Trained though she was by her music-teacher father Harihar Pathak, Rekha's singing languished for nearly 19 years after her marriage to transporter Pankaj Jha. It was her husband, however, who would push her into pursuing her career more seriously. She had been singing (mostly folk numbers) for stage shows and Doordarshan in Patna. A chance audition got her picked up by music composer Sneha Khanwalkar for one of the two lead voices in the iconic song that playfully spoke to women about how to one-up their men.

In contrast to the manner she assumes in rendering '*Womaniya*', 45-year-old Rekha sounds far from assertive in real life. She is matter-of-fact, however, and reveals a certain resolve in her world view and choices. A career, it seems, was never her goal or ambition while she was in the thick of domesticity, raising her five children. She looks back at the past and wonders if, perhaps, by deferring marriage to a later stage in her life, she would have had the freedom to pursue her singing career with more tenacity and commitment.

'But by 25, I had given birth to all my five children,' she observes. '*Agar tab* career *ke baare mein sochte to hamare bachche nahin pal paate. Woh ladkhada jaate*. Had I focussed on my career at the time, I wouldn't have been able to bring up our children with the care they deserved. They would've gone astray.'

She is still unable to believe in and process her instant stardom.

'*Kabhi socha nahin tha ki meri awaaz itna door tak jaa paayegi*. I had never even dreamt that my voice could have such a wide-ranging impact.'

That too with just one song. '*Womaniya*' has brought her fame and greater opportunities to perform back at home. It's a reluctant stardom, though; she hasn't really been able to capitalize on it in Bollywood in a big way as yet. Not because the Hindi film industry hasn't been interested, but because her home and hearth still hold her back.

'I have always been a housewife. *Baahari duniya ka anubhav bhi nahin hai humko*. I'm far from experienced in the ways of the outside world,' she admits candidly.

Rekha can't simply take the first train to Mumbai the moment an offer to sing comes in. In fact, Jackie Shroff and Ekta Kapoor had wanted her to sing for their films, but she couldn't just up and leave.

'I need to know at least three-four days in advance,' she says.

On the positive side, her children, aged between 14 and 21, are all grown up now and less dependent on her. They, along with the family in general, are interested in seeing her pursue a career in playback singing. The keenest of them all is her husband Pankaj who, at one time, had nurtured dreams of becoming an actor himself.

Says Rekha: '*Apna shauk aur sapne ab mere gaane se poora kar rahe hain*. He is now fulfilling his dreams through my singing.'

For him, Bollywood has become just a '*Womaniya*' away from Kankarbagh. All that Rekha needs to do is get on a train.

For Ramkumar Singh, Mumbai is just an hour and a half away. He prefers to fly there, hold his meetings, have narrations and discussions, and come back home to Jaipur to work on his scripts – all in the comfort of his personal space. The rapid march of technology – in the form of mobile phones, the Internet and Skype – has made it easy.

'Mumbai might be the centre of Bollywood, but filmmaking is getting increasingly decentralized,' Singh declares.

Zed Plus, the 2014 feature film which marked his debut as a screenplay writer from Jaipur, also involved others who weren't originally from Mumbai: the lead actor Adil Hussain is from Delhi, one of the heroines Ekavali Khanna comes from Kolkata and the cinematographer H.M. Ramachandran belongs to Bengaluru.

Familiarity and comfort apart, another reason to work from home, I gather, is to remain rooted when it comes to Singh's storytelling. The journalist-writer-columnist grew up in a village in the Shekhawati area of Rajasthan, which is quite similar to the Fatehpur he depicts so realistically in *Zed Plus*, a departure from the usually touristy portrayals of Rajasthan presented in film after film. Instead of highlighting the havelis and *baori* (stepwell), Singh focusses his attention on the region's politics and demographics.

'I could have placed the film in any small town in UP or Bihar. But I wanted to dedicate the film to the region I grew up in,' he explains.

Owing to his familiarity with the area and its people, his portrayal of the lower and lower middle-class Muslim families living there is a faithful and realistic one.

'It was a Muslim-majority area,' Singh recalls. 'The political representatives here have also always been Muslim. We had many Muslim friends; we used to visit and eat in their homes regularly. An MLA who ran buses in the region would offer free rides to all the girls of the village.'

Later, for his high-school education, he was sent to a boarding school in Lakshmangarh. Those were the late '80s, the years of growing up watching Govinda and Mithun Chakraborty on screen, and falling hopelessly in love with a Sanjay Dutt–Salman Khan–Madhuri Dixit – starrer called *Saajan*, of watching films on the sly on hired VCRs or in illegal video parlours.

'Cinema *dekhne ke saath ek apradh bodh juda hota tha*. Socially frowned upon where youngsters were concerned, watching films afforded a guilty pleasure,' Singh confesses.

But being an only child whose whims were often indulged, he could bulldoze his way into watching films and choosing an atypical career: journalism and writing. An unexpected meeting with filmmaker Chandraprakash Dwivedi in Delhi and a chance narration of a story idea to him in Mumbai, while Dwivedi was waiting for his house help to return from Sunday Mass, helped turn the idea into a full-fledged film.

There are many who dream of cinema, dream of becoming a part of it.

'But it is rare for someone from a village to come face-to-face with filmdom the way I have,' Singh admits.

His next two scripts are also rooted in his reality. One involves the journey of a man from a rural world to an urban one, and the financial and cultural conflicts it triggers. Another is about a person from Rajasthan who moves for business purposes to Europe, but continues to maintain his ties with home. Just like Singh himself, who seeks to work in Bollywood, without having to let go of his ties with Jaipur.

Six months after meeting him at the cosy Sonapani Film Festival, I bump into Amit Dutta at another festival in the hills with the same friendly, intimate vibes: the Dharamshala International Film Festival. India's most reclusive and retiring filmmaker cheerfully informs me that he has shifted base from Jammu, where he had, all the while, been thinking, reading, researching, writing, making and editing his films, to an area near Palampur in Himachal Pradesh

The country's cinema-consuming masses might know little about Dutta, but film buffs, both in India and abroad, regard this 2004 graduate of Pune's FTII as one of the most exciting and elusive filmmakers today. His films have won several awards. A retrospective of his work was held at Germany's Oberhausen Film Festival in 2010. A selection of his films has been archived by the Oberhausen Film Festival and screened at Austria's Viennale, New York's Museum of Modern Art (MoMA), the Tate Modern in London, the Venice Architecture Biennale and the Centre Georges Pompidou in Paris. Most recently, his 22-minute short *Field Trip* (2013) on art historian B.N. Goswamy's visits to the many sources of art and *Saatvin Sair* (The Seventh Walk), 2013, on celebrated Indian landscape painter Paramjit Singh, were shown at the Rome Film Festival to much acclaim.

The most internationally fêted of Indian filmmakers never wanted to be part of the film 'industry', as we know it. So his work has never been about stories or stars, song-and-dance routines or high-pitched histrionics. Grounded in the theories of art, aesthetics and culture, his films make references to history, myth and legend, and are steeped in literature and nature. No wonder he refuses to work out of big cities. In fact, he wants to create cinema as far away from the urban chaos and madness as possible.

'You get poorer in the city,' he declares with conviction.

He reads, absorbs and internalizes an enormous amount of material on the subjects of his films (even trying his hand at painting) before embarking on the actual shoot.

'For doing all this, a middle-class, simple, quiet life of anonymity is bliss,' he believes.

It aids his intensive research and documentation, and also allows his imagination to take flight. The equipment and basic studio set-up are all in place. He carried on with his work for a long time in Jammu, but the town, with its mounting power problems, was proving difficult to live in and had ceased to creatively inspire him. As a result, Dutta has had to move to the peace and immersive isolation of the mountains in Palampur.

The solitude of the creative space within which he functions is reflected in his films. It helps him in his attempt to distil cinema to its purest: evading words, but embracing the sights and sounds, making the films highly experiential. His cinema is about a poetic play between nature and spaces, music and quietude. There is a breathtaking stillness and meditative touch in the composition of his shots. His is a rare cinema of rhythm and cadence.

Gurvinder Singh, a friend of Dutta's and the helmsman of path-breaking, alternate Punjabi films like *Anhe Ghode da Daan* (Alms for a Blind Horse), 2011, and *Chauthi Koot* (The Fourth Direction), 2015, works out of Bir in Himachal Pradesh. He also runs Café Cloud Door there, named after a film directed by his mentor Mani Kaul, a leading light of the parallel film movement of the '70s and '80s.

Anhe Ghode da Daan, about the subordination of Dalits in Punjab, is the first Punjabi-language film to have travelled to numerous international film festivals; it premiered in the Orizzonti (Horizons) section at the 68th Venice International Film Festival. *Chauthi Koot*, set in the Sikh militancy era of the 1980s, is the first Punjabi film to have been screened in the prestigious Un Certain Regard section at the 2015 Cannes Film Festival.

Does the long distance from the competitive and commercial urban hubs of filmmaking inspire him to create the profound, artistic films he does, I'd asked when I last met him in 2016 in the chaos of Mumbai at Andheri's Cinepolis multiplex, where his film *Chauthi Koot* was being screened.

'Life is not only about filmmaking. Why should we put all our eggs in one basket?' he had replied with his characteristic Zen-like calmness (which I am sure also derives from his life in Bir). '*Theek hai, ek* film *banayi; kal main wahan jaa ke kheti kar sakta hoon.* Okay, I have made a film; tomorrow, I could be farming there in Bir... I could forget about it [filmmaking] and wonder why the ladyfinger and eggplant are not flowering.'[24]

Isn't it too idyllic a life, I had wondered aloud, mystified by his lack of anxiety over when his next film would be made.

'The idea is to be relaxed. It will get made when it has to get made,' Singh had shot back.

His aim is to be completely immersed in the world around him. For a month, he could just be painting and not think about cinema at all. Another month could be entirely devoted to reading.

Singh's cinema is organic; shunning drama, it is pivoted on silences and pauses. Most of all, it is about creating multiple layers of meanings, using metaphors, signs and symbols, to open up the work to various readings, interpretations and personal experiences. The life he leads in Bir allows him to embrace it in his cinema.

'If you are creating multiple narratives in film,' he had explained, 'you need to create multiple narratives in your own life.'

Last heard, Singh had cast – along with many other Bir residents in secondary roles – the 17-year-old boy who works in his café as the main protagonist of *Khanaur* (Bitter Chestnut), his new feature film that will be about the changing Bir, a quiet hill town caught between its pastoral past and Himachal Pradesh's emerging ambition as a paragliding hub of the future.[25]

For Singh and Dutta, the cinema they create, its stories, myths and language are rooted in the way they have chosen to live – in little idylls far away from the stress and strain of urban chaos. They are content in the bucolic spaces they have chosen for themselves. Ramkumar Singh is firm in his resolve to tell tales of Rajasthan in Bollywood, while staying connected with his home state. For Rekha Jha, it is about coming to terms with the wide chasm between Bihar and Bollywood that circumstances have not allowed her to bridge so far. Bhagi and Kapoor, on the other hand, while having severed their fragile ties with Bollywood, must still make a conscious effort not to look back with regret. Some have emerged famous and successful. Others may appear to have lost out in the celluloid race. But they all have something in common: regardless of their circumstances and the eventual outcome of the choices they made, they have nurtured hope in their hearts and dreamed of cinema from close and afar.

Heartland Connections

ONE OF BOLLYWOOD'S BIGGEST successes in the last four years has been actor Pankaj Tripathi, with stellar performances in films like *Masaan* (2015), *Newton, Gurgaon*, and *Bareilly ki Barfi* – all 2017 releases – and *Stree* (2018), among others. Belonging to a farming family in the village of Belsand, near Gopalganj, Bihar, Tripathi still remembers the day he first landed in Mumbai – 16 October 2004 – after travelling on the Golden Temple Express. But you can sense that 14 years later, the immigrant within him is still alive and kicking when he looks back at the early days with fondness – performing small roles in the amateur plays put up during the Chhath festival in his village; displaying his storytelling skills at students' union functions in Patna in the '90s; being the high-jump champion at Patna's Magadh University; spending seven days in jail in 1993 for participating in an agitation as a right-wing students' union member and doing a course in hotel management in Patna, while working night shifts as a trainee cook in a hotel.

Belsand still resides in his heart. No wonder when I last interviewed him for *The Hindu*, he spoke fondly of his house in Andheri's Charkop, which faces a huge pond and a temple, recreating the familiar rural feel that feeds his nostalgia for Belsand.[26] I recently got to know that he has moved on from the idyll to a new home in Madh Island, in step with his new-found success. But I have often reasoned that the rootedness of his environment and his own personality are also reflected in the organic nature of his roles and performances.

Like Tripathi, another recent star Sohum Shah, who made an impression with his performances in *Ship of Theseus* (2012) and *Tumbbad* (2018), likes his office in Aram Nagar, because it doesn't feel like Mumbai. The surrounding greenery and the absence of tall buildings remind him of his home back in Rajasthan's Sri Ganganagar, where he dabbled in several businesses before deciding to zero in on acting and filmmaking. It was because of his small-town roots that he would take a long while to adjust to Mumbai's fast-track ways. He first moved here in 2010 and spent two years in the city.

'I didn't even have the confidence to order a cappuccino. I used to be on the backfoot, felt suffocated,' he confided to me during an interview for *The Hindu*.[27]

Shah moved to Jaipur, shuttling between the Pink City and the Maximum City for four years, till he finally decided to confront Mumbai and set up base there in 2016.

According to him, there were only two things of consequence in Sri Ganganagar – cricket and Bollywood.

'Aamir, Shah Rukh and Salman have been Brahma–Vishnu–Mahesh for me,' he said.

And it was from films, not books, that he derived his real education.

'Aamir Khan inspired me to put my heart and soul in work,' he said. 'To do one thing at a time, but do it well. *Hum Aapke Hain Koun...!* made me value my family.'

And Shah Rukh Khan's charm and lack of inhibitions helped Shah realize that there was an urgent need for the socially inhibited person that he was to open up.

An MD in ayurveda and a national-level basketball player, Varanasi boy Vineet Kumar Singh had to wait for 17 long years – filled with inconsequential films and performances – to eventually land a lead role in *Mukkabaaz* (2017). He first came to Mumbai in

1999–2000 and still remembers witnessing the most heartbreaking part of an outsider's struggle as aspiring actor friends gave up trying to gain a foothold in the industry and decided to go back home. He also recalls being seized by the consequent overarching dread that it could happen to him as well.

'We used to get emotional while packing. There used to be silence. It felt like I was packing their dreams away,' he recollects in an interview for *The Hindu*.[28]

Like Tripathi, Shah and Singh, some of the biggest names of Bollywood have travelled all the way from the heartland and landed in the urban jungle that is Mumbai. There is Manoj Bajpayee, who was born in the small village of Belwa in Bihar, named after actor Manoj Kumar by his film-buff farmer parents and did his early schooling in Bettiah, where he also saw the earliest movies of his life.

They all bring with them trunkloads of memories, cultures, lingos and experiences, along with an ethos that is peculiar to each one of them. Some of these may have faded with time, but most have irrevocably influenced their work, both consciously and unconsciously. Some of their experiences may be congruent and others entirely at a tangent from each other, but they yield a treasure trove of anecdotes, heard and unheard, about how they experienced the magic of cinema while growing up at a distance from the dream factory that is Mumbai and how, eventually, they made their own journeys into Bollywood.

We spoke to a few of them and who better to start with than the biggest star of them all – Amitabh Bachchan – who was born in Allahabad in 1942 and would live there till 1956, moving to New Delhi when his father was transferred there?

'Those were my wonder years…' he tells us in an interview conducted over emails.

He still has vivid memories of the places his family lived in, the schools he and his brother, Ajitabh, went to, their neighbours…

Back then, the films that younger members of a family could watch were vetted by their parents. So the Bachchan boys saw Disney cartoons, *Laurel and Hardy* at the Capitol and later, a 1954 Hindi film *Jagriti*, directed by Satyen Bose.

'Cinema was a fascination,' Bachchan writes. 'Fascination for the visuals, the darkened halls and later, much later, for an air-conditioned theatre, the only one in the city.'

The swashbuckling heroes of those '50s' films and, of course, Dilip Kumar, were big stars back then. But cinema did nothing to influence Bachchan into becoming a film actor. There was the stage, the school plays he participated in every year, but the idea of acting in films was nowhere on his horizon in those days, he declares in an email.

The ambience, the décor and the whole process of watching a film would become more elaborate in the bigger cities, he writes.

'In small towns, visibility was the main attraction. In its absence, the stars became these elusive beings, perceived as living in some wonderland. So, when Kamini Kaushal, a huge star at that time, was passing through Allahabad in a train in the early '50s, the entire city came to a standstill,' he recalls. 'Those fortunate to have had a glimpse of her (among the millions that thronged the railway platform), had stories to tell. How her air-conditioned compartment's glass was broken by the eager crowds became the talking point for years. I remember it even now.'

Information and visibility have improved a millionfold through media and television in recent years. Personal contact with a star is just a picture away on the mobile. You can directly interact with them on social-media sites. So the enigma, the elusive aura around a star has been significantly watered down. But the small towns still retain a great passion for cinema and its stars, Bachchan believes.

According to him, small towns are an obvious attraction for our films and filmmakers because a majority of those connected with the medium all migrated from these places to Mumbai.

'Remembering one's roots is a genetic necessity and joy. We can never be too far away from our own "*mitti*"," he acknowledges, adding that every film of his that portrayed small-town culture and was steeped in that particular ambience has been among his greatest joys to work in. 'The essence of the small town breathes through our performances, willingly or unwillingly [consciously or unconsciously].'

From Big B's erudite, well-articulated recollections, we come to Anupam Kher's colourful ones. Perhaps, not many are aware that Kher's onscreen debut happened much before he starred in the 1984 Mahesh Bhatt–directed *Saaransh* that not only pushed him into the limelight but fetched him and the film's director a Filmfare Award each. It was, in fact, in Yash Chopra's 1973 film *Daag* that was being shot in Shimla, with Rajesh Khanna, Sharmila Tagore and Raakhee in the lead, that Kher made his very first screen appearance as part of the 500-strong starstruck crowd that had gathered at the shoot, only to unwittingly become part of the film.

'There is one trolley shot in *Daag*, which I often freeze to show people what was unofficially my first break in films,' Kher says with a smile.

Though originally from Kashmir, the actor was born and raised in Simla (now Shimla), one of Bollywood's favourite locales in those days. It was here that Sikander Khanna was shooting his 1975 film *Umar Quaid*, with Sunil Dutt, Vinod Mehra, Jeetendra, Moushumi Chatterjee, Reena Roy and Asrani. Since Kher was learning drama at the time, he was cast as an extra.

'I was mesmerized by the whole experience, by even the food we used to eat on the sets every day,' Kher recalls. 'I boasted endlessly to my friends: that I was doing one of the main roles, how I was friendly with the big stars. So my entourage of friends and *chamchas* [hangers-on] became even bigger than what it already was.'

One day, Kher was hanging out with his group on the Mall Road when the stars of the film walked past.

'I was petrified that they'd ignore me and the cat would be out of the bag,' the actor remembers. 'But Asrani remembered me and gave me a wide smile. That acknowledgment made me an even bigger star amongst my friends.'

Shimla had practically no source of entertainment back then, other than the four cinema halls – Shahi, Ritz, Rivoli and Regal.

'These halls were our pilgrimage points and films were our fantasies, our dream world,' Kher remembers.

There was not much to do; life was slow and monotonous, and cinema provided a release, some much-needed excitement and a sense of adventure.

'Our lives depended on films,' Kher declares. 'In fact, there was such a passion for movies in Shimla that there is this tale about how a landslide struck Rivoli during a show of *Do Chor*. The right-hand wall broke down, but the film continued to be shown.'

The government also organized open-air film screenings on the streets around residential neighbourhoods. A dirty white screen would come up from nowhere and most of the films shown were educational – like Dev Anand's 1960's release *Ek ke Baad Ek*, which was on family planning.

'Later, when I got educated in cinema, saw world cinema, I realized how much the Italian film *Cinema Paradiso* reflected our own quirky way of growing up with cinema,' says Kher.

The seed of the desire to become an actor was planted in those years, but at a subconscious level.

'When three of us friends watched *The Good, the Bad and the Ugly*, we all wore hats and whistled along [with the popular theme music],' the actor reminisces.

He still remembers watching *Jagriti*, *Dil ek Mandir* and *Dosti* (1964) in Shimla. There was Manoj Kumar's *Shaheed* (1965), *Upkar* (1967) and *Balidaan* (1971).

'These films affected us for days together,' Kher admits.

Dara Singh's 1965 releases *Lootera* and *Tarzan 3003* were also big hits. It was for Dilip Kumar's 1970 film *Gopi* that Kher bunked class for the first time to watch a movie.

'We were caned in school, but that didn't deter us from [going out to watch] the films,' Kher confesses.

He also remembers that in college, the best way to date a girl was to take her out for a horror film. There was always this unspoken promise that she'd hold your hand and cling to you in fear.

'I took mine for *The Exorcist*. And in the iconic scene in which the girl's head turns 180-degrees, not only did she hold my hand, but bit my finger out of fear,' he smiles.

For Nawazuddin Siddiqui, life in a farmer's family in Budhana, about 40 km from Muzaffarnagar, was more banal than scintillating. It was all about fields (of *gehoon* and *ganna*, wheat and sugarcane), the harvest, the cows and buffaloes they would feed, the *kheera* and *kakdi* (cucumbers) they used to steal from adjoining fields. His most powerful memories of growing up in Budhana are those of people who were somewhat like the films themselves – brilliant at telling stories.

'They were the locals; they used to gather in the neighbourhood, sit in the shops and tell interesting tales in their inimitable style,' he recalls. 'They gave Mahabharata and Ramayana their own interpretation and spin. They gave the impression as though the real understanding of Indian politics started and ended with them. They were our main source of entertainment.'

However, in the name of cinema, all they had was a semi-built structure with a tin roof, which showed C-grade films, 'the *khoon ka badla khoon* variety,' as he puts it.

Joginder, Dada Kondke and later, Kanti Shah were the popular filmmakers; and Mahendra Sandhu was the big hero.

'I could only see these fringe films in Budhana, not the mainstream Bollywood [ones]. In fact, I never saw Bollywood [films] in my younger days. After moving to the National School of Drama, all I got to watch was [Jean-Luc] Godard and [Federico] Fellini. I grew up between these two extremes of filmmaking: world cinema and the substandard fare,' he confides.

Budhana falls in a belt known for its aggression and gun culture;

it's a crime-prone zone. The films that do well here are also those with action, stunts and fights.

'So my *Gangs of Wasseypur* gets accepted, but there are no takers for a *Miss Lovely*,' Siddiqui explains.

As for himself, the one film of his that he could identify a lot with was Ketan Mehta's *Mountain Man*, because it emerges from the real, mofussil India that he belongs to. Shot in actual locations in Gaya district's Gehlore, it's a biopic on Dashrath Manjhi, the poor, low-caste villager from Bihar who spent 22 years of his life carving a road out of a mountain. With just a hammer and sickle in hand he was determined to open up his isolated village to the world because the absence of hospitals in the vicinity and even an access road to medical facilities further away had prevented him from taking his seriously injured wife, Falguni Devi, to a doctor in time following an accident. Falguni's death had set her grieving husband on this extraordinary path.

Living and growing up in four cities has given lyricist, writer and comic Varun Grover a varied experience at the movies. His first exposure to film was as a four or five year old in Sundarnagar, Himachal Pradesh. All he remembers of the 1982 release *Nikaah* is a scene where Raj Babbar bumps into a cow, making everybody in the audience laugh.

It was in Dehradun that Grover started taking serious note of film for the first time. Going to cinemas – perhaps, three or four times a year – was a big occasion for them. *Tridev*, released in 1989, starring Naseeruddin Shah, Sunny Deol, Jackie Shroff and Madhuri Dixit, had created a buzz and that was the first time ever that Grover and his family bought tickets at black-market rates – that too for stall seats.

As for *Maine Pyar Kiya*, he overheard somebody at school recounting how he had thrown coins at the screen when the '*Kabootar ja ja*' song came on screen.

'I wanted to go and watch the film just to do this,' Grover admits. 'My younger brother and I were ready with two–three coins each when the song [sequence] came [was shown]. Over the loud sound of music, one could still hear the clinking of coins being thrown and, on cue, we also threw ours. I don't think they even reached the screen. We were in balcony [seats] and we were just seven and nine-year-old kids; but still, it was a community exercise, almost [like a] religious [ritual], like how we would throw coins in [the] Ganga or Yamuna on every rail trip [when the train crossed the bridges] over these rivers.'

The first film they saw in the next city they moved to – Lucknow – marked Ajay Devgn's debut – *Phool aur Kaante*. It was probably the first 'adult' film Grover would watch.

'I still feel uncomfortable thinking about the vulgarity, misogyny (though I didn't know the term or concept then) and violence it had,' he says.

It was in Lucknow that he also graduated to going out for movies with friends, away from the watchful eyes of his parents. When three of them went to watch the 1997 Govinda–Karisma Kapoor–starrer *Hero No. 1*, there was a lucky draw based on seat numbers and their seat numbers were J7, 8, and 9.

'A friend of mine (Sandeep Singh) said, "Let me sit on J9, as 9 is my lucky number." And amazingly, we did win that contest,' Grover remembers. 'More fascinating for me was that seat number J9 was flashed on [the] big screen during the interval. It was like seeing your name on the big screen for the first time, though it was just a seat number one of us was sitting on. We won a T-series ceiling fan, which we gave back to the theatre owner and he gave us ₹300 in its stead. With my share of ₹100, I treated my younger brother to the first ever fancy Chinese dinner of our lives.'

Within a week of landing in Varanasi for his engineering course at the Indian Institute of Technology (BHU), Grover went to watch his first ever porn film at Ganga Talkies, which had a huge Shiva statue engraved on its outer wall. It was a theatre infamous for screening such movies. In Varanasi, he further graduated to the joy of watching films alone.

'Probably, the greatest self-realization any movie-buff stumbles upon – a lot of movies reveal their full gifts [potential] only when seen alone,' Grover believes.

He watched Govind Nihalani's 1999 release *Thakshak* alone at Saajan Cinema, as no friend was willing to go for a film with such a boring art-house title.

Having lived in both UP cities, just a few hundred kilometres apart, Grover feels impelled to compare the film-viewing cultures of Lucknow and Varanasi.

'Cinema in Lucknow was (and still is, as far as I know) a family affair,' he tells me. 'Films are judged not just by their quality, but by how "*saaf suthri*" (clean) they are. A lot of people (even youngsters) would ask that question first: "*Saaf suthri* film *hai, na*?"'.

Varanasi, owing to its huge student and migrant population, offers more of a bachelor's (though mostly male bachelors) viewing experience, along with a more liberal view of themes and genres.

'I remember watching [2001 release] *Aks* [starring Amitabh Bachchan] in a house-full theatre in Banaras [now Varanasi] and then again, in Lucknow, in a nearly empty hall,' says Grover.

In Lucknow, the 1997 Hollywood blockbuster *Titanic* created a huge buzz, especially the scenes of the ship sinking and the epic story behind it. The small problem, however, was talk circulating about the nude scene. So Grover's parents went to watch the film on their own first, to decide if their offspring should be allowed to see it. Grover and his brother were eventually sent off to see *Titanic* in the second week following its release in town.

'It was a clear moment, if there can ever be, of being told that you've grown up,' he acknowledges. 'Me and my brother, alone in the hall, watching that nude scene (it was *not* cut out [censored] to our amazement and [that] they [his parents] still sent us [to watch the film]), is a landmark memory in my movie-watching life.'

As compared to how it used to be in Lucknow and Varanasi, Grover feels movie-watching in Mumbai rarely evokes the feeling of a community experience. He is of the view that cinema should open up a new world or reveal new layers to a world we are already familiar with.

'And all this I probably learned from the collective sighs, catcalls, claps and yawns observed in so many of those single screens in these four cities,' he tells me.

Like Grover, actor Nimrat Kaur also grew up in several places across India. As the offspring of an army man, home for her was in the cantonments of several small towns – Yingkiong in Arunachal Pradesh, and Bhatinda (or Bathinda, as it is now known) and Patiala in Punjab. The first film she saw was the 1976 Hollywood horror film *The Omen* screened in an open-air theatre in Pune. It was in Bhatinda that she was fed on a diet of Hindi films: *Qayamat Se Qayamat Tak, Dil, Beta*... She recalls watching *Mr India* 40 times.

'Life in [the] army is protected and insulated,' Kaur explains. 'The Lux ads with film heroines then felt like dreams from a different planet. I was fascinated by the number of times the hero–heroine would change their clothes in a song on *Chitrahaar*. They didn't seem real, but mythical. They intrigued me, made me curious.'

She looks back at herself as an impressionable, exhibitionistic kid, who would slavishly copy Madhuri Dixit in '*Ek do teen*...' right down to the side ponytail.

In a chat with me back in 2015, Kaur had recalled a visit to the New Majestic cinema hall in Ajmer, one of the oldest theatres in India. They were showing Akshay Kumar's 1996 release *Sapoot*.

'It felt as though one was caught in some kind of time warp,' she muses.

New Majestic is totally rundown and shows only old films of the '80s and '90s. There are still spools and reels used here.

'It felt like a world that does exist, but not really. It was an eye-opener for me,' she reveals.

Kaur echoes Big B's sentiment that in the theatres in small places, you can sense the awe and anticipation in the audience.

'Actors are demigods that they pray to,' she says. 'Cinema is [a] religion. In big cities, the world gets bigger; these same stars feel more accessible. You can spot an Arjun Rampal on a bike on Carter Road and say a casual "hi" to him.'

Actor Randeep Hooda, who was born in Rohtak and spent his early years in a boarding school – Motilal Nehru School of Sports in Rai, Sonepat – says that the campus had its own unique world within the small town. Cloistered, like the kids in the army cantonments mentioned by Kaur, Hooda and his schoolmates were shown an English film every Saturday; a Hindi film was a monthly treat. He grew up on the films of Charlton Heston, Alec Guinness and Harrison Ford.

'I guess those early films have been the reason why I have gravitated more towards realistic [rather] than larger-than-life films,' he says.

Big B's 1978 film *Don*, with Zeenat Aman as his leading lady, the 1985 Dharmendra–Mithun Chakraborty–starrer *Ghulami*, the 1987 Ketan Mehta–directed *Mirch Masala* were family favourites; and Dharmendra was the unrivalled household superstar.

'He had the macho look that went down well with the Jats,' Hooda explains.

The leap from Haryana to the North East might seem a huge one; not, however, when it comes to the love for cinema. So you have actor Adil Hussain growing up in the picturesque, but neglected, district town of Goalpara in Assam. It's a little town on the Brahmaputra, where the newspaper would arrive three days after it had been published. Hussain distinctly remembers the two cinema halls in the town and his earliest memory is of watching Raj Kapoor's *Mera Naam Joker*.

'Like the young kid in the film, I also instantly fell in love with Simi Garewal back then,' he confesses. 'Through the high school [years], I remember bunking classes every Friday to watch films of Hema Malini, Dharmendra and Randhir Kapoor. Films like [the 1973 Dharmendra–Hema Malini–starrer] *Jugnu*, *Rickshawala* [released the same year, with Randhir Kapoor and Neetu Singh as the lead pair], *Yaadon ki Baraat* [with Zeenat Aman and Vijay Arora, 1973].'

Once he bunked classes for five consecutive Fridays. There were also Bengali and Assamese films on offer and, once in a while, some

English-language sex movies that were screened during the morning shows, which they were barred from. But there was no avenue at all for thought-provoking, alternate Hindi films. It was only the commercial stuff which travelled all the way to Goalpara.

As Hussain remembers it, films shaped their mindsets, determined their social equations and helped them express their feelings in relationships.

'We imbibed our ideas and beliefs from them. We still do,' he affirms.

Unlike, say, Kolkata, Mumbai or Delhi, where people are more committed to their own culture, are more aware of and exposed to other cultures, the Assamese are more innocent and naive, generous and gullible, he feels.

'Therefore, perhaps, the impact of films on us has been much deeper and life-altering,' is how the actor sees it.

Hussain also looks back at Hindi films as the medium that ensured their exposure to the Hindi language.

'We learnt it by watching films. So by the time I enrolled in the National School of Drama in Delhi, my Hindi enunciation had become pretty good, except, perhaps, the eternal problem between "d" and "r". I used to pronounce "*gaadi*" as "*gaari*" for quite a while,' he confesses.

Hindi films were their bridge to the world outside.

Later, politics would take over. The United Liberation Front of Assam, along with the All Assam Students Union (AASU), took up cudgels against the 'linguistic and cultural imperialism' that Hindi films represented for them and imposed restrictions on their public screening.

You may have taken lyricist, writer and actor Swanand Kirkire out of his hometown, Indore, but Indore hasn't quite left him. He tells us how living in a state surrounded by other states, he was exposed to a mix of the neighbouing Marathi, Gujarati and Marwari cultures. There was lots of Indian classical music around and good Marathi theatre.

'It's a well in itself. An island in its own prosperity and progress,' he observes.

Indore had been modelled and built like Mumbai and Ahmedabad. It had yarn mills and a cloth market, and was referred to as 'mini Mumbai'.

'We never figured time by our watches; it was always by the sirens of the mills,' Kirkire informs me.

That was a time – the '70s and '80s – when Indore had 29 cinema halls. Of them, two screened only Hollywood films.

'I saw all my Chaplins there,' says Kirkire.

A lot of films from the parallel-cinema genre were also screened. MP Film Development Corporation put in a great deal of effort between 1985–90 to get good films to Indore.

'I saw the Indian panorama there, films like *Nayakan* [Mani Ratnam's 1987 release, with Kamal Haasan in the lead], Adoor [Gopalakrishnan] and Sudhir [Mishra] retrospectives,' he recalls, elaborating further on the town's film literacy. 'I would see Govinda, Mithun films like *Sahhas* [Chakraborty's 1981 release with Rati Agnihotri as his leading lady], *Wanted* [the 2009 Salman Khan film with Govinda in a special appearance], *Heeron ka Chor* [Mitun Chakraborty's 1982 action film] alongside Jabbar Patel's [1982 Marathi film] *Umbartha* [with Smita Patil in the lead], [Shyam] Benegal's *Nishant* and [Govind] Nihalani's *Aakrosh*. I could figure how Naseer's performance would vary in [Goutam Ghose-directed 1984 feature film] *Paar* from that in [Naseeruddin Shah's 1987 action film] *Jalwa*. I also saw many old black-and-white classics on [the] big screen. Like [the 1949 Raj Kapoor–Nargis–starrer] *Barsaat* and [the 1958 Kishore Kumar comedy] *Chalti ka Naam Gaadi* [where both the actor-singer's brothers, along with leading lady Madhubala, were his co-stars]. The entire spectrum of movies was available to us.'

In the '70s and '80s, Indore fell within Bollywood's CP-CI distribution territory and served as the testing ground for commercial Hindi films. They would release a day earlier here, that is, on a Thursday, to check market response. Subsequently, films began being released on Fridays, as in the rest of the country.

'Film-viewing was a serious business there,' Kirkire remembers. 'It was not a routine, but a celebration, a big moment of life. I remember my shirt had got torn in the mad rush for booking tickets for first day, first show of [Amitabh Bachchan's 1984 release] *Sharaabi*, but the joy of finally managing to get them [the tickets] in my hand was unforgettable. That madness for movies has now gone.'

Actor Manav Kaul was born in Baramulla, Kashmir, and spent his childhood in Hoshangabad, Madhya Pradesh. College, the beginnings of his interest in theatre and his general coming-of-age happened in Bhopal, after which he moved to Mumbai in 1998.

Kaul recalls watching *Do aur Do Paanch*, the 1980 release with Amitabh Bachchan heading the multi-star cast, in Baramulla, completely mesmerized by what was unfolding on screen: 'There was this lovely two-storey military theatre there, where we were taken to watch films.'

Another favourite memory is of a particular audio cassette of the film *Sholay* his father once bought them: 'It had all the songs, of course, but also all the dialogues. Basically, it was the entire film in audio format. We couldn't really afford another cassette, so my brother and I learnt the entire film by heart. I loved imagining what the scenes must be like and would listen to it every day without fail.'

Cinema was the most fantastical thing that could have happened to them.

'I believed everything that was happening onscreen. This larger-than-life element really shook me. It was as if some invisible god was telling us the story of this man, how he lived this life, with songs and women and, sometimes, tragedy,' he recalls.

Happiness was a ticket and a seat. Watching a film was a really big deal; it happened rarely and they were privileged if they got to watch a show on its opening weekend. It was all very real; it never occurred to them that this could have anything to do with the world of make-believe.

'We were so far away from Bombay that the reality behind [the] cameras never hit us,' he remembers. 'We never met, in our day-to-day lives, people who worked as, say, extras or spot boys or, you know, a dresswalla. The sense of wonder was intact – which I am very thankful for.'

Amitabh Bachchan was huge, then, and Kaul was a crazy fan of his, like everyone else. He remembers the hand-painted posters from that time and how they highlighted the actor's hair with a hint of blue.

'I thought that suited him and seriously considered dyeing my hair blue!' he confesses.

Later, Bruce Lee, Jackie Chan and Shah Rukh Khan would enter his world.

The kind of cinematic exposure they were getting wasn't something he could participate in.

'It was an unreal fantasy – far away and inaccessible,' he recalls.

His understanding of cinema as a child and as an adult has been very different.

'It was an alternate universe – no one could imagine being a part of it,' he muses. 'We would watch a movie once in a blue moon and then reminisce about it for ages.'

He watched a movie with friends for the first time in Bhopal and still relishes that sense of freedom. But understanding films was still far away. That happened much later, when he came to Mumbai.

His favourite still remains that two-storey Military Talkies in Khojabad, his small village in Baramulla district. Years later, he was visiting a small town called Itarsi and went to watch *Bade Miyan Chote Miyan*, a 1998 release with Amitabh Bachchan and Govinda in the lead roles, on its opening weekend at a single-screen there.

'They had put a string of lights around the screen which would light up and sparkle during the songs; it was eating up corners of the screen, but people did not mind,' he tells me. 'They were going crazy dancing and shouting. It was the most jubilant thing! Every theatre put their [its] own energy into the screening of a film and that kind of made it special.'

In Mumbai, Kaul got to learn that there were two sides to the camera – one in front of it and one behind it. And, of course, he witnessed the insane circus around it.

'The sense of wonder gradually diminished, but a very strong love for the form took its place,' he says.

He realized that cinema was its own world – so many genres, so many countries, so many different styles, so many different cultures of storytelling. He began to pick and choose – the director whose films he would go and watch, actors he liked to watch, stories he wanted to see interpreted on screen. He became an active viewer and participant. What he misses now is the all-consuming awe for what is showing.

'No one is wonderstuck!' he says ruefully.

Kaul loves the way small towns allow one to make discoveries, big or small.

'These gentle surprises are precious; they make for a more fulfilling adventure and, for me, that is what life is... I am [a] slave to a sense of adventure,' he admits.

Big cities tend to make one jaded and he is not the one for tiresome tales; he likes to stay mesmerized.

Having said that, one has to acknowledge that small towns today are very different from how they were half a decade ago. Everyone now has access to the Internet and a vast array of entertainment options. This will inevitably dilute, to some extent, the excitement that films bring with them. But Kaul would like to believe that this will lead to a newer culture of storytelling.

Says he: 'Someone who is growing up in a tiny town far away from Mumbai and watching Hrithik Roshan on his computer screen will, perhaps, have a whole new experience to share. Distance from anything makes you either worship it or gives you enough clarity to see it for what it really is. These are both very intriguing points to start a story from!'

They are indeed.

Small Towns on Big Screens

ON 1 MARCH 2019, two Hindi films, both set in the same region of north India, were released: *Sonchiriya*, starring Sushant Singh Rajput, Manoj Bajpayee, Bhumi Pednekar and Ranvir Shorey, and *Luka Chuppi*, with Kriti Sanon of *Bareilly ki Barfi* fame and Kartik Aaryan in the lead. The films' approach to their locations and how they used them offer an interesting insight into the extent to which the heartland narrative has been embraced and the manner in which our notion of it is evolving in Hindi cinema, especially in the last three or four years.

Laxman Utekar's *Luka Chuppi* is ostensibly about negotiating a live-in relationship in Uttar Pradesh's Mathura and Madhya Pradesh's Gwalior, but it hardly has anything 'lived in' about it when it comes to the two towns it features. There are barely any discernible cultural nuances or local flavours to speak of, other than the Yamuna River, a sprinkling of temples in the background and the incantation of 'Radhe, Radhe' – typical of the Braj region – interspersing the dialogues. These apart, the film could well have been set and shot just about anywhere – in Delhi, Mumbai or New York.

Sonchiriya, on the other hand, has the veritable boondocks as its backdrop; it has been shot in the ravines of the Chambal region. Its itinerant filmmaker Abhishek Chaubey, who has travelled to the interiors of India for all his films till date – from Gorakhpur in *Ishqiya* and Lucknow in *Dedh Ishqiya*, to the small towns and villages of Punjab in *Udta Punjab* – calls the area 'gobsmackingly beautiful', but it wasn't so much its picturesque appeal as the quest for authenticity that drew him, along with his cast and crew, to Dholpur, Rajasthan, and Gwalior.

A combination of two genres – the 'Western' and the Indian dacoit drama – *Sonchiriya* is about the fate of a group of bandits in the Chambal during the state of Emergency imposed on the country by the Indira Gandhi–ruled administration between 1975 and 1977. With a huge political upheaval taking place across India, how were the badlands and their infamous residents affected? Was there a shift in the power play between the state, the police and the dacoits during those turbulent times? These are some of the questions that *Sonchiriya* addresses.

In the telling of this particular tale, the film draws from many real-life stories, issues and actual people, but most crucial for Chaubey was the specificity of the locale where the tradition and culture of dacoity had existed for decades without inspiring very many serious films about them, other than a rare *Bandit Queen* (Shekhar Kapoor) in 1996 or *Paan Singh Tomar* (Tigmanshu Dhulia) 16 years later.

It is in a particular location and milieu, steeped in patriarchy and caste, social and gender discrimination, that the theme of *Sonchiriya* is entrenched. Be it the smothered, abused, violated women, seething with inner rebellion, or the rough, brutal men and their misplaced notions of masculinity – both belong to the Chambal as much as the Chambal lives on in them.

In *Sonchiriya,* Chaubey evokes a sense of place by moving beyond the region's stark, arid, larger-than-life landscape. It is apparent in the Bundeli the dacoits conduct their conversations in, the raw, risqué humour that sparks their interchanges. Their body language and attire, their mindsets and perceptions are rich in local flavour. The region's shared culture emerges in the minutest of details – whether it's the reference to the guns used in the 1962 war between India and China or the Special Task Force set up to capture the dacoits in the region, the morning crackle of the radio with AIR's signature tune or then Prime Minister Indira Gandhi's declaration of the Emergency over the air waves.

It is between these polarities – the token realism of *Luka Chuppi* and a deep sense of rootedness in the local culture that *Sonchiriya* conveys – that a clutch of Bollywood films with a small-town backdrop remains suspended.

Luka Chuppi is just one in the long line of recent Hindi films where a small town has been turned into a formula with its own defined arcs – the heartland serving as a visually appealing backdrop in a desperate attempt to pump novelty into an otherwise ho-hum plot and painfully familiar love story. So you have the small town looking resplendent in Eastman colour, packaged in all its panoramic grandeur, proving that visually, Lucknow and Bareilly can be just as fetching as Switzerland.

'District tourism' is how media commentator Sudheesh Pachauri describes the perspective and intent of these films, but is careful to add that none of them attempt a 'radical exploration of a rapidly changing and modernizing world that it is set in'.

The usual token 'supporting' characters, distinguished by one over-the-top quirk or another, are rounded up to serve as friends and family members of the hero and heroine. The room for nuance is kept tightly on a leash in these 'light-hearted, small-town romcoms'. If there is any discernible attempt at infusing local colour, it is quite superficial, emerging in a turn of phrase here, a display of attitude there, in the ethnic attire of a character or two, or in the expression of a worldview popularly believed to be in keeping with the social mores of the place. There is no serious effort to explore in depth the social realism underlying their environment.

The small town depicted in a film like this one is intended to serve as a pretty backdrop for some romance and fun; the spice, as it were, to enhance the flavour of the whole package, ready for consumption in urban multiplexes. Writer and columnist Santosh Desai believes that the specificity of a small town and the accompanying realism, however cosmetic, do still manage to add 'textures' and 'grains' to a film and are often, along with its rawness and freshness of emotion, an appealing counterpoint to the tired big-city narratives of love and romance that almost always turn out to be about the multiplicity of choices on offer in contemporary urban man–woman relationships and the inevitable fallout – commitment phobia.

A film's provincial setting is meant to be offered as a surprise gift to urban viewers in whose imagination small towns continue to be insular and 'conservative', even regressive, whereas in reality, a 'sexual revolution' could well be in full swing there.

'[A] small town offers more cinematic room, becomes a shorthand to project change, explore and measure it,' Desai observes.

What better examples of this phenomenon than *Manmarziyaan* (Anurag Kashyap, 2018), with Taapsee Pannu cast opposite Vicky Kaushal and Abhishek Bachchan, and *Running Shaadi* (Amit Roy), also featuring Pannu, released a year earlier? But that awareness of social realities remains, at best, facile; it fails to cut deep. So while the seemingly progressive, non-interfering parents of the heroine in *Bareilly ki Barfi* (Ashwini Iyer Tiwari, 2017) may have no objections to her smoking and drinking, her need to hang out with boys, getting her married off to a 'suitable boy' still remains the ultimate goal of their lives.

Badrinath ki Dulhania (Shashank Khaitan, 2017), a Karan Johar production starring Varun Dhawan and Alia Bhatt, barely skims the surface of small-town realism, emerging in the surnames, in the wit that comes through some of the dialogues, in the middle-class preoccupation with provident funds and loans, and in the *maata ka jagrata,* a religious ritual devoted to the Goddess Durga and observed by the Hindu faithful. The intercity Kota–Jhansi (via Mumbai and Singapore) love story about patriarchy and gender inequity is careful about not venturing too far. It is content to gently nudge the societal system, instead of daring to take a radical stand against it. While minor negotiations in this regard do take place, the larger framework – the problem of patriarchy – is left unaddressed, intact. In short, it's all about a rebellion within permissible limits.

The boundaries get defined for the woman, in particular. In *Luka Chuppi*, for instance, the heroine chooses to live in with a man, but can't shake off the weight of the *sindoor-mangalsutra* combo – the traditional symbols of matrimony to which a young bride is yoked in conservative households. Interestingly enough, she is eager to accept it; getting married is, eventually, mandatory. In *Badrinath ki Dulhania*, on the other hand, it is the woman who is the heartening initiator of change. The smart, educated girl from Kota wants to fly high, rather than allow her restricted life to clip her wings, tether her to humdrum routine. She opts for a career of her choice over marriage with someone she can't relate to. All of which is totally understandable. But the contrived and entirely unconvincing twist at the interval turns her, rather unfairly, into the villain of the story. For the rest of the film, she has to keep fighting the guilt of putting herself before family, society and Badri.

Filmmaker Aanand L. Rai, known for fathering recent mainstream small-town narratives like *Tanu Weds Manu* (2011), starring Kangana Ranaut, R. Madhavan and Jimmy Shergill, and *Raanjhana* (2013), with Sonam Kapoor and Dhanush in the lead, looks at these films as successors to the Sai Paranjape–Basu Chatterjee–Hrishikesh Mukherjee school of filmmaking, with one difference – the locales have shifted from cities to small towns, perhaps because the urban middle class that used to be the focus of the earlier films has undergone too radical a metamorphosis to serve as an appropriate milieu for such stories any more.

'It's nostalgia for a world gone by,' says Rai.

He remembers life in a laidback, unhurried Delhi, sleeping on the terrace under the stars, listening to Hindi film songs on the transistor radio late into the night.

'Those were the days when parents had time to spend with their children,' he recalls, 'and even if families could barely make ends meet, there was always enough food on the table, even for guests. We have become more formal in our interactions now.'[29]

According to him, it's these little joys that he consciously seeks out in the worlds he creates in his stories.

Over the years, he has come to be known for bringing alive the Hindi heartland on the big screen – the bylanes of Varanasi, Kanpur, Haridwar, Lucknow, Agra and Amritsar. He has created his own updated, contemporary, colourful version of 'small-town cinema' that runs parallel to Bollywood's metro and NRI-centred flicks.

'I am a true-to-life location kind of person, someone who wouldn't have even seen film sets,' he acknowledges.

Abhishek Chaubey's small-town aesthetic might be diametrically opposite to Rai's – that is, far from romantic or steeped in nostalgia – but he does echo the other filmmaker's thoughts when he describes the location as a 'necessary crutch'.

'I won't be able to make a film unless it's about a place,' he tells me. 'It's very difficult for me to imagine a film that is not rooted strongly in a milieu or space.'

So his *Ishqiya* was all about Gorakhpur, *Dedh Ishqiya* romanced Lucknow and *Udta Punjab* highlighted the location in its very title.

In an earlier interview with me, Chaubey had said, 'If I had placed *Ishqiya* [2010] in Mumbai, it would not have worked. It is in a world like that of rough and rustic Gorakhpur – a world of arms smuggling and gang wars, of anarchy and violence, and of castes and clans, the Thakurs, Yadavs, Pandeys – that Krishna, the wily, deceitful, manipulative and exploitative widow played by Vidya Balan, comes across as truly emancipated. In Mumbai, her liberated ways would not have been as striking.'

Ishqiya and *Dedh Ishqiya* may seem similar in the way they deal with deceit and deception, but the resemblance is merely a cosmetic one. *Dedh Ishqiya* that released four years after *Ishqiya* is more about a subculture in the Awadh region. Here, crime is served, sodden in nostalgia, in Awadh's Mahmoodabad. It is an arcane world of *sher-o-shairi* and mushairas, ghazals and qawwalis and magnificent, crumbling havelis. Here, crime abides by its own unique etiquette, underscored by an unwritten code that rides high on *adab*, *tehzeeb* and *saleeka*.

'I did not go for realism, but created an alternate world, a world that was there, but is now no more,' Chaubey had taken pains to explain to me. 'The elaborate achkans were worn once upon a time; people did quote Mirza Ghalib. But the nawabs don't have any money in their pockets now. The mushairas have become more like noisy political rallies. This sense of loss makes things poignant.'

Each of his films spoke in its own local Hindi dialect. As Mihir Pandya, a professor of Hindi from Delhi University, points out, Chaubey has used different language families in each of his films: Magadhi Apabhransha in *Ishqiya*, Ardh Magadhi Apabhransha in *Dedh Ishqiya*, Paishachi/Lahanda Apabhramsha in *Udta Punjab* and now, Shauraseni Apabhramsha in *Sonchiriya*.

Anurag Kashyap is another filmmaker who gets the nuances of language pitch-perfect.

'North India is like a home ground,' he explained to me during an interview for *The Hindu*, referring to the dialogues and lyrics in *Mukkabaaz*, a 2017 Indian sports drama that he had co-written, directed and produced.[30] 'I know the language so well. It is so ingrained in me. Someone pointed out the dialogues from *Shool*, the Lallan dialogues in *Yuva*, [Gangs of] *Wasseypur*, *Gulaal* and this [*Mukkabaaz*]; that I should keep making films in north India. "*Bahut hua samman*" is borrowed from a very popular parlance in the university; you will see a very abusive version of it there. [Poet, writer and lyricist] Hussain Haidry came up with "*Aisi ki taisi*" and it became something else. "*Mushkil hai apna meil priye*" is a very popular 2001 poem by Sunil Jogi [a writer with a special talent for comic verses]. All we did was contemporize it.'

Chaubey has been unofficially anointed Hindi cinema's heartland filmmaker, along with Kashyap (*Dev D* and *Gulaal*, both released in 2009, *Gangs of Wasseypur*, 2012, *Mukkabaaz* and *Manmarziyaan*), Tigmanshu Dhulia (*Haasil*, 2003, *Saheb, Biwi aur Gangster*, 2011, *Paan*

Singh Tomar, 2012) and Vishal Bhardwaj (*Omkara*, 2006, *Matru ki Bijli ka Mandola*, 2013, *Pataakha*, 2018) as the other two members of the quartet. And we have Aanand L. Rai (*Tanu Weds Manu, Raanjhana)* bringing up the rear in the more commercial mainstream zone.

In fact, Chaubey's engagement with hinterland politics owes a lot to his guru and mentor in filmmaking, Vishal Bhardwaj. It was Bhardwaj's *Omkara* – Shakespeare's *Othello*, set in the badlands of western UP – that is often held up as a precursor to the more rooted, contemporary explorations of the heartland in Bollywood. A true blue Indian Wild West, of which *Sonchiriya* could well be a progeny.

During an interview with me for *Outlook* in 2006, around the time *Omkara* released, Bhardwaj had confided how he originally thought of the jealous Moor as captain of the Indian cricket team, with the credulous Cassio and the scheming Iago jostling for the slot of vice-captain. It didn't work. He then considered setting the tragedy in a submarine during one of the Indo–Pak wars, but eventually dismissed the concept as too gimmicky.[31]

Shakespeare's plays, with their dramatic power and the impact of the universal truths that emerge from their delineation of human nature, have always lent themselves well to adaptation, however different the era, the geographical location or the social milieu.

'It would have been easy to place it in the period setting of Rajasthan,' Bhardwaj had admitted, 'but I wanted an unseen, exciting, striking place.'

He then decided to turn to the environment he had grown up in and, in the process, brought alive a whole new landscape and culture on screen, authentic to the last detail: a world ensconced in the mores of the past, yet caught in the throes of change; a world invaded by Sumos, television sets and mobile-phone mania.

'We need to create new worlds in our cinema,' Bhardwaj had reflected during the interview.

To that end, he relocated *Othello* in the rustic, violence-prone districts of western UP. The brutality of this world came alive on screen in a myriad ways. It was manifest not only in its harsh, rugged landscape or in the blood and gore that accompanied the killings, but also in the rough dialect and relentless flow of cusswords. In a way, the film magnified the scope of Shakespeare's story, turning one man's private tragedy into that of an entire community and region, and Bhardwaj's ingenuity lay in faithfully capturing the minutiae of contemporary small-town society and politics. In keeping with the tempo and tenor of such a world, Desdemona became the docile, vulnerable, waif-like Dolly, who could well have been Bharati Yadav of the infamous, real-life Nitish Katara murder case. Fine detailing went into the transformation of the central protagonist: Othello became Omkara Shukla or Omi, the '*adha*-Baaman', a half-Brahmin born of a low-caste mother and a high-caste father – the reason why he is unacceptable to the girl's family as a prospective son-in-law.

'Every Othello has been made black. I felt I could [draw an Indian] parallel [by portraying] the Moor as a half-caste,' Bhardwaj had explained, while discussing the issue of casteist politics in his film.

Abhishek Chaubey gets a different kind of high from heading to the interiors. He describes it as one of the joys of being a filmmaker: 'You go to a new place and completely do a new thing.'

For him, every film then becomes a fresh endeavour, not the same old job he had on hand two or three years ago. It's also as much about the discovery of India and its people as it is about trying to understand them.

This kind of engagement with the heartland has not been a conventional Bollywood trait. Filmmakers from regional-language cinema originating in places as diverse as Tamil Nadu, Kerala and West Bengal, for instance, have enjoyed a distinct advantage in being truer to their culture. In contrast, Hindi commercial films, following the brief post-Independence wave of grassroots, village-centric cinema, gradually evolved into a vehicle of entertainment for a society that has, traditionally, been deeply divided, not just in terms of beliefs, but also in terms of culture and language.

'Hindi cinema is like Rajasthan *mein bhi dekho*, Kolkata *mein bhi dekho*, Guwahati *mein bhi*. They [the films] have to become generic,' says Chaubey.

The growing pool of urban and NRI audiences has taken it further ahead, into a pleasurable *La La Land*. No wonder a filmmaker like Chaubey pitches himself as a 'regional Hindi filmmaker', rather than as a 'pan-India Bollywood filmmaker'.

Much of the heartland churn in recent times is due to the influx of talent into Bollywood from remote corners of India. These individuals emanating from small towns have brought with them their own stories, experiences, beliefs, mindscapes and ethos. Like Chaubey, 'a Tier 2-town kid,' as he describes himself, who grew up in UP, Bihar and Jharkhand, and is more than familiar with many Hindi dialects to boot.

For him, it has also been a reaction to the kind of cinema he grew up watching.

'It was set in this Bollywood Neverland that I was never convinced by,' he observes during my conversation with him. 'I realized early that the [a] film should have a great sense of place and geography. Where do the characters come from? What society do they belong to?'

Timangshu Dhulia shares a similar aversion to the idea of India's Tinseltown serving as a film's backdrop. During an interview, he had made it quite clear to me that he would never set a film in Mumbai.

'[The] urban mess of Mumbai just doesn't interest me. So much of it has already been shown on [the] big screen, anyhow. For me, a romance set in Mumbai is eminently fake, lacks complexity. What conflict can I show in it as a filmmaker? Rich versus poor, Bandra versus Bhayander?'

Instead, he had probed the issue of student politics in Allahabad in *Haasil*; explored the drug cartels of Kasol in *Charas* (2004); offered insights into love, betrayal and politics in a royal family on the decline in a small UP town in *Saheb Biwi aur Gangster*; depicted the lives of the bandits of Morena and the Chambal ravines in *Paan Singh Tomar*; and trained his astute gaze on the political mafia of Lucknow in *Bullet Raja*.

'Small town is a space I understand better. Also, there are more stories there,' says Dhulia. Elaborating further on the idea, he had explained, 'Small-town portrayals are, however, a lot more about detailing. For example, the caste and surnames – Mishra, Shukla, Yadav, Tripathi – matter. Gupta *ho ki* Brahman *ho* decides your love, job and friendships.'

Dhulia grew up in Allahabad between 1967 and 1986, before going off to study at the National School of Drama, in Delhi. Allahabad, as he had known it then, was an educational hub and culturally vibrant, be it in theatre, music, politics or literature.

'During my days [in the city] there was blatant violence in the Allahabad city, but not so much in the university itself, as I showed in my debut film *Haasil*,' he would tell me. 'It happened [the violence flared up at the university] much later.'

The basic idea of the film about the love of a gangster for a girl was inspired by the experience of a friend in Mathura, though Dhulia situated his own story in Allahabad and shot 80 per cent of the film there.

'I don't think college politics in Mumbai – or anywhere else in India – is as volatile as it is in the Hindi belt,' he had declared. 'In UP, if you are a university, president, you are bound to become a politician some day. There's a lot of violence and money involved in college politics, which is just like mainstream politics – albeit on a much smaller scale.'

He had witnessed this for himself as a student and even become involved with a leftist political group. It seemed inevitable that he would base his first film in a university-centric milieu in Allahabad.

'I had to show how religious and caste-based parties have entered our universities and are killing the culture and ethos of our campuses and the cities,' he had observed during his conversation with me.

Knowing Allahabad intimately, Dhulia needed to do no research for *Haasil*. For *Paan Singh Tomar*, on the other hand, he had to strive to achieve a certain level of authenticity in depicting the film's terrain and characters, their language and emotions to lend the film its raw, rustic feel.

'I had to work at packing in the finer details and nuances, like the film's Bhind–Morena dialect,' Dhulia would recall. 'The research about the bandit-turned-sportsman was back-breaking work, especially tracing Paan Singh's family, army colleagues and gang members. His gang member, dacoit Balwanta, insisted on meeting me in the night in a chai shop on the highway.'

Saheb Biwi aur Gangster also required serious research.

'I was familiar with some members of such a crumbling old royalty [as portrayed in the film], trying desperately to hold on to [their] fading glory and seeking refuge in crime, business and politics,' he had confided. 'I had seen their *ainth aur tevar* [conceit and attitude] very closely.'

Given the passion and efforts of filmmakers like him and several others with a yen for setting their stories and characters in provincial society and culture, little-known places – some we haven't even heard of – are leaping off the map and on to the screen. In the past few years, with Hindi cinema starting to explore diverse terrain – from Uttar Pradesh to Gujarat via Madhya Pradesh, Jharkhand and Chhattisgarh – Haryana seems to be emerging as the favourite onscreen dystopia. It's the heart of darkness, a bit like the Bihar we glimpsed in films such as *Shool* (E. Niwas, 1999), *Gangaajal* (Prakash Jha, 2003) and *Gangs of Wasseypur*. The precursor to it could well be Vishal Bhardwaj's anarchic *Matru ki Bijlee ka Mandola* that dealt with the illegal acquisition of agricultural land and the attempt to turn cultivated green fields into Special Economic Zones (SEZ).

Ordinary Joes and Janes are becoming the heroes and heroines of Bollywood's current silver-screen stories. If earlier, it had been left to the actors in the alternative-cinema zone – like Naseeruddin Shah (in *Nishant*, 1975, and *Manthan*, 1976, [both by Shyam Benegal] for example) and Om Puri (in *Aakrosh*, [Govind Nihalani, 1980]) – to embrace the hinterlands, mainstream actors are doing it now with a relatively deeper level of engagement than they had demonstrated earlier. The hero and heroine of *Sui Dhaaga* (Sharat Katariya, 2018) –

played by Varun Dhawan and Anushka Sharma – are from Chanderi; the hero Mauji is into a profession as banal as tailoring. In *Stree* (Amar Kaushik) too, released the same year, the hero (Rajkummar Rao) is 'Chanderi *ka* Manish Malhotra', 'Bhagwan *ka darzi roopi avtaar* – god incarnated as a tailor'.

For his 2016 film *Dangal* (Nitesh Tiwari), a superstar like Aamir Khan based his onscreen character Mahavir Singh Phogat, a real-life champion wrestler and estranged father, at Balali village in Bhiwani, Haryana, for the sake of lending authenticity to the story. Salman Khan also rooted himself in Haryana for *Sultan* (Ali Abbas Zafar), released the same year.

Akshay Kumar became a denizen of Maheshwar by the Narmada in *Padman* (R. Balki 2018), and in *Toilet: Ek Prem Katha* (Shree Narayan Singh 2017), the character he played very rightly took Prime Minister Narendra Modi's mission 'Clean India 2019' all the way to Mathura district, a place barely 150 km from the capital, but apparently lost to civilization when it comes to matters of sanitation; where morning ablutions have been a trial for years, what with basic sewage lines arriving late in the area; where the consumption of meals and the act of defecation have been taking place almost side by side, right there in the narrow lanes by the temples.

Even Shah Rukh Khan, with his otherwise larger-than-life persona, managed to blend with the motley Meerut crowd in *Zero* (2018); his wicked, obnoxious, self-obsessed, crude Bauua was quite in consonance with the internalized aggression, irreverence and rough manner associated with the town's denizens.

In recent times, however, it was Subhash Kapoor's *Jolly LLB 2*, a 2017 release, that managed to marry the opposites – the mainstream dramatic tropes and a realistic tapestry – most persuasively, before it started mutating into a done-to-death formula.

In the world of *Jolly LLB 2*, the landscape and local flavour, language and culture of Lucknow, Kanpur and Jhansi, along with the speech and enunciation, are highlighted to the same degree as the cheap sneakers and tericot trousers and shirts that Jolly (played by Akshay Kumar) sports. It's a world encompassing the paan-stained walls and seedy environs of Zila Evam Satr Nyayalaya (District and Sessions Court), where surnames are more defining than first names, cheating in exams is a legitimate business, class divides take precedence over religious ones and a 15th assistant is treated like house help by the senior lawyer. It's where professions are inherited, but also broken into and broken away from by more ambitious youngsters and a munshi's son dreams of having a lawyer's chamber of his own, even if he has to pay a bribe of ₹12 lakh for it. Here, women negotiate their own space within the larger male bastion. The film shows women chipping away at conservatism from within – be it by drinking surreptitiously within the confines of home or wearing daring outfits while out with the husband in the relative anonymity of Lucknow's Hazratganj, away from the watchful, censorious eyes of their own neighbourhood. In the Jolly household, it's the Gucci-obsessed wife, Pushpa, with an MA in Sanskrit under her belt, who seems to wear the pants and even takes on the goons in times of crisis. Her husband manages a balancing act with the area's religious realities as well. The fun lies in the throwaway details that help make the place become a significant character in itself.

In fact, in several recent off-mainstream films, we have seen the grassroots setting acquire the magnitude of a character. *A Death in the Gunj* (2016), written and directed by Konkona Sen Sharma, starring an ensemble cast of fine actors, evokes a place, a period and its people, bringing alive McCluskieganj as it used to be in the Bihar (now Jharkhand) of the '70s – comfortingly lived in on the surface, but with disturbingly melancholic undercurrents. The place itself is instrumental in creating the brooding, disquieting, unsettling mood that pervades the film.

The landscape is similarly harnessed to evoke fear and an eerie anticipation of the diabolical in *Tumbadd* (2018), a film in the horror genre directed by debutants Rahi Anil Barve and Adesh Prasad. The ambience of rural, period Maharashtra, the Konkani Brahmin culture and class, caste and gender exploitation are underscored by a strange, Gothic dread and the sense of unrelenting gloom that comes with incessant rain.

The 2017 film *Ashwatthama*, directed by Pushpendra Singh, is rooted in a rural milieu – in this case, the rough ravines around Agra and the many intersections of mythology, folk culture and religion. The searing quietude of its stark, still, spartan visuals and the geometry of its frames bring to the fore the secrets, repressions and rebellions simmering in the hearts of rural families. Violence is omnipresent and implicit, even while affections are explicit.

And what better place to set a film about the cycle of life and death than Varanasi? In *Mukti Bhawan* (Shubhashish Bhutiani, 2016), starring Adil Hussain, the much-mythologized image of Varanasi is tempered down with scenes of the utter banalities of life on the streets: the revered ritual of Ganga *arti*, seen through a bhang-induced haze, death viewed as a money-making process and salvation as business. This particular perspective on the holy town colours the film's ambience and defines its attitude – ritualism is observed with a distanced gaze and, at times, a sarcastic, even wicked, smile, without compromising the understanding of and receptivity to faith as a mode of reconciliation with the cycle of life.

It's also fascinating to see the hinterlands becoming the platform on which the most contentious and fractious political and social issues of the day are engaged. Anurag Kashyap's *Mukkabaaz* takes a hard-nosed look at the rampant corruption, nepotism and casteist politics that lie at the core of sports in Uttar Pradesh, underscoring how central these elements are even to life in general.

'I wanted to address that and, in the process, everything around us that was bothering me – casteism and nepotism,' he had explained, when I interviewed him. 'It's [the film] not about any political party, but society at large… I thought we had dealt with caste and it was all over. But it has resurfaced all over again. It is back in everyday conversation, in newspaper headlines. Even sports is about caste divides. Education is. You can't escape caste politics, gender politics. You are conditioned by it. It is ingrained. The whole dynasty culture is ingrained in us. It is not about just the Gandhi family. It's everywhere. Whose son or daughter you are has always mattered to normal, everyday persons also.'

Other issues too have been jostling for attention. Like the blood-bank scam in dusty, grimy Karnal that the 2016 Randeep Hooda-starrer *Laal Rang* (Syed Ahmed Afzal) brought to the fore. The expressions of male bonding, the ready wit and loud, rustic humour, the restlessness that torments small-town youth, the intricacies of their dating and mating games, their obsessions, even with something as inconsequential to an outsider as a Yamaha RX100, their shared aspiration for mofussil cool – these are the elements that the film brings out rather well. It takes us closer to a hedonistic subculture; except that in this particular world, the young don't rock 'n' roll in a big city, but swing to folk numbers in Haryana.

Udta Punjab exposes us to the frightening dystopia the state seems to have degenerated into in the past few years because of a canker eating away at its heart – the drug menace afflicting the young. What we see here is not the prosperous, happy, gregarious, gung-ho, outgoing and all-embracing bhangra Punjab of our collective imagination, but more like a lawless Mexico, with uncounted casualties.

Caught between state machinery and insurgency, Dandakaranya in conflict-ridden Chhattisgarh and its tribal community become an embodiment of the nation's own dilemmas, contradictions and paradoxes, and impel us to examine not only the polling process in a new light, but democracy itself in the much-acclaimed *Newton* (Amit Masurkar), a 2017 black comedy drama featuring Rajkummar Rao, Raghubir Yadav and Pankaj Tripathi, that ended up with two Filmfare Awards and was selected as the Indian entry for the Best Foreign Language Film at the 90th Academy Awards.

More overtly political small-town films include *Mulk* (Anubhav Sinha, 2018), a Taapsee Pannu–Rishi Kapoor starrer that captures Varanasi's culturally and communally concordant Ganga–Jamuni *tehzeeb*, even while offering a glimpse of the hidden flashpoints, the discords and fissures that can tear the fabric apart. Similarly, *Mohalla Assi* (Chandraprakash Dwivedi, 2018), a Sunny Deol film whose release was stayed by the courts for three years, purportedly for hurting religious sentiments, deals with the changing cultural dynamics and social fabric at Varanasi's Assi Ghat at the time of the Mandal Commission and Babri Masjid–Ram Janmabhoomi dispute.

Aligarh (2016), a critically acclaimed Hansal Mehta film, starring Manoj Bajpayee – whose performance won him the Filmfare Critics' Award for Best Actor – and *Ek Ladki Ko Dekha Toh Aisa Laga* (Shelly Chopra Dhar, 2019), featuring Sonam Kapoor in an avatar that is a radical departure from the image she seems to have appropriated for herself over the years – of the stylish, lightweight, upper-class brat with attitude – have dared to take sexuality issues to small towns. The cramped, shabby homes, the wintry, foggy, sinister air of the small north Indian town portrayed in *Aligarh* are symptomatic of the town's warped public moral compass, of the gloomy university that had taken the lead in bringing progressive thinking and the scientific spirit of enquiry to the Muslim community, but eventually started going downhill because of internal politics.

Then there is an entire genre of small-town films dealing with the gender issue. Behind their seemingly prosaic existence, four ordinary women in Bhopal lead secret lives as a reaction against the everyday repression they face in the Ratna Pathak–Konkona Sen Sharma–starrer *Lipstick under my Burkha* (Alankrita Shrivastava, 2016). A domestic help in Agra wants her daughter to study and do well in life in *Nil Battey Sannata*. Released in 2016, the film won Ashwini Iyer Tiwari a Filmfare Award for Best Debut Director. Swara Bhaskar, the lead actress, along with her child co-star, picked up Screen awards. A flamboyant singer-dancer, also played to perfection by Bhaskar in *Anaarkali of Aarah* (2017), refuses to be cowed down by the diktats society has imposed on her simply because she is in the business of entertainment and is perceived as a commodity. While she may not be a '*sati savitri*', she believes that she has the first right to her body and dignity, and ensures that men understand the meaning of consent. In the film, the rough, provincial, plain-speaking world of the bawdy singer-dancers of Aarah is painted with subversive little brushstrokes, as are Delhi's marginalized, blue-collar Bihari pockets, due to filmmaker Avinash Das's own familiarity with and understanding of these spaces.

Of the lot, *G Kutta Se* (Rahul Dahiya), based on a true story and released in 2017 after being held up for a year because of censorship-related issues, is one of the most relentlessly horrifying films – from the first frame to the last – one has seen in recent times, primarily because it presents the patriarchal reality of Haryana in a shockingly stark, straightforward and unembellished way. No sugar-coating of the bitter pill here. The realism lies in the specificity of the raw, rustic locale, the authenticity of its crude lingo and the sexual innuendoes that the dialogue is peppered with. It comes through in the inherent swagger and attitude of the characters, in the unflinching documentary style in which the film has been shot and, especially, in the way it lays bare the unquestioning manner in which this particular society's conservative values have been accepted and internalized by its members, and its legacy of patriarchy, along with the cycle of violence it perpetuates, resolutely passed on from one generation to the next.

What now, one might well ask. Will these hinterland narratives evolve to take centre stage or lose their shine after the novelty has worn off? Abhishek Chaubey feels the change has mostly been a positive one.

'Ultimately, it's about how you choose to tell your story, what content you plan to make,' he declares. 'Yes, we are going to Rajinder Nagar from Golf Links. *Stree* and *Sui Dhaaga* were shot in Chanderi. That's great; but ultimately, what's important is the kind of story you are telling.'

He also feels that people are essentially the same everywhere; it is societies that are different. If you try and explore in depth the compulsions and quirks that define the social set-up of the place where your film is set, chances are that its concerns and issues will find resonance with everybody across the world, regardless of nationality.

'If my film is about social discrimination, then there is no society in the world that has not faced it,' says Chaubey. 'Only if I am going to go completely local, am I going to be able to say anything that has a global meaning.'

Notes

1. Namrata Joshi, 'Bunty Babli aur Bollywood', *Outlook*, 13 October 2008.
2. Dola Mitra, 'Calling Jimmy', *Outlook*, 28 April 2014.
3. ——, 'Ma Mati Mamta', *Outlook*, 12 May 2014.
4. Namrata Joshi, 'Stalking Mrigayas', *Outlook*, 10 September 2017.
5. ——, 'We felt we were in an alternate universe,' *Outlook*, 27 October 2014.
6. Shohini Ghosh, 'The Irresistible Badness of Salman Khan,' *Caravan*, 1 October 2012.
7. Namrata Joshi, 'Sallu Boti, Anyone?' *Outlook*, 20 September 2010.
8. ——, 'For Shah Rukh's biggest fan today is maha kumbh', *The Hindu*, 2 November 2015.
9. Ajeet Mahale, 'Apta sought-after by filmmakers, highest revenue generator for CR', *The Hindu*, 9 May 2016.
10. Namrata Joshi, 'Great Expectations[Live]', *Outlook*, 9 August 2010.
11. Manu Joseph, 'Parallel Cinema', *Outlook*, 21 July 2003.
12. Namrata Joshi, 'From farmer to filmmaker', *The Hindu*, 22 October 2015.
13. ——, 'By the people, for the people', *The Hindu*, 23 June 2017.
14. Ibid.
15. Namrata Joshi, 'With Village Rockstars going to the Oscars, director Rima Das is on a high', *Outlook*, 30 November 2018.
16. Sankhayan Ghosh, 'Nomads of cinema', *The Hindu*, 27 April 2016.

17. Namrata Joshi, 'The Less Visible', *Outlook*, 25 October 2010.
18. ——, 'Syncretic cinema in saffron city', *The Hindu*, 25 March 2017.
19. ——, 'A Marquee in Gorakhpur, *Outlook*, 6 April 2015.
20. ——, 'BYOFF reinvents at 15', *The Hindu*, 22 February 2018.
21. ——, 'In Aurangabad, a woke film festival at the grass roots', *The Hindu*, 8 January 2019.
22. ——, 'The Unsung', *Outlook*, 13 January 2014.
23. Ibid.
24. Namrata Joshi, 'Life is not about filmmaking', *The Hindu*, 4 August 2016.
25. Sankhayan Ghosh, 'Gurvinder Singh's cafe in the mountains becomes the setting of his new film', *Film Companion*, 26 November 2018.
26. Namrata Joshi, 'The Storyteller Within,' *The Hindu*, 21 April 2016.
27. ——, 'Tumbbad felt like once in a lifetime opportunity', *The Hindu*, 9 October 2018.
28. ——, 'After 17 years of struggle Vineet Kumar lands the lead role in Mukkabaaz', 8 January 2018.
29. ——, 'It all boils down to the loyalty to the story: Aanand L. Rai', *The Hindu*, 11 August 2018.
30. ——, 'Not just another sports movie', *The Hindu*, 21 October 2017.
31. ——, 'Moor of Meerut', *Outlook*, 14 August 2006.

Acknowledgements

There are many people I want to thank for having helped in this journey. To begin with, Manas, Anjali and Maggie for being there and generously letting the most senior and junior members of the Joshi family edge their way into the dedication.

All the people who shared their lives, stories, accounts and opinions that can be found in the pages of this book.

Nandini Mehta and Anjali Puri for setting me off on the assignment to Saharanpur and Muzaffarnagar that paved the way for more adventures. Udayan Mitra, who first spotted the possibility of a book in a 700-word story on Saharanpur. Manishadi for guiding me to Anubhadi, who provided a home, meals and sources in Saharanpur. Nirmalda and Deepa Bhabhi for helping with the Muzaffarnagar end and Priyata, Anup and Nalin for the Bengaluru sojourn.

Sanjay Mehta, who has always been my guide to the single screens in the interiors of north India, besides being the one to introduce me to the *dahi bhalle* of Natraj in his film distribution office in Old Delhi.

Pavan Jha for being ever so generous with his knowledge, anecdotes and contacts, especially when it came to Hindi film music.

Pravesh Bhardwaj and his family for providing a home, chaat and a compelling character and story in Bareilly.

Abhivyakti Patil and her aayi and baba for being my anchors in Malegaon.

Svetlana Naudiyal for the travels, company and base camp in

Mumbai, long before it became home for me. Manish Rathore, who has been my Lucknow companion on several assignments to the city. Sai Prasad Narendran for being the able guide and support in Coimbatore. Soma Basu for showing me the other facet of Madurai.

Kalpana for Bhopal and Neeraj Mishra for Raipur contacts. Utpal Borpujari for being the window into cinema from the North East. Avijit Ghosh for the discussions and debates on cinema and small towns. Velu Shankar for the critical inputs in bridging the North–South divide, and maintaining it too.

My mentors in journalism – Sadanand Menon, Shailaja Bajpai, Madhu Jain, Sandipan Deb, VM a.k.a Vinod Mehta, Malini Parthasarathy, Mukund Padmanabhan.

Outlook and *The Hindu* – all former and current colleagues who provided nurturing soil – where many of these stories found their first home.

Friends who have become a family through this enterprise – Chitra, Aarti, Shubhra, Suparna, Poonam, Anna, Arnab, Suanshu, Mihir, Suman, Aseem, Yasser.

Amish, Prerna, Ansila and Poulomi at Hachette for bearing with the many headaches I gave them over the years.

Kanishka Gupta, my agent at Writer's Side, for the thousands of emails and calls he had to make to keep me at it when I had almost given up on the project. And Sheela Reddy for putting me in touch with him.

Lastly, all the stories and people who couldn't make it in this book – Bhaskar Hazarika's Guwahati-based *Aamis*, Pradip Kurbah's *Iewdah* set in Shillong, Ridham Janve's *The Golden Laden Sheep and the Sacred Mountain* about the Gaddi community in Himachal Pradesh in their Gaddi dialect and the several web series set in mofussil India.

Meanwhile, as we go to press, I hear Farogh from Malegaon will be starting a comic YouTube channel of his own. At the end of one story lies the beginnings of several others.